THE NEW
PSYCHO-CYBERNETICS

The Original Science of Self-Improvement and Success that Has Changed the Lives of 30 Million People

MAXWELL MALTZ, M.D., F.I.C.S.
EDITED AND UPDATED BY DAN S. KENNEDY AND THE PSYCHO-CYBERNETICS FOUNDATION, INC.

Prentice
Hall Press

 A member of Penguin Putnam Inc.
375 Hudson Street
New York, New York 10014

www.penguinputnam.com

Copyright © 2001 by Penguin Putnam Inc.
Prentice Hall® is a registered trademark of Pearson Education, Inc.
Cover art: Original watercolor by Salvador Dali used by permission of
The New Psycho-Cybernetics Foundation, Inc.
Cover design by Nicola Evans
Text design by Shelly Carlucci

Prentice Hall Press hardcover edition published 2001
Prentice Hall Press trade paperback edition: December 2002

The Library of Congress has catalogued the
Prentice Hall Press hardcover edition as follows:

Maltz, Maxwell, 1899–1975.
  The new psycho-cybernetics: the original science of self-improvement and success that
has changed the lives of 30 million people / by Maxwell Maltz : edited and updated by
Dan S. Kennedy and the Psycho-Cybernetics Foundation, Inc.
    p. cm.
Rev. ed. of : Psycho-cybernetics.
Includes index.
ISBN 0-7352-0275-3
    1. Success—Psychological aspects.   I. Kennedy, Dan S., 1954.   II. Maltz, Maxwell,
    1899–1975. Psycho-Cybernetics.   III. Psycho-Cybernetic Foundation.   IV. Title.

  BF637.S8 M25 2001
  158.1—dc21   2001036799

Printed in the United States of America

10   9

"*Psycho-Cybernetics* changed my destiny. From a small farm-house nearly 2 miles from a major road in Chucketauck, Virginia, to a successful career as an author, consultant, lecturer to organizations like NASA, Disney, AT&T . . . Dr. Maltz's suggestions gave me the confidence to bring out my talents and go for my dreams."
—LEE MILTEER, author, *Success Is An Inside Job*

"I was flunking out of college when I first read *Psycho-Cybernetics*, and it literally turned my life around."
—MARSHALL REDDICK, PH.D.

———

The late **DR. MAXWELL MALTZ** received his doctorate in medicine from the College of Physicians and Surgeons of Columbia University. After post-graduate work in plastic surgery in Europe, Dr. Maltz headed several departments of reparative surgery in New York hospitals. He was a prominent international lecturer on the physical and psychological aspects of plastic surgery, and published two books on these subjects: *New Faces, New Futures* and *Dr. Pygmalion*. The original ideas that formed the basis of *Psycho-Cybernetics* grew out of ideas he developed in his very successful private practice in New York, where he treated patients from all over the world, including many celebrities.

DAN S. KENNEDY is a marketing consultant, popular professional speaker, and author of nine books. He is the CEO of the Psycho-Cybernetics Foundation and author of *The New Psycho-Cybernetics* audio program.

Contents

Chapter Seven

Chapter Eight

Chapter Nine

Chapter Ten

Chapter Eleven:

Chapter Twelve:

Chapter Thirteen:

Chapter Fourteen:

CHAPTER FIFTEEN:

CHAPTER SIXTEEN:

Acknowledgments

The Psycho-Cybernetics Foundation's founding board members:
    William Brooks
    Matt Oeschsli
    Jeff Paul

Jeff Herman, the Foundation's hard-working literary agent, Eugene Brissie and Ellen Schneid Coleman at Prentice Hall Press, who have been consistently and enthusiastically supportive of the "renaissance" of Dr. Maltz's works.

Introduction

*T*he year 2000 was the 40th anniversary of the publication of Dr. Maltz's original *Psycho-Cybernetics*. The book has sold over 30 million copies in all of its different editions worldwide, inspired a number of audio cassette programs for individuals as well as complete training programs created for corporations, sales organizations, even sports teams. In the 2000 Olympics, for example, the coach of the U.S. equestrian team used Psycho-Cybernetics techniques, as she has with other teams for many years.

In many ways, Psycho-Cybernetics is *the* original *science* of self-improvement. I make that statement for three principal reasons:

First, Dr. Maltz was the first researcher and author to understand and explain how the *self-image* (a term he popularized for certain processes within the subconscious mind) has *complete control* over an individual's ability to achieve (or fail to achieve) any goal.

Second, everything written, said, recorded or taught about self-improvement since Maltz wrote has derived from his work. Try and find any book on success or self-improvement written since 1960, right through to yesterday, that does not include a discussion of self-image and the techniques for improving and managing it—notably including visualization, mental rehearsal, and relaxation—and you'll realize how crucial the work of Maltz still is. The relatively young "science" of sports psychology, relied on heavily by professional golfers, sports franchises, coaches, and Olympians, owes an enormous debt, occasionally acknowledged, to Psycho-Cybernetics.

Third, unlike philosophical musings about success, Psycho-Cybernetics is, in fact, scientific: It provides practical things to do (not just think about), that yield quantifiable results. What is unique about Psycho-Cybernetics is that it offers techniques that help make whatever was once difficult easy.

In short, whether you set out to lose weight and keep it off, lower your golf score, double your income in selling, become a confident public speaker, write the great American novel, or achieve any other imaginable goal, in order to succeed, you will use Psycho-Cybernetics techniques, either directly from Dr. Maltz or some other source influenced by his work. By acquiring this book, you have gone to the first and still foremost source.

It is significant that, with very little publicity or marketing, the original *Psycho-Cybernetics* book has had such amazing longevity, and is now a classic in its field. Today, just as ten, twenty, and thirty years ago, sales managers tell recruits, coaches tell athletes, consultants tell clients: Get and read this book.

Now I dare to update the classic. In doing so, I have set out to preserve much of the original content; much of it, in fact, is unchanged; some has been modestly updated in language or example. To integrate it with other works of Dr. Maltz, I have added my own observations and lessons learned from teaching Psycho-Cybernetics techniques along with examples and stories submitted by many users of these techniques and culled from others' books referencing these techniques. Throughout, I have tried to maintain Maltz's original voice. Over the years since 1960, Dr. Maltz and those who followed him devoted increasing emphasis to translating the principles and concepts of Psycho-Cybernetics into actual, practical "mental training exercises," and I've included a number of those as well. All things combined, this is the most complete Psycho-Cybernetics work ever published.

* * *

My own experiences with Psycho-Cybernetics began in childhood, when I used it to conquer a stubborn, rather severe stuttering problem. I've gone on to enjoy a 20-year career as a professional speaker, in recent years addressing audiences as large as 35,000 and, in total, over 200,000 people annually. In adult life, I returned repeatedly to these techniques in my sales, consulting, and business activities, to assist me in my prolific writing career—nine published books, a monthly newsletter, over 50 different audio cassette programs, and as an advertising copywriter, my primary vocation.

For example, using Psycho-Cybernetics, I am able to give my subconscious mind certain instructions and put it to work on a writing assignment before going to sleep at night or taking a nap, wake up, instantly put fingers to keyboard and "download," pour out what the subconscious wrote while I slept. Not long ago, I climbed into a sulky and became a harness racing driver (at age 46), and found myself relying heavily on Psycho-Cybernetics.

In my business life, I have worked with many millionaire and multimillionaire entrepreneurs, including some who have risen from poverty or financial disaster and others who have started from scratch and rapidly built empires. Most of them use these techniques. Many trace their understanding of them directly to Dr. Maltz, as I do.

I first began working directly with Psycho-Cybernetics as a writer, editor, and publisher in the late 1980s. At the time, I worked with Dr. Maltz's widow, Anne Maltz, and a university associated with her, to develop a collection of audio tapes featuring Dr. Maltz's lectures, radio broadcasts, and interviews. Since then, I've been directly involved in the first book ever written featuring Psycho-Cybernetics specifically for salespeople, titled *Zero Resistance Selling*, an audio program *The New Psycho-Cybernetics*, book-on-tape programs, a 12-week home study course, and a monthly newsletter as well as special editions of programs for certain professions, industries, corporations, and international translation.

My point is that I've lived and worked with—and benefited from—Psycho-Cybernetics my entire life. I was told by Anne Maltz that she had difficulty telling my writing on this subject apart from her late husband's. That was an enormous compliment. I hope she was right, and that this expanded and updated version of the original comes across to you seamlessly, in one voice, Dr. Maltz's, as if he were here to prepare it himself.

If you have comments, I would enjoy hearing from you via fax at 602-269-3113, or mail c/o The Psycho-Cybernetics Foundation, 5818 N. 7th Street, Suite #103, Phoenix, AZ 85014. If you would like to read back issues of the Foundation's newsletters, you may access them at www.psycho-cybernetics.com.

I sincerely believe that you hold in your hands one of the most powerful tools for self-improvement and goal achievement available anywhere, at any time, at any price. It has been my privilege to have a small part in bringing it to you.

Dan S. Kennedy

CHAPTER ONE

The Self-Image: Your Key to Living Without Limits

*Nothing splendid has ever been achieved except by those
who dared believe that something inside them
was superior to circumstance.*

—Bruce Barton

A revolution in psychology began in the late
1960s and exploded in the 1970s. When I
wrote the first edition of Psycho-Cybernetics in 1960, I was at the
forefront of a sweeping change in the fields of psychology, psychiatry,
and medicine. New theories and concepts concerning the "self" began
emerging from the work and findings of clinical psychologists, practicing psychiatrists, and even cosmetic or so-called "plastic surgeons"
like myself. New methods growing out of these findings resulted in
dramatic changes in personality, in health, and even in basic abilities
and talents. Chronic failures became successful. "F" students changed
into "straight A" pupils with no extra tutoring. Shy, retiring, inhibited
personalities became happy and outgoing. At the time, I was quoted
in the January 1959 issue of *Cosmopolitan Magazine*, in which T. F.
James summarized these results obtained by various psychologists and
MDs as follows:

Understanding the psychology of the self can mean the difference between success and failure, love and hate, bitterness and happiness. The discovery of the real self can rescue a crumbling marriage,
recreate a faltering career, transform victims of "personality failure."
On another plane, discovering your real self means the difference
between freedom and the compulsions of conformity.

This was barely predictive of everything that has occurred in the four decades that followed.

When *Psycho-Cybernetics* was first published, if you visited a bookstore to obtain a copy, you might have found it nestled on an obscure shelf with only a dozen or so other so-called "self-help" books. Today, of course, "self-help" is one of the largest sections in the entire bookstore. Psychologists, psychiatrists, and therapists have proliferated, new specialists have emerged, such as sports psychologists and corporate performance coaches, and the stigma of seeking such help has disappeared to such an extent that in some circles doing so is trendy. Self-help psychology has become so popular it even has found a place in television infomercials!

Once Difficult, Now Easy!

I'm gratified that much of this modern explosion of ideas, information, and people to assist you with everything from conquering procrastination to shaving strokes off your golf score appears to be based on Psycho-Cybernetics. You might say that my original work was ahead of its time, or you might say that it has aged well. Whatever you conclude, the most important thing for you, personally, is that the fundamental promise of Psycho-Cybernetics has been proven true beyond any doubt or argument—that is, "once difficult, now easy." Whatever is now difficult for you, whatever may have prompted your reading of this book, can be transformed from difficult to easy through the use of certain sound psychological concepts, easily understood and mastered mental training techniques, and a few practical steps.

Your Secret Blueprint

I would argue that the most important psychological discovery of modern times is the discovery of the self-image. By understanding your self-image and by learning to modify it and manage it to suit your purposes, you gain incredible confidence and power.

Whether we realize it or not, each of us carries within us a mental blueprint or picture of ourselves. It may be vague and ill-defined to our conscious gaze. In fact, it may not be consciously recognizable at all. But it is there, complete down to the last detail. This self-image is our own conception of the "sort of person I am." It has been built up from our own beliefs about ourselves. Most of these beliefs about ourselves have unconsciously been formed from our past experiences, our successes and failures, our humiliations, our triumphs, and the way other people have reacted to us, especially in early childhood. From all these we mentally construct a *self* (or a picture of a self). Once an idea or a belief about ourselves goes into this picture it becomes "truth," as far as we personally are concerned. We do not question its validity, but proceed to act upon it *just as if it were true.*

The self-image then *controls* what you can and cannot accomplish, what is difficult or easy for you, even how others respond to you just as certainly and scientifically as a thermostat controls the temperature in your home.

Specifically, all your actions, feelings, behavior, even your abilities, are always consistent with this self-image. Note the word: *always*. In short, you will "act like" the sort of person you conceive yourself to be. More important, you literally cannot act otherwise, in spite of all your conscious efforts or willpower. (This is why trying to achieve something difficult with teeth gritted is a losing battle. Willpower is *not* the answer. Self-image management is.)

The Snap-Back Effect

The person who has a "fat" self-image—whose self-image claims to have a "sweet tooth," to be unable to resist "junk food," who cannot find the time to exercise—will be unable to lose weight and keep it off no matter what he tries to do consciously in opposition to that self-image. You cannot long outperform or escape your self-image. If you do escape briefly, you'll be "snapped back," like a rubber band, extended between two fingers, coming loose from one.

The person who perceives himself to be a "failure type person" will find some way to fail, in spite of all his good intentions or his willpower, even if opportunity is literally dumped in his lap. The person who conceives himself to be a victim of injustice, one "who was meant to suffer," will invariably find circumstances to verify his opinions.

You can insert any specific into this: your golf game, sales career, public speaking, weight loss, relationships. The control of your self-image is absolute and pervasive. The snapback effect is universal.

The self-image is a "premise," a base, or a foundation upon which your entire personality, your behavior, and even your circumstances are built. As a result, our experiences seem to verify and thereby strengthen our self-images, and either a vicious or a beneficent cycle, as the case may be, is set up.

For example, a student who sees himself as an "F"-type student, or one who is "dumb in mathematics," will invariably find that his report card bears him out. He then has "proof." In the same manner, a sales professional or an entrepreneur will also find that her actual experiences tend to "prove" that her self-image is correct. Whatever is difficult for you, whatever frustrations you have in your life, they are likely "proving" and reinforcing something ingrained in your self-image like a groove in a record.

Because of this objective "proof," it very seldom occurs to us that our trouble lies in our self-image or our own evaluation of ourselves. Tell the student that he only "thinks" he cannot master algebra, and he will doubt your sanity. He has tried and tried, and still his report card tells the story. Tell the sales agent that it is only an idea that she cannot earn more than a certain figure, and she can prove you wrong by her order book. She knows only too well how hard she has tried and failed. Yet, as we shall see, almost miraculous changes have occurred both in grades of students and the earning capacity of salespeople—once they were prevailed upon to change their self-images.

Obviously, it's not enough to say "it's all in your head." In fact, that's insulting. It is more productive to explain that "it" is based on certain ingrained, possibly hidden patterns of thought that, if altered, will free you to tap more of your potential and experience vastly different results. This brings me to the most important truth about the self-image: It *can* be changed.

Numerous case histories have shown that you are never too young or too old to change your self-image and start to live a new, amazingly different life.

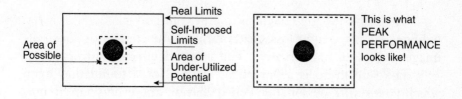

EDITOR'S NOTE: Here is another illustration of how the self-image operates. Picture us living inside two boxes. The line farthest out, the solid line, represents real or realistic limits. The dotted line, in the first drawing shown tightly confining Self, represents self-imposed limits. The area between the two is your area or range of under-utilized potential. As you discover the means of strengthening and liberating your self-image, you move the dotted line closer to the solid line, permitting greater use of your true potential.

Success from the Inside Out, Not the Outside In

One of the reasons it seems so difficult for a person to change habits, personality, or a way of life has been that nearly all efforts at change have been directed to the circumference of the self, so to speak, rather than to the center.

Numerous patients have said to me something like the following: "If you are talking about 'positive thinking,' I've tried that before, and it just doesn't work for me." However, a little questioning invariably brings out that these individuals employed positive thinking, or attempted to employ it, either on particular external circumstances or on some particular habit or character defect ("I will get that job," "I will be more calm and relaxed in the future." "This business venture will turn out right for me." And so on.) But they never thought to change their thinking of the self that was to accomplish these things.

Jesus warned us about the folly of putting a patch of new material on an old garment or of putting new wine into old bottles. "Positive thinking" cannot be used effectively as a patch to the same old self- image. In fact, it is literally impossible to really think posi-

tively about a particular situation, as long as you hold a negative concept of self. Numerous experiments have shown that, once the concept
of self is changed, other things *consistent* with the *new* concept of self
are accomplished easily and without strain.

A System of Ideas

One of the earliest and most convincing experiments along this line
was conducted by the late Prescott Lecky, one of the pioneers in self-
image psychology. Lecky conceived of the personality as a *system of
ideas*, all of which must be consistent with each other. Ideas that are
inconsistent with the system are rejected, "not believed," and not
acted on. Ideas that seem to be consistent with the system are
accepted. At the very center of this system of ideas—the keystone, or
the base on which all else is built—is the individual's self-image, or his
conception of himself.

Lecky was a school teacher and had an opportunity to test his
theory on thousands of students. He theorized that if a student had
trouble learning a certain subject, it could be because (from the student's point of view) it would be inconsistent for him to learn it. Lecky
believed, however, that if the student could be induced to change his
self-definition, his learning ability should also change.

This proved to be the case. One student, who misspelled 55
words out of 100 and flunked so many subjects that he lost credit for
a year, made a general average of 91 the next year and became one of
the best spellers in school. A girl who was dropped from one college
because of poor grades, entered Columbia and became a straight "A"
student. A boy who was told by a testing bureau that he had no apti-
tude for English won honorable mention the next year for a literary
prize.

The trouble with these students was not that they were dumb or
lacking in basic aptitudes. The trouble was an inadequate self-image
("I don't have a mathematical mind"; "I'm just naturally a poor
speller"). They "identified" with their mistakes and failures. Instead of
saying "I failed that test" (factual and descriptive), they concluded "I
am a failure." Instead of saying "I flunked that subject," they said "I am
a flunk-out." (For those who are interested in learning more of

Lecky's work, try to find a copy of his book: *Self Consistency, A Theory of Personality.*)

Lecky also used the same method to cure students of such habits as nail biting and stuttering.

My own files contain case histories just as convincing: the woman who was so afraid of strangers that she seldom ventured out of the house and who now makes her living as a public speaker. The salesman who had already prepared a letter of resignation because he "just wasn't cut out for selling" and six months later was number one man on a force of one hundred salespeople. The minister who was considering retirement because "nerves" and the pressure of preparing a sermon every week were getting him down, and who now delivers an average of three "outside talks" a week in addition to his weekly sermons and doesn't know he has a nerve in his body.

Following Dr. Lecky's breakthrough thinking on this subject, born from observation, as well as my own observations and thoughts chronicled in the earlier editions of this book, a mountain of more sophisticated scientific research and anecdotal evidence has led to the acceptance of the controlling self-image by most of the academic psychological community.

How a Plastic Surgeon Became Interested in Self-Image Psychology: My Story

Offhand, there would seem to be little or no connection between surgery and psychology. Yet, it was the work of the plastic surgeon that first hinted at the existence of the self-image and raised certain questions that led to important psychological knowledge.

When I first began the practice of plastic surgery many years ago, I was amazed by the dramatic and sudden changes in character and personality that often resulted when a facial defect was corrected. Changing the physical image in many instances appeared to create *an entirely new person*. In case after case, the scalpel that I held in my hand became a magic wand that transformed not only patients' appearance, but their whole life. The shy and retiring became bold and courageous. A "stupid" boy changed into an alert, bright youngster who went on to become an executive with a prominent firm. A salesman who had lost his touch and his faith in himself became a model of self-confidence. And perhaps the most startling of all was the habitual "hardened" criminal who changed almost overnight from an incorrigible—who had never showed any desire to change—into a model prisoner, who won a parole and went on to assume a responsible role in society.

Some sixty years ago I reported many such case histories in my book *New Faces—New Futures*, written more for my peers than the public. Following its publication, and similar articles in leading magazines, I was besieged with questions by criminologists, psychologists, sociologists, and psychiatrists. They asked questions that I could not answer, but they did start me on a search. Strangely enough, I learned as much from my failures as from my successes, if not more.

It was easy to explain the successes. The boy with the too-big ears, who had been told that he looked like a taxi cab with both doors open, had been ridiculed all his life—often cruelly. Association with others meant humiliation and pain. Why shouldn't he avoid social contacts? Why shouldn't he become afraid of people and retire into himself? Terribly afraid to express himself in any way, he became known as "stupid." When his ears were corrected, it would seem only natural that since the cause of his embarrassment and humiliation had been removed, he should assume a normal role in life, which he did.

Or consider the salesman who suffered a facial disfigurement as the result of an automobile accident. Each morning when he shaved he could see the horrible disfiguring scar on his cheek and the grotesque twist to his mouth. For the first time in his life he became painfully self-conscious. He was ashamed of himself and felt that his appearance must be repulsive to others. The scar became an obsession with him. He was "different" from other people. He began to wonder what others were thinking of him. Soon his self-image was even more mutilated than his face. He began to lose confidence in himself. He became bitter and hostile. Soon almost all his attention was directed toward himself, and his primary goal became the protection of his ego and the avoidance of situations that might bring humiliation. It is easy to understand how the correction of his facial disfigurement and the restoration of a "normal" face would overnight change this man's entire attitude and outlook, his feelings about himself, resulting in greater success in his work.

The mystery inspired me: If the scalpel was magic, why did some people who acquired new faces go right on wearing their old personalities?

What about the exceptions, those who didn't change? What about the Duchess who all her life had been terribly shy and self-conscious because of a tremendous hump in her nose? Although surgery gave her a classic nose and a face that was truly beautiful, she continued to act the part of the ugly duckling, the unwanted sister who could never bring herself to look another human being in the eye. If the scalpel itself was magic, why did it not work on the Duchess?

Or what about all the others who acquired new faces but went right on wearing the same old personality? How to explain the reaction of people who insist that the surgery has made *no difference whatever* in their appearance? Every plastic surgeon has had this experience and has probably been as baffled by it as I was. No matter how drastic the change in appearance may be, certain patients will insist that "I look just the same as before—you didn't do a thing." Friends, even family, may scarcely recognize them, may become enthusiastic over their newly acquired "beauty," yet the patients themselves insist that they can see only slight or no improvement, or in fact deny that any change at all has been made. Comparison of before and after photographs does little good, and may even arouse hostility. By some strange mental alchemy the patient will rationalize: "Of course, I can see that the hump is no longer in my nose—but my nose still *looks* just the same." Or, "The scar may not show any more, but it's *still there*."

Scars That Bring Pride Instead of Shame

Still another clue in search of the elusive self-image is the fact that not all scars or disfigurements bring shame and humiliation. When I was a young medical student in Germany, I saw many a student proudly wearing his "saber scar," much as an American might wear the Medal of Honor. The duelists were the elite of college society and a facial scar was the badge that proved you a member in good standing. To these boys, the *acquisition* of a horrible scar on the cheek had the same psychologic effect as the eradication of the scar from the cheek of my salesman patient. I began to see that a knife itself held no magical powers. It could be used on one person to inflict a scar and on another to erase a scar with the same psychological results.

The Mystery of Imaginary Ugliness

To a person handicapped by a genuine congenital defect, or suffering an actual facial disfigurement as a result of an accident, plastic surgery can indeed seemingly perform magic. From such cases it would be easy to theorize that the cure-all for all neuroses, unhappiness, failure, fear, anxiety, and lack of self-confidence would be wholesale plastic surgery to remove all bodily defects. However, according to this theory, persons with normal or acceptable faces should be singularly free from all psychological handicaps. They should be cheerful, happy, self-confident, free from anxiety and worry. We know only too well this is not true.

Nor can such a theory explain the people who visit the office of a cosmetic surgeon and demand a face lift to cure a purely imaginary ugliness. There are, for example, the 35- to 45-year-old women who are convinced that they look "old" even though their appearance is perfectly normal and in many cases unusually attractive.

There are the young girls who are convinced that they are ugly merely because their mouth, nose, or bust measurement does not exactly match that of the currently reigning Hollywood celebrity, teen pop star, or the most popular girl in their school. There are men who believe that their ears are too big or their noses too long.

Such imagined ugliness is not at all uncommon. Surveys of everyone from teenagers and college students to mature men and women consistently show high numbers—70%, 80%, even 90%—dissatisfied in some way with their appearance. If the words "normal" or "average" mean anything at all, it is obvious that 90% of our population cannot be "abnormal" or "different" or "defective" in appearance. Yet surveys have shown that approximately the same percentage of our general population find some reason to be ashamed of their body image.

Of course, in some cases, this becomes constructive dissatisfaction that motivates healthy weight loss and exercise. Many other times, though, it either stimulates attempts at weight loss or fitness doomed to failure (because of strong self-image-based restrictions) or simply cause people profound unhappiness.

These people react *just as if* they suffered an actual disfigurement. They feel the same shame. They develop the same fears and anxieties. Their capacity to really "live" fully is blocked and choked by the same sort of psychologic roadblocks. Their "scars," though mental and emotional rather than physical, are just as debilitating.

Why Are the Rich and Powerful Unhappy?

Why do the popular, successful, wealthy "beautiful people" of Hollywood, athletes awarded megamillion-dollar contracts and set for life, and enormously influential and powerful business or political leaders engage in amazingly unhappy and self-sabotaging acts of alcohol or drug abuse and addiction, or in all manner of publicly humiliating and destructive behavior? You see it reported everyday.

"They've bought the BMW and they have the $3-million Mill Valley house. And they still wake up in the morning and say 'I don't feel good about myself.'" That's a quote from Dr. Stephen Goldbart, a psychologist treating many dot.com and tech industry millionaires in Silicon Valley for what is characterized as "undeserved wealth syndrome."

Wealth, success, power, and celebrity are no more guarantees of happiness and peace of mind than surgical improvement of some personal appearance flaw.

The Self-Image—The Real Secret

Discovery of the self-image explains *all* the apparent discrepancies we have been discussing. It is the common denominator—the *determining factor* in all our case histories, the failures as well as the successes.

The secret is this: To really live, that is to find life reasonably satisfying, you must have an adequate and realistic self-image that you can live with. You must find your self acceptable to you. You must have a wholesome self-esteem. You must have a self that you can trust and believe in. You must have a self that you are not ashamed to be, and one that you can feel free to express creatively, rather than hide or cover up. You must know yourself—both your strengths and your weaknesses—and be honest with yourself concerning both. Your self-image must be a reasonable approximation of "you," being neither more nor less than you are.

When this self-image is intact and secure, you feel good. When it is threatened, you feel anxious and insecure. When it is adequate and one that you can be wholesomely proud of, you feel self-confident. You feel free to be yourself and to express yourself. You function at your optimum. When the self-image is an object of shame, you attempt to hide it rather than express it. Creative expression is blocked. You become hostile and hard to get along with.

If a scar on the face enhances the self-image (as in the case of the German duelist), self-esteem and self-confidence are increased. If a scar on the face detracts from the self-image (as in the case of the salesman), loss of self-esteem and self-confidence result.

When a facial disfigurement is corrected by plastic surgery, dramatic psychologic changes result *only* if there is a corresponding correction of the mutilated self-image. Sometimes the image of a disfigured self persists even after successful surgery, much the same as the "phantom limb" may continue to feel pain years after the physical arm or leg has been amputated.

I Begin a New Career

These observations led me into a new career. In 1945 or so, I became definitively convinced that many of the people who consult a plastic surgeon need more than surgery and that some do not need surgery at all. If I were to treat these people as patients, as a whole person rather than as merely a nose, ear, mouth, arm or leg, I needed to be in a position to give them something more. I needed to be able to show them how to obtain a psychological, emotional, and spiritual face lift, how to remove emotional scars, how to channel their attitudes and thoughts as well as modify their physical appearance.

This determination launched me on a continuing process of pointed observation, documenting my own case histories, lecturing both to peers and to the public, then writing this book, first published in 1960. This book caught the public's imagination in a special way. It was excerpted in popular magazines including *Reader's Digest* and *Cosmopolitan*, purchased by the thousands by corporations for their salespeople and other employees, adopted by top athletes, coaches and teams, including the Vince Lombardi-coached Green Bay Packers. Its success led quickly to many speaking engagements, seminar tours, radio and television interviews, even my own radio program. Invitations to speak about my discoveries came from churches, colleges, and corporations. Ultimately, I also wrote several other books, extensions of this one, including *The Magic Power of Self-Image*. Late in my life, three decades after its first publication, I was gratified that *Psycho-Cybernetics* continues to sell tens of thousands of copies each year, almost entirely thanks to word-of-mouth recommendations, and is inspiring new interpretations.

With each passing year, as I accumulated more experience teaching the power of self-image, counseling, and monitoring the results people achieved with this information, I became more convinced than ever that what each of us really wants, deep down, is more *life*—something I termed *aliveness*, the experience of living a life unrestricted by self-image-imposed, artificial limits. Happiness, success, peace of mind—whatever your own conception of supreme good may be—is experienced in its essence as more life. When we experience expansive emotions of happiness, self-confidence, and success, we enjoy more life. And to the degree that we inhibit our abilities, frustrate our God-given talents, and allow ourselves to suffer anxiety, fear, self-condemnation and self-hate, we literally choke off the life force available to us and turn our back on the gift that our Creator has made. To the degree that we deny the gift of life, we embrace death.

Your New Program for Liberated Living

In my opinion, the professions of psychology and psychiatry are often far too pessimistic regarding people and their potential for self-directed change, even greatness. Since psychologists and psychiatrists deal with so-called "abnormal" people, the literature is almost exclusively taken up with various abnormalities, with some people's tendencies toward self-destruction. Many people, I am afraid, have read so much of this type of viewpoint that they have come to regard such things as hatred, the destructive instinct, guilt, self-condemnation, and all the other negatives as normal human behavior. Average persons feel awfully weak and impotent when they think of the prospect of pitting their puny will against these negative forces in human nature, in order to gain health and happiness. If this were a true picture of human nature and the human condition, self-improvement would indeed be a rather futile thing.

However, I believe—and the experiences of my many patients have confirmed the fact—that you do not have to do the job alone. There is within each one of us a *life instinct*, which is forever working toward health, happiness, and all that makes for more life for the individual. This life instinct works *for you* through what I call the Creative Mechanism or, when used correctly, the Automatic Success Mechanism that is built into each human being.

In this book, I will endeavor to give you very practical ideas and instructions for liberating your own self-image, fully activating your own Automatic Success Mechanism. If you will give all this a reasonable chance, I'm confident you too will be pleasantly amazed at all the positive changes you will experience.

New Scientific Insights into the Subconscious Mind

There is admittedly debate about the actual, structural makeup of the human mind. Crammed into your brain are more neurons than there are stars in the Milky Way, hundreds of billions of them—an unimaginable number. Each of these neurons receives input from tens of thousands of the other neurons and sends messages to tens of thousands of others, adding up to over one million-billion connections. In his book about the brain, *Bright Air, Brilliant Fire*, neuroscientist Gerald Edelman speculated that if you were to attempt counting the links, one per second, you might finish 32 million years later.

The operation is something roughly akin to your clicking on the "you've got mail" beeping icon on your computer and finding 10,000 or 20,000 e-mail messages that require sorting, prioritizing, organizing, and responding to, just to get everything right so that you can accomplish the first simple task of your day, such as tying your shoelaces. You would "melt down" at the prospect, but your brain handles it in nanoseconds with aplomb.

The brain is roughly three pounds, yet it contains the equivalent of entire cities full of giant buildings full of computer circuitry. It is surely the most complex and amazing thing we will ever discover. And it is still a frontier because research keeps uncovering new revelations about how the human mind operates.

On top of the "mechanical" aspects, there are psychological and spiritual matters, the issue of mind as the pathway to the soul, the conscious and subconscious, the Freudian concept of id, the idea of three operating systems rather than two (reptilian, limbic, and cerebral), left brain-right brain, and on and on.

My take on all this has been criticized by some as simplistic. It's possible that research continuing long after my departure will eventually demonstrate that I've been partly right and partly wrong, and will produce even better insights into practical self-improvement. If and when that occurs, I'd applaud. But for now, let me just say that to you it shouldn't matter much whether some professor of psychology with lots of letters after his name looks down his nose at what we are discussing as oversimplistic. Let's you and I focus on the most important point: *what works*. And I can assure you that what we are discussing here has worked for thousands and thousands and thousands of people, and will work for you. By "work" I mean empower you to get more of what you want out of life.

My exploration of the science of cybernetics convinced me that the so-called "subconscious mind" is not a mind at all, but a goal-striving *servo-mechanism* consisting of the brain and nervous system, which is *used and directed* by the mind. The most usable concept is that man does not have two minds, but rather a mind (or consciousness), which operates an automatic, goal-striving machine. This automatic, goal-striving machine functions in much the same way as electronic servo-mechanisms function, but it is much more marvelous, much more complex, than any electronic brain, computer, or guided missile ever conceived by man.

The Creative Mechanism within you is impersonal. It will work automatically and impersonally to achieve goals of success and happiness, or unhappiness and failure, depending upon the goals you set for it. Present it with "success goals" and it functions as a "Success Mechanism." Present it with negative goals, and it operates just as impersonally and just as faithfully as a "Failure Mechanism." Like any other servo-mechanism, it must have a clear-cut target, objective, or problem to work upon.

In short, the goals you attempt to convey to this mechanism are filtered through the self-image, and if they are inconsistent with the self-image, they are rejected or modified. By discovering how to alter your self-image, you end its conflict with your goals. Then if you can communicate your goals directly to your Creative Mechanism, it will do what is necessary for you to achieve them.

Like any other servo-mechanism, our Creative Mechanism uses the information and data that we feed into it (our thoughts, beliefs, interpretations). Through our attitudes and interpretations of situations, we describe the problem to be worked on.

If we feed information and data into our Creative Mechanism to the effect that we ourselves are unworthy, inferior, undeserving, incapable (negative self-image), this data is processed and acted on as any other data in giving us the "answer" in the form of objective experience. When someone we know acts—or when we behave—in a way that is astoundingly "wrong" and wonder why, the answer is basically miscommunication with the servo-mechanism; the servo-mechanism is functioning perfectly but acting on a severe misunderstanding.

In the excellent book *Battling the Inner Dummy (ID)—The Craziness of Apparently Normal People*, David Weiner and Dr. Gilbert Hefter state, "It is apparent that even the most civilized among us have an inner craziness, a potential for irrationality with which we must contend." The computer jargon, usually used by computer experts shrugging their shoulders at some wild malfunction, is GIGO— Garbage In, Garbage Out. In other words, if neuron channels process enough "garbage" and link together in a certain way, the outcome or output is "garbage behavior."

Like any other servo-mechanism, our Creative Mechanism makes use of stored information, or "memory," in solving current problems and responding to current situations. Sometimes this "stored data" can remain in control long after any truth or usefulness has evaporated. Again quoting from *Battling the Inner Dummy*, this example:

> "You are no good, you will never amount to anything" we might be told by our father at the age of ten, after we just failed a math quiz in school. This is the kind of statement that might become a limbic memory within our id, our Inner Dummy, and remain with us for years, if not for a lifetime ..."

The reason it would remain with us rather than just bounce off like water off a duck's back is what they call *limbic memory*, or what I view only slightly differently as self-image imprinting. This is most controlled by three factors: authoritative source, intensity, and repetition. What we hear from a source we accept as authoritative—such as the father we see as omnipotent, from whom we desperately seek acceptance as a child—is given far more weight than the same statements if heard from what is to us at the time a less credible source. What we see, hear, or experience with intensity—such as the father yelling it at us, in front of others, making us humiliated—has added weight. And what we hear repetitively from authoritative sources has even more weight. Years after this "programming" has ceased, it may still be governing all sorts of behavior, because the servo-mechanism continues acting upon it as current.

Your program for more liberated living consists in, first of all, learning something about this Creative Mechanism, or automatic guidance system within you. In the process, you will learn how to use it as a Success Mechanism, rather than as a Failure Mechanism. Second, you will actually "program," and "reprogram," or "engineer," the personality and the life experiences you desire.

It is not widely known, but the controversial Dr. Timothy Leary, a 1960s hippie icon but also a scientist, was as fascinated with the link between mechanical cybernetics and the workings of the human mind as I. In an interview in 1992, Leary stated, "It is a genetic imperative to explore the brain. Because it's there. If you're carrying around in your head 100 billion mainframe computers, you just have to get in there and learn how to operate them." I think it is your personal imperative to invest the time, energy, and study needed to better understand and use your mind power, including your self-image power.

He also said, "We can only understand our inner workings in terms of the external mechanical or tele-logical models that we build." This program now in your hands is exactly that: a path to greater understanding of your own mind, based on tele-logical models, such as guided missile and computer technologies.

The method itself consists in *learning*, *practicing*, and *experiencing* new habits of thinking, imagining, remembering, and acting in order to (1) develop an adequate and realistic self-image and (2) use your Creative Mechanism to bring success and happiness in achieving particular goals. While the human mind is an endlessly complex creation, and while you could read hundreds of texts by neuroscientists and be no further along in improving your use of your own mind, self-improvement with Psycho-Cybernetics can be remarkably simple and it offers rapid results.

**If you can remember, worry, or tie your shoe,
you can succeed with Psycho-Cybernetics!**

As you will see later, the method to be used consists of creative mental picturing, creatively experiencing through your imagination, and the formation of new automatic reaction patterns by "acting out" and "acting as if." You may already have read or heard quite a bit about such techniques and tried them with mixed or disappointing results. If so, it does *not* necessarily mean that you used them improperly, nor does it mean that you are somehow unable to use them successfully. It more likely means that you attempted applying the techniques in conflict with your self-image. Once you use them in concert with modifying, managing, and strengthening your self-image, you will see positive results.

I often told my patients that "If you can remember, worry, or tie your shoe, you will have no trouble applying this method." The things you are called upon to do are simple, but you must practice and "experience." Visualizing—creative mental picturing—is no more difficult than what you do when you remember a scene out of the past or worry about the future. Acting out new action patterns is no more difficult than "deciding," then following through on tying your shoes in a new and different manner each morning, instead of continuing to tie them in your old habitual way, without thought or decision.

All Those Who Have Benefited from Psycho-Cybernetics

You might be encouraged by a quick list of those who use these methods exactly as I am going to describe them to you as we proceed through this book.

Athletes

Psycho-Cybernetics and athletes have long been linked. In 1967, the newspapers reported that "the big thing now with the Green Bay Packers is Psycho-Cybernetics." This was the Vince Lombardi-era Packers, and Coach Lombardi, as well as famous players Jerry Kramer and Bart Starr, all carried their copies of the book with them and shared it with their teammates. A *New York Times* article from July 1968 reported on Yankee great Mickey Mantle uncovering Jim Bouton's copy of *Psycho-Cybernetics* and finding it full of handwritten margin notes.

Jack Nicklaus, the late Payne Stewart, and many other top golfers have made very specific statements about their reliance on "the mental side of golf." In a foreword to the book *Mind over Golf*, referring to his victories in the 1989 PGA Championship and the 1991 U.S. Open, Payne Stewart wrote, "With my old mind-set I don't think I would have been able to prevail in either of those major championships. But with my new mental approach, I was able to raise my game to the highest level when I had to." (*Mind over Golf*, incidentally, is written by Dr. Richard Coop, a professor of educational psychology at the University of North Carolina, a contributing editor to *Golf Magazine*, and a coach to many golfers. I recommend his book as a companion to this one, should golf be your recreation or vocation.)

In this book, you will also discover rodeo riders, Olympic athletes, football players, and many coaches who rely on Psycho-Cybernetics strategies in general, or specifically by name, to succeed.

Coaches

In 1997, The Psycho-Cybernetics Foundation received a letter from Linda Tyler Rollins, assistant athletic director for academic affairs at the University of North Texas. She wrote that she had been teaching from Psycho-Cybernetics for years and that, in a course for incoming scholarship athletes, "the vocabulary they become accustomed to during their academic and athletic careers at UNT is based on the concepts presented by Dr. Maltz before these students were born!"

A Boston psychologist now coaching pro golfers, profiled in *Golf Magazine*, Dr. Gloria Spitalny, says: "By my calculations, the average golfer spends about 86% of their time doing nothing but wrestling with their thoughts and emotions, feeling one way or another about what is taking place, feeling exhilaration or anger, struggling to keep focused, worrying about what's happened or what is up ahead." It only stands to reason that if 86% of the time spent playing the game is dominated by thought and emotion, not physical action, that 86% of the success/failure determination is due to management of thoughts and emotions, not swing mechanics or putting prowess. This same thing is true in every athletic activity, so more and more coaches are devoting more and more time and energy to mental preparation and psychological motivation. Several top coaches have written their own books about these subjects, notably including Pat Riley and Phil Jackson of the NBA. Brendan Suhr, former assistant head coach with Chuck Daly at the Detroit Pistons and the Orlando Magic, is a fan of Psycho-Cybernetics and, in a video program about Psycho-Cybernetics, explained that he used the principles in suggesting new "mental pictures" to players struggling with different aspects of the game.

Entrepreneurs and Business Leaders

Consider Ray Kroc, the milkshake machine salesman who looked at the McDonald brothers' little hamburger stand and envisioned something amazing. Long after McDonald's hamburger shops were everywhere, Mr. Kroc was asked in an interview how he felt about the tendency of competitive fast food restaurant chains to copy every new McDonald's idea, product, or promotion so quickly. He replied, "We can invent faster than they can copy." He was making a statement of self-image—an affirmation of confidence, initiative, and power—in regard to a set of circumstances that many people would complain about and feel threatened by. Every business visionary and leader of note has a similar "bring it on!" approach which, from a Psycho-Cybernetics standpoint, I admire.

Let me tell you one quick story about a remarkable young business leader by the name of Joe Polish. Joe is a carpet cleaner by trade, who discovered certain effective, albeit unorthodox, methods for marketing and promoting such a business, and used that as a springboard to develop a company that teaches and assists other carpet cleaners with their marketing. At last count, Joe's organization had nearly 4,000 carpet-cleaners as members from all over the United States and several foreign countries, with combined sales of over $800 million in cleaning services and products each year! Several hundred of those carpet-cleaning business owners belong to Joe's "telephone coaching program" too. Joe is a young man who has risen above a difficult family background, without a college education, and with no formal education in marketing, to become the leading figure in his entire industry. In fact, he was named the Person of the Year by the number one industry trade journal. Joe says that he has "worn out" his copy of *Psycho-Cybernetics* and recommends it to all his members, and has even held a special seminar for his members built around Psycho-Cybernetics, with the editor of this book as a guest speaker. The reason? As Joe says, "all the business and marketing knowledge and technical skills in the world coupled with the best products, prices and positioning are of far less value than they should be if the person who possesses them lacks the inner confidence needed to use them."

"One of the things we teach," Joe adds, "is how to sell at prices higher than your competition, and that has more to do with the individual business owner's self-image than it does with anything else."

Sales Professionals

Bill Brooks, a Founding Member of the Board of the Psycho-Cybernetics Foundation, has devised complex and sophisticated sales training systems for sales forces of some of America's biggest corporations. His High Impact Sales System has been the subject of several very fine books, including *You're Working Too Hard to Make a Living*. Bill has succeeded personally as a salesman and assisted thousands of others. And, while he is very focused on methodology, he freely admits that the most sophisticated, perfectly engineered system for selling cannot produce results in the hands of salespersons attempting to function in conflict and combat with their own self-images.

Zig Ziglar is arguably America's most celebrated motivational speaker and sales trainer. In his book *Secrets of Closing the Sale*, which has sold well over 250,000 copies, Zig writes: "The salesman's self-image has a direct bearing on his sales success... when your self-image is solid, you can go from one prospect to the next, regardless of the reception you get. As a salesperson it will help you enormously to understand that nobody on the face of this earth can make you feel inferior without your permission. Once you get your image right, then your sales world and your personal world will improve. Dr. Maxwell Maltz, author of Psycho-Cybernetics, said the purpose of all psychotherapy is to build the self-esteem, that is, the image of the patient … your self-image is important, so build a good one and you will be able to build your sales career bigger, better and faster."

• • •

In this book, you'll be privy to a handful of case histories involving sales professionals, including the man with the too-big nose and too-big ears. You will see that Psycho-Cybernetics crosses all occupational, vocational, educational, or situational borders to work almost as reliably and consistently as gravity! (Note: Chapter 16 of this book features five amazing stories of individuals' successes with Psycho-Cybernetics.)

But What About Genetics or "Natural Talent"?

The argument of genetic predestination is utterly without merit. Bunk.

In his outstanding book, *Profiles of Power and Success,* Dr. Gene Lundrum provides in-depth analytical, psychological profiles of fourteen extraordinarily successful visionaries and achievers, and flatly concludes that nurture, not nature, is the basis for success. "Based on the family histories of these visionaries, heritage had little or nothing to do with their success." Instead he identifies certain characteristics with which, he says, they were "programmed" and they "programmed themselves."

If genetic talent were the barrier to success you cannot overcome or the ultimate secret behind achievement, you would expect Walt Disney to have come from "breeding stock" evidencing extraordinary creativity and entrepreneurial accomplishment. Walt Disney's father failed in five different businesses, including a Florida motel. Master architect Frank Lloyd Wright's "sire" was an unemployed, itinerant minister, so inept he never kept any one job for more than a year.

Picasso's father was a mediocre artist at best. No, this isn't like breeding horses or show dogs.

Evidence abounds that the conditioned, programmed, nurtured, and directed self-image controls success, not a genetic transfer over which you have no control. You cannot select your parents. You can select your self-image with Psycho-Cybernetics.

Someone can argue this by pointing a finger at Michael Jordan or Tiger Woods. While it is true they each exhibit exceptional raw physical talent, that talent alone would surely have gone to waste without the healthy self-image conditioned through a variety of influences, not the least of which were "authoritative sources," such as Tiger's father or Michael's college coach, Dean Smith. And for every Jordan, I can point my finger to an athlete of admittedly "average" physical talent who rises to the very top of his sport. In baseball, Ty Cobb and Pete Rose come to mind. In football, Fran Tarkenton or Doug Flutie, both erroneously judged by the experts as "too small" to play the game, are examples.

Do not tolerate for a minute the idea that you are prohibited from any achievement by the absence of in-born talent or ability. This is a lie of the grandest order, an excuse of the saddest kind.

PRESCRIPTION

Begin collecting scrapbooks on persons, past or present, who exhibit both the qualities of character and personality and the life achievements to which you aspire. Select a different representative for each characteristic, each aspiration. Become the reigning expert in these peoples' lives by collecting and reading their biographies, autobiographies, articles about them, speeches made by them, others' analyses of them that can be found in books like Dr. Lundrum's, Napoleon Hill's, and others. Discover the almost universal absence of predisposition (from genetics and often from their early environment and upbringing) for the personality they developed and the accomplishments of their lives. Ferret out the forces, thoughts, and influences that actually shaped them. By making this your hobby, you will feed your imagination with valuable raw material that it can utilize to build the stronger, more goal-oriented self-image you require to achieve your life aspirations.

In *Mind over Golf,* Coop tells golfers:

If you've attended a PGA or LPGA Tour event and found your own swing seemed to contain a little more rhythm and tempo than usual the next time you played, it was no accident. By watching the tour professionals swing their clubs with proper pace, you were able to absorb some of their talent and it showed in your game. This is common for many golfers of all talent levels. Even the most disjointed golfer begins to look rhythmical after observing smooth swingers such as Mark O'Meara, Gene Littler, or Nancy Lopez. The problem is that the newfound tempo doesn't last very long unless you're able to reinforce your visualization by regularly watching the tour pros.

This is exactly what I'm suggesting you do: "watch" the people who best exemplify the characteristics you wish to strengthen and who are living as you aspire to live by studying them through every media and source available.

MENTAL TRAINING EXERCISE

Pick someone to thoroughly study for a month, to get so intimately familiar with the way he or she thinks that you can sit down and have a conversation with the person and solicit advice and coaching in your imagination.

CHAPTER TWO

How to Awaken the Automatic Success Mechanism Within You

If one advances confidently in the direction of his dreams,
and endeavors to live the life which he has imagined,
he will meet with a success unexpected in common hours.
—Henry David Thoreau

When I first began getting serious about pondering the inner workings of the mind, I was amused to read an article by R. W. Gerard, in the June 1946, issue of *Scientific Monthly* on the brain and imagination, in which he stated that it was sad but true that most of our understanding of the mind would remain as valid and useful if, for all we knew, the cranium were stuffed with cotton wadding.

Since then, of course, understanding of how the human mind operates has expanded exponentially. Much of the thanks goes to the computer industry. When humans set out to build an "electronic brain" and to construct goal-striving mechanisms within computers, we *had* to discover and utilize certain basic principles. Having discovered them, scientists began to ask themselves: Could this be the way the human brain works also? Could it be that in making man, our Creator had provided us with a servo-mechanism more marvelous and wonderful than any electronic brain or guidance system ever dreamed of by man, *but operating according to the same basic principles?* In the opinion of famous cybernetic scientists like Dr. Norbert Weiner, Dr. John von Newmann, and others, the answer was an unqualified "yes."

Your Built-In Guidance System

Every living thing has a built-in guidance system or goal-striving device, put there by its Creator to help it achieve its goal—which is, in broad terms, to "live." In the simpler forms of life, the goal to live simply means physical survival for both the individual and the species. The built-in mechanism in animals is limited to finding food and shelter, avoiding or overcoming enemies and hazards, and procreating to ensure the survival of the species.

In humans, the goal to live means more than mere survival. Humans have certain emotional and spiritual needs that animals do not have. Consequently, for them to "live" encompasses more than physical survival and procreation of the species. It requires certain emotional and spiritual satisfactions as well. The built-in human Success Mechanism is also much broader in scope than an animal's. In addition to avoiding or overcoming danger, and the "sexual instinct" that helps keep the race alive, the human Success Mechanism can help him get answers to problems, invent, write poetry, run a business, sell merchandise, explore new horizons in science, attain more peace of mind, develop a better personality, or achieve success in any other activity that is intimately tied in to "living" or that makes for a fuller life.

It is important to accept that you possess just such a Success Mechanism.

The Success "Instinct" in Action

A squirrel does not have to be taught how to gather nuts, nor does it need to learn that it should store them for winter. A squirrel born in the spring has never experienced winter. Yet in the fall of the year it can be observed busily storing nuts to be eaten during the winter months when there will be no food to be gathered. A bird does not need to take lessons in nest-building, nor does it need to take courses in navigation. Yet birds navigate thousands of miles, sometimes over open sea. They have no newspapers or TV to give them weather reports, no books written by explorer or pioneer birds to map out for them the warm areas of the earth. Nonetheless the bird "knows" when cold weather is imminent and the exact location of a warm climate even though it may be thousands of miles away.

In attempting to explain such things, we usually say that animals have certain "instincts" to guide them. Analyze all such instincts and you will find they assist the animal to successfully cope with its environment. In short, animals have a "success instinct."

We often overlook the fact that humans also have a success instinct, much more marvelous and much more complex than that of any animal. Our Creator did not short-change us. On the other hand, we are especially blessed in this regard. Animals cannot select their goals. Their goals (self-preservation and procreation) are preset, so to speak. And their Success Mechanism is limited to these built-in goal images, which we call "instincts." Humans, on the other hand, have something animals haven't: Creative Imagination. Thus humans, of all creatures, are more than creatures; they are also creators. With imagination, they can formulate a variety of goals. They alone can direct their Success Mechanism by the use of imagination or imaging ability.

You might say that animals are hard-wired, and that is that. But we operate with software and can continually alter our output.

Thus, a formula emerges:

You, As Creator of Your Own Life Experiences

(1) Conscious Mind Decision + (2) Imagination
Communicates Goal/Target to (3) Self-Image
= (4) "Work Order"Instructions to
Servo-Mechanism

We often think of Creative Imagination as applicable only to poets, inventors, and the like. But imagination is creative in everything we do. Although they did not understand why or how imagination sets our creative mechanism into action, serious thinkers of all ages, as well as hard-headed practical men, have recognized the fact and made use of it. "Imagination rules the world," said Napoleon. "The faculty of imagination is the great spring of human activity, and the principal source of human improvement ... Destroy this faculty, and the condition of man will become as stationary as that of the brutes," said Dugold Stewart, the famous Scottish philosopher.

"You can imagine your future," said hard-nosed industrialist Henry J. Kaiser, who attributed much of his success in business to the constructive, positive use of creative imagination.

Contemporary business leaders also acknowledge the importance and power of imagination:

Consider the role of imagination in the remarkable rise of Starbucks Coffee. In his book *Pour Your Heart into It: How Starbucks Built a Company One Cup at a Time*, its CEO Howard Schultz talks of strolling the streets of Italian towns and having his imagination captured by the little sidewalk coffee or espresso bars, packed with happy people, infused with energy, even romance. Schultz saw an opportunity, as he puts it, to reinvent a routine commodity—coffee. He noted: *"If it captures your imagination, it will captivate others."*

The Starbucks shop you visit today is the result of Schultz' imaginative efforts to replicate the romantic, happy experience of the Italians and their espresso bars in your downtown or your shopping center.

Mr. Schultz writes: "Every Starbucks store is carefully designed to enhance the quality of everything the customers see, touch, hear, smell or taste ... what's the first thing you notice when you approach a Starbucks store? Almost always, it's the aroma. Aroma triggers memories more strongly than any of the other senses, and it obviously plays a major role in attracting people to our stores. Keeping that coffee aroma pure is no easy task." He goes on to describe how they banned smoking before it became the norm and do not sell certain foods in deference to the purity of the aroma, how they carefully select only certain kinds of background music over which the hiss of the espresso machine and the swish of the metal scoop shoveling out fresh beans can be heard, and on and on. Such intense attention to every minute detail requires imagination!

Howard Schultz' "creation" of the Starbucks experience echoes the phenomenal imagination-to-reality leadership of Walt Disney. Pick just about any Disney attraction and look closely, and you will notice amazing attention to detail born of the imagination. Former Disney confidante and creative thinking consultant to companies like Apple Computer and GE, Mike Vance gives us this insight into the creation of the Blue Bayou restaurant inside Disneyland, then replicated at Disney World, in his book *Think Outside The Box*:

> If you were designing a restaurant with a New Orleans theme, the Blue Bayou restaurant, *what would you picture in your mind?* The Louisiana bayou country? Shadowy swamps? And what else? No shadowy, mysterious swamp is complete without fireflies darting about ... what about the

distinctive aromas lingering in the air of Old New Orleans? Roasting coffee with chicory adulterating the brew adds to the unmistakable ambiance of the French Quarter. The chicory aroma of fresh coffee was circulated through the restaurant's air conditioning system ... the strains of that Dixieland band in the background, combined with the distinctive sounds of crickets chirping and a lone banjo, picking out a lazy melody in the distance.

Mike notes that you may not identify each of these and other details but that, combined, they transport you to a different place and time.

Virtually every person who visits Disneyland or DisneyWorld once, as a child or adult, returns more than once—a 100% retention of customers! It is no happy accident. It is imagination power put to the most practical of uses, for corporate profit.

Of course, many people waste much of their imagination power, frittering it away on aimless daydreaming and fantasy, with no real appreciation for what it might do if applied purposefully.

The sun's light, diffused, is gentle warmth; directed through a magnifying glass in a certain way, it is incendiary.

The imagination, aimless, may provide pleasant entertainment. Applied purposefully, it can effectively program your self-image and, in turn, your Automatic Success Mechanism to realize whatever goals you choose.

How Your Automatic Success Mechanism Works

You are not a machine, not a computer.

But in a very real sense, you have an awesomely powerful computer-like success machine at your disposal. Your physical brain and nervous system make up a servo-mechanism that you use and that operates very much like a computer, a mechanical goal-seeking device. Your brain and nervous system constitute a goal-striving mechanism that operates automatically to achieve a certain goal, very much as a self-aiming torpedo or missile seeks out its target and steers its way to it. Your built-in servo-mechanism functions both as a "guidance system" to automatically steer you in the right direction to achieve certain goals or to make correct responses to environment, and also as an "electronic brain," which can function automatically to solve problems, give you needed answers, and provide new ideas or inspirations.

The word *cybernetics* comes from a Greek word meaning literally "the steersman." Servo-mechanisms are so constructed that they automatically "steer" their way to a goal, target, or "answer." In 1948, the physicist Dr. Norman Weiner began using "cybernetics" to denote the field of study of control and communication in animals, humans, and machines. In Psycho-Cybernetics, we are learning to more effectively communicate with and through the self-image so as to better control the servo-mechanism within.

Your servo-mechanism is capable of being an Automatic Success Mechanism or an Automatic Failure Mechanism. That depends on what marching orders or programming it gets through your self-image.

When we conceive of the human brain and nervous system as a form of servo-mechanism, operating in accordance with cybernetic principles, we gain a new insight into the why and wherefore of human behavior.

I chose to call this new concept "Psycho-Cybernetics": the principles of Cybernetics as applied to the human brain.

I must repeat. Psycho-Cybernetics does not say that a human being is a computer. Rather, it says that we *have* a computer that we use. Let us examine some of the similarities between mechanical servo-mechanisms, such as computers, and the human brain:

Understanding the Two General Types of Servo-Mechanisms

Servo-mechanisms are divided into two general types: (1) where the target, goal, or "answer" is *known* and the objective is to reach it or accomplish it; (2) where the target or "answer" is *not known* and the objective is to discover or locate it. The human brain and nervous system operate in both ways.

An example of the first type is the self-guided torpedo or the interceptor missile. The target or goal is known—an enemy ship or plane. The objective is to reach it. Such machines must "know" the target they are shooting for. They must have some sort of propulsion system that propels them forward in the general direction of the target. They must be equipped with "sense organs" (radar, sonar, heat perceptors, etc.), which bring information from the target. These "sense organs" keep the machine informed when it is on the correct course (positive feedback) and when it commits an error and gets off course (negative feedback). The machine does not react or respond to positive feedback. It is doing the correct thing already and just keeps on doing what it is doing.

There must be a corrective device, however, that responds to negative feedback. When negative feedback informs the mechanism that it is off the beam—e.g., too far to the right—the corrective mechanism automatically causes the rudder to move so that it will steer the machine back to the left. If it overcorrects and heads too far to the left, this mistake is made known through negative feedback, and the corrective device moves the rudder so it steers the machine back to the right. The torpedo accomplishes its goal by *going forward, making errors, and continually correcting them.* By a series of zigzags, it literally "gropes" its way to the goal.

Dr. Norbert Weiner, who pioneered the development of goal-seeking mechanisms in World War II, believes that something very similar to the foregoing happens in the human nervous system whenever you perform any purposeful activity, even in such a simple goal-seeking situation as picking up a pencil from a table.

We are able to accomplish the goal of picking up the pencil because of an automatic mechanism, not by "will" or conscious thinking alone. All that the conscious thought does is to select the goal, trigger it into action by desire, and feed information to the automatic mechanism so that your hand continually corrects its course.

In the first place, said Dr. Weiner, only an anatomist would know all the muscles involved in picking up the pencil. And if you knew, you would not consciously say to yourself, "I must contract my shoulder muscles to elevate my arm, now I must contract my triceps to extend my arm, etc." You just go ahead and pick up the pencil and are not conscious of issuing orders to individual muscles, nor of computing just how much contraction is needed.

When "you" select the goal and trigger it into action, an automatic mechanism takes over. First of all, you have picked up a pencil or performed similar movements before. Your automatic mechanism has learned something of the correct response needed. Next, your automatic mechanism uses feedback data furnished to the brain by your eyes, which tell it "the degree to which the pencil is not picked up." This feedback data enables the automatic mechanism to continually correct the motion of your hand, until it is steered to the pencil.

Picking up a pencil probably isn't very exciting.

But it should be, because the little process just described that we use to pick up a pencil or perform any number of other routine, unchallenging tasks is exactly the same process we can use to achieve much more complex and seemingly challenging goals. What's exciting is that you "own" the process and use it constantly. No new goal-achieving capabilities are needed and none are lacking.

In other words, if you can pick up a pencil, you can speak confidently and persuasively to large audiences, or write compelling advertising, or start a business, or play golf or— you name it. You already "own" the "process."

In a baby, just learning to use its muscles, the correction of the hand in reaching for a rattle is very obvious. The baby has little stored information to draw upon. Its hand zigzags back and forth and gropes obviously as it reaches. As learning takes place, correction becomes more and more refined. We see this in a person just learning to drive a car, who overcorrects and zigzags back and forth across the street.

Once, however, a correct or successful response has been accomplished, it is remembered for future use. The automatic mechanism then duplicates this successful response on future trials. It has learned how to respond successfully. It remembers its successes, forgets its failures, and repeats the successful action as a habit.

This is why the most adept, successful achievers in different fields appear to be succeeding so effortlessly. Top-performing sales professionals respond to prospects' objections or concerns without missing a beat, say just the right thing at just the right time. Their responses have become habits—instinctive, in a way.

You already have reached this point with any number of things you do well. This fact, that you have done so, guarantees that you can do so again, for any other purpose you choose.

How Your Brain Finds Answers to Problems

Let's return to our examination of "the process." Now let us suppose that the room is dark so that you cannot see the pencil. You know, or hope, there is a pencil on the table, along with a variety of other objects. Instinctively, your hand begins to grope back and forth, performing zigzag motions (or "scanning"), rejecting one object after another, until the pencil is found and "recognized." This is an example of the second type of servo-mechanism. Recalling a name temporarily forgotten is another example. A "scanner" in your brain roams through your stored memories until the correct name is recognized.

An electronic brain solves problems in much the same way. First, a great deal of data must be fed into the machine. This stored, or recorded, information is the machine's "memory." A problem is posed to the machine. It scans back through its memory until it locates the only answer that is consistent with and meets all the conditions of the problem. Problem and answer, together, constitute a "whole" situation or structure. When part of the situation or structure (the problem) is given to the machine, it locates the only "missing parts," or the right size brick, so to speak, to complete the structure.

You are familiar with this in search engines on the Internet and search functions within computer software. The earliest versions of these in computers were relatively slow, awkward, and inefficient. Today's versions are lightning fast by comparison, but still very limited in scope and power if compared to the equivalent "search engine" included in your own mind. People who become very committed practitioners of Psycho-Cybernetics get very, very good at using their internal search engines. Many writers and speakers, for example, tell me of giving their subconscious instructions about their need for a good anecdote, story, joke, or forgotten details of a story for a writing task or speech, then taking a nap, to awake with exactly the material they wanted "on their minds."

A Look at the Automatic Mechanism in Action

We marvel at the awesomeness of interceptor missiles that can compute in a flash the point of interception of another missile and be there at the correct instant to make contact. The "smart bombs" we witnessed during the Desert Storm conflict utilized technology of this kind. Today's technology is far superior to what guided torpedoes in World War II submarines, and it is arguably possible for the so-called Star Wars defense system advocated by President Reagan to eventually become reality.

Yet are we not witnessing something just as amazing each time we see a center fielder catch a fly ball? To compute where the ball will fall or where the "point of interception" will be, he must take into account the speed of the ball, its curvature of fall, its direction, windage, initial velocity, and the rate of progressive decrease in velocity. He must compute just how fast he must run, and in what direction in order to arrive at the point of interception at the same time or before the ball does. The center fielder doesn't even think about this. His built-in goal-striving mechanism computes it for him from data that he feeds it through his eyes and ears. The computer in his brain takes this information, compares it with stored data (memories of other successes and failures in catching fly balls). All necessary computations are made in a flash and orders are issued to his leg muscles—and he "just runs."

Science Can Build the Computer but Not the Operator

Dr. Weiner said that at no time in the foreseeable future will scientists be able to construct an electronic brain anywhere near comparable to the human brain. "I think that our gadget conscious public has shown an unawareness of the special advantages and special disadvantages of electronic machinery, as compared with the human brain," he says. "The number of switching devices in the human brain vastly exceeds the number in any computing machine yet developed, or even thought of for design in the near future."

His prophesy remains true as of this writing. To be sure, many miraculous computer-type machines and gadgets have come into our hands since Dr. Weiner first tinkered with cybernetics. What once consumed rooms of space now fits in a hard drive that sits on your desk top. Still, nothing compares with your system of imagination, self-image, servo-mechanism.

But even should such a computer be built, it would lack a programmer. A computer cannot pose problems to itself. It has no imagination and cannot set goals for itself. It cannot determine which goals are worthwhile and which are not. It has no emotions. It cannot feel. It works only on new data fed to it by an operator, by feedback data it secures from its own "sense organs" and from information previously stored.

Are You Connected to an Infinite Storehouse of Ideas, Knowledge, and Power?

Many great thinkers of all ages have believed that a human being's "stored information" is not limited to personal memories of past experiences and learned facts. "There is one mind common to all individual men," said Emerson, who compared our individual minds to the inlets in an ocean of universal mind.

Thomas Edison believed that he got some of his ideas from a source outside himself. Once, when complimented for a creative idea, he disclaimed credit, saying that "ideas are in the air," and if he had not discovered it, someone else would have.

Dr. J. B. Rhine, once head of Duke University's Parapsychology Laboratory, has proved experimentally that people have access to knowledge, facts, and ideas other than their own individual memories or stored information from learning or experience. Telepathy, clairvoyance, and precognition have been established by countless scientific laboratory experiments. Our government, the Russian government, and other nations have quietly invested huge sums and many years of ongoing research into such matters.

In recent years people have brought these subjects to the public more as entertainment than science, such as Uri Geller or The Amazing Kreskin. While much of what passes for telepathy in magicians' and mentalists' stage performances is nothing but trickery, both Geller and Kreskin have had their abilities documented in laboratory settings. Kreskin himself insists that everybody possesses the same abilities as he does; the difference is in development and use.

I am admittedly more interested in the thinking of a Thomas Edison than a Kreskin on this, but if you look at the entire span of research and relevant writings from the 1920s to the present, you'll find one common thread of great potential use to you, and directly related to Psycho-Cybernetics:

You can give problem-solving or idea-getting tasks to your servo-mechanism, send it off on a search while you do other things, even while you sleep, and have it return with useful material you didn't know you knew and might never have obtained through conscious thought or worry.

This becomes a common experience and great benefit for those of us who regularly rely on Psycho-Cybernetics. It occurs because the servo-mechanism has access to a much more expansive storehouse of information than the conscious mind.

The famous composer Schubert is said to have told a friend that his own creative process consisted in "remembering a melody" that neither he nor anyone else had ever thought of before. Many creative artists, as well as psychologists who have made a study of the creative process, have been impressed by the similarity between creative inspiration, sudden revelation, or intuition, and ordinary human memory.

Searching for a new idea or an answer to a problem is, in fact, very similar to searching memory for a name you have forgotten. You know that the name is "there" or else you would not search. The scanner in your brain scans back over stored memories until the desired name is "recognized" or "discovered."

The Answer Exists Now

In much the same way, when we set out to find a new idea or the answer to a problem, we must *assume that the answer exists already some-*

where and set out to find it. Dr. Norbert Wiener has said, "Once a scientist attacks a problem which he knows to have an answer, his entire attitude is changed. He is already some fifty per cent of his way toward that answer" (Norbert Wiener, *The Human Use of Human Beings*).

When you set out to do creative work—whether in selling, managing a business, writing a sonnet, improving human relations, or whatever—you begin with a goal in mind, an end to be achieved, a "target" answer, which, although perhaps somewhat vague, will be "recognized" when achieved. If you really mean business, have an intense desire, and begin to think intensely about all angles of the problem, your creative mechanism goes to work and the scanner we spoke of earlier scans back through stored information or gropes its way to an answer. It selects an idea here, a fact there, a series of former experiences, and relates them—or ties them together into a meaningful whole that will fill out the incomplete portion of your situation, complete your equation, or solve your problem. When this solution is served up to your consciousness—often at an unguarded moment when you are thinking of something else, or perhaps even as a dream while your consciousness is asleep—something clicks and you at once recognize this as the answer you have been searching for.

In this process, does your creative mechanism also have access to stored information in a universal mind? Numerous experiences of creative workers would seem to indicate that it does. How else, for example, can you explain the experience of Louis Agassiz, told by his wife?

> He had been striving to decipher the somewhat obscure impression of a fossil fish on the stone slab in which it was preserved. Weary and perplexed, he put his work aside at last and tried to dismiss it from his mind. Shortly after, he waked one night persuaded that while asleep he had seen his fish with all the missing features perfectly restored.
>
> He went early to the Jardin des Plantes, thinking that on looking anew at the impression he would see something to put him on the track of his vision. In vain—the blurred record was as blank as ever. The next night he saw the fish again, but when he waked it disappeared from his memory as before. Hoping the same experience might be repeated, on the third night he placed a pencil and paper beside his bed before going to sleep.
>
> Towards morning the fish reappeared in his dream, confusedly at first, but at last with such distinctness that he no longer had any doubt as to its zoological characters. Still half dreaming, in perfect darkness, he traced these characters on the sheet of paper at the bedside.

In the morning he was surprised to see in his nocturnal sketch features which he thought it impossible the fossil itself would reveal. He hastened to the Jardin des Plantes and, with his drawing as a guide, succeeded in chiseling away the surface of the stone under which portions of the fish proved to be hidden. When wholly exposed, the fossil corresponded with his dream and his drawing, and he succeeded in classifying it with ease.

You're No Einstein

Sometimes a parent or teacher, frustrated at a young person's seeming inability to grasp mathematics, will utter the critical, disparaging, negative affirmation "He's no Einstein," walking away in disappointment and frustration. Well, it turns out that Einstein was no Einstein either! In the book *Sparks of Genius*, researchers and authors Robert and Michele Root-Bernstein disclose that Einstein's peers knew that Einstein was relatively weak in mathematics, often needing the assistance of mathematicians to do the "detail work" to push his ideas forward. Einstein wrote to one such person, "Do not worry about your difficulties in mathematics. I can assure you that mine are far greater."

Much of Einstein's celebrated success came about in his imagination, in very "unscience-like" ways. He once described an experiment in which he imagined himself to be a photon moving at the speed of light, imagined what he as a photon saw and *felt*, then imagined himself as a second photon pursuing the first. What kind of scientific experimentation is this? Where is the blackboard filled with chalky logarithms and formulas we typically associate with Einstein?

My own analysis of everything I've read about Albert Einstein is that he was a great practitioner of Psycho-Cybernetics. He acted as if a theoretical idea was a factual conclusion, then turned the "figuring out" over to his own servo-mechanism as well as to other "worker bees." I am convinced he connected with intelligence outside the realm of his own stored data through his imagination. He was a brilliant target setter. His accomplishments stand as testament to an individual's opportunity to rise above and beyond his or her stored knowledge, education, experience or skill through the power of imagination. You can too.

So What Exactly Is Psycho-Cybernetics?

You might think of Psycho-Cybernetics as a collection of insights, principles, and practical methods that enable you to do all of the following:

1. Conduct an accurate inventory and analysis of the contents of your self-image.

2. Identify erroneous and restrictive programming imbedded in your self-image and systematically alter it to better suit your purposes.

3. Use your imagination to reprogram and manage your self-image.

4. Use your imagination in concert with your self-image to effectively communicate with your servo-mechanism, so that it acts as an Automatic Success Mechanism, moving you steadily toward your goals, including getting back on course when confronted with obstacles.

5. Effectively use your servo-mechanism as something like a giant search engine, to provide precisely the idea, information, or solution you need for any particular purpose—even reaching beyond your own stored data to obtain it.

In a way, Psycho-Cybernetics is a communication system, for effectively communicating with yourself.

Get a New Mental Picture of Yourself

The unhappy, failure-type personality cannot develop a new self-image by pure willpower or by arbitrarily deciding to. There must be some grounds, some justification, some reason for deciding that the old picture of self is in error and that a new picture is appropriate. You cannot merely imagine a new self-image, unless you feel that it is based upon truth. Experience has shown that when people change their self-image, they have the feeling that, for one reason or another, they "see" or realize the truth about themselves.

The truth in this chapter can set you free of an old inadequate self-image—if you read it often, think intently about the implications, and "hammer home" its truths to yourself.

In her book *Revolution from Within: A Book of Self-Esteem*, Gloria Steinheim tells the story of the Royal Knights of Harlem, a prize-winning, championship school chess club improbably made up of a dozen "toughs" from Spanish Harlem. These kids were hanging out on the street, engaging in minor crime and violence, one foot mired in delinquency, experimenting with drugs. Most people who observed them quickly concluded they were useless, hopeless, dangerous, very unlikely to achieve anything much beyond a jail sentence, and unworthy of any investment. But Bill Hall, an "ordinary" school teacher, somehow saw potential here that no one else could see. And through the activity of a chess club, he engineered an environment and a series of experiences that changed the way these kids saw themselves.

Quite often, a person voted unlikely to succeed by others and by him- or herself fortunately encounters someone who sees a potential no one else sees, believes in him far more than he does in himself, and literally directs a change in that person's self-image through a determined influence. However, there is no need to wait for someone else to do this for you. You can do it for yourself with Psycho-Cybernetics, and, as you'll discover in this book, thousands have.

The fundamental message of Psycho-Cybernetics is that every human being has been literally "engineered for success" by the Creator. Every human being has access to a power greater than him- or herself. This means *you*.

If you were engineered for success and happiness, then any old picture of yourself as unworthy of happiness or inherently unable to excel in a certain aspect of life—of a person who was "meant" to fail—must be in error.

PRESCRIPTION

Read this chapter through at least three times per week for the first 21 days. Study it and digest it. Look for examples, in your experiences and in the experiences of your friends, that illustrate the creative mechanism in action. Think about limiting ideas about yourself that may be held firmly in the self-image, that may be the "cause" of "effects" you no longer desire.

MENTAL TRAINING EXERCISE

Memorize the following basic principles by which your Success Mechanism operates. You do not need to be a computer genius or a neurophysicist to operate your own servo-mechanism, anymore than you have to be able to engineer an automobile in order to drive one or become an electrical engineer in order to turn on the light in your room. You do need to be familiar with the following, however, because, having memorized them, they will throw "new light" on what is to follow:

1. = AIM Your built-in success mechanism must have a goal or "target." This goal, or target, must be conceived of as "already in existence now," either in actual or potential form. It operates either (1) by steering you to a goal already in existence or (2) by "discovering" something already in existence.

2. = TRUST The automatic mechanism is tele-logical; that is, it operates on, or must be oriented to, "end results," goals. Do not be discouraged because the means may not be apparent. It is the function of the automatic mechanism to supply the means when you supply the goal. Think in terms of the end result, and the means will often take care of themselves.

3. = RELAX Do not be afraid of making mistakes or of temporary failures. All servo-mechanisms achieve a goal by negative feedback, or by going forward, making mistakes, and immediately correcting course. Automatic course correction is one of the many benefits of Psycho-Cybernetics.

4. = LEARN Skill learning of any kind is accomplished by trial and error, mentally correcting your aim after an error, until you achieve a "successful" motion, movement, or performance. After that, further learning and continued success are accomplished by *forgetting the past errors*, and *remembering the successful response*, so that it can be "imitated."

5. = DO You must learn to trust your creative mechanism to do its work and not "jam it" by becoming too concerned or too anxious as to whether it will work or not, or by attempting to force it by too much conscious effort. You must let it work, rather than make it work. This trust is necessary because your creative mechanism operates below the level of consciousness, and you cannot "know" what is going on beneath the surface. Moreover, its nature is to operate spontaneously according to the present need. Therefore, you have no guarantees in

advance. It comes into operation as you act and as you place a demand on it by your actions. You must not wait to act until you have proof. You must act as if it is there, and it will come through. "Do the thing and you will have the power," said Emerson.

With all this in mind, select a "target"—whether that is a thinner, healthier you; a more confident, persuasive you; a you free of constant worry; a sales professional free of procrastination who begins each day with an organized to-do list and ends each day with it completed; or a golfer who hits perfectly straight drives. Devote just ten or fifteen minutes every day to taking that mental picture from a vague idea to a good sketch to a finely detailed, fully fleshed out and colored vision that occurs to you exactly the same way whenever called upon. If it helps to write out descriptions, or to draw illustrations on paper, or to collect relevant pictures from magazines, do so. Just stick to ten- or fifteen-minute sessions, when you close your eyes to the outer world and open them only to this picture's continuing development. Try this little experiment for 21 days, and see what happens.

The Strengthened and Empowered Automatic Success Mechanism

The ASM at Work

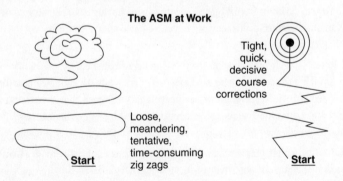

You accelerate personal development and goal achievement by providing your ASM with a clear, precisely detailed, vividly imagined, and perfectly communicated "target." As the target gets clearer, the ASM responds by doing its job more efficiently.

CHAPTER THREE

Imagination: The Ignition Key to Your Automatic Success Mechanism

To carry on a successful business a man must have imagination.
He must see things as in a vision, a dream of the whole thing.
—Charles M. Schwab, Industrialist

*I*magination plays a far more important role in our lives than most of us realize.

I have seen this demonstrated many times in my practice. A particularly memorable instance concerned a patient who was literally forced to visit my office by his family. He was a man of about 40, unmarried, who held down a routine job during the day and kept to himself in his apartment when the work day was over, never going anywhere, never doing anything. He had had many such jobs and never seemed able to stay with any of them for any great length of time.

His problem was that he had a rather large nose and ears that protruded a little more than normal. He considered himself "ugly" and "funny looking." He imagined that the people he came into contact with during the day were laughing at him and talking about him behind his back because he was so "odd." His imaginings grew so strong that he actually feared going out into the business world and moving among people. He hardly felt "safe" even in his own home. The poor man even imagined that his family was ashamed of him because he was "peculiar looking," not like "other people."

Actually, his facial deficiencies were not serious. His nose was of the classical Roman type, and his ears, though somewhat large, attracted no more attention than those of thousands of people with

43

similar ears. In desperation, his family brought him to me to see if I could help him. I saw that he did not need surgery, only an understanding of the fact that his imagination had wrought such havoc with his self-image that he had lost sight of the truth. He was not really ugly. People did not consider him odd and laugh at him because of his appearance. His imagination alone was responsible for his misery. His imagination had set up an automatic, negative failure mechanism within him and it was operating full blast, to his extreme misfortune. Fortunately, after several sessions with him and with the help of his family, he was able gradually to realize that the power of his own imagination was responsible for his plight, and he succeeded in building up a true self-image and achieving the confidence he needed by applying creative imagination rather than destructive imagination.

You might say he needed emotional surgery, not physical surgery with an actual scalpel.

In the latter years of my surgical practice, I became quite skilled at talking myself out of business!

This is an analogy for the experiences of thousands of people, quite possibly, in one way or another, including you. No, you may not feel ashamed of your nose or ears or any other physical feature, and you may not be a recluse. But many people believe there is something about them that causes others to look down on them, to ridicule them behind their backs, to reject them—something that prevents them from progressing in certain ways.

One of the smartest, most successful and prolific idea men I've ever known in the advertising field has had a lifelong pattern of rising to high income, then suddenly experiencing circumstances that "pull the rug out from under him," so that he must rebuild from scratch his reputation and his finances. One month he was living in a mansion, the next in a motel. He has admitted to me and to others that he has spent his entire life trying to escape the iron-fisted grip of what he calls his "white trash ancestry" and, to paraphrase Al Pacino in one of the Godfather movies, just as he gets out, he is again pulled back. Of course, this "thing" that keeps pulling him back does not exist in the physical world, only inside his own self-image. It is *his* "ugly nose and big ears." What's yours?

Ironically, even though his entire business is "the imagination business," he has yet to discover how to use his imagination as a scalpel in emotional surgery, to rid his self-image of its "big nose."

Creative imagination is not something reserved for the poets, the philosophers, the inventors. It enters into our every act. Imagination sets the goal picture that our automatic mechanism works on. We act, or fail to act, not because of will, as is so commonly believed, but because of imagination.

This is *the* most important statement to be gleaned from this entire book:

Human beings *always* act and feel and perform in accordance with what they *imagine* to be *true* about themselves and their environment.

You cannot long escape or outperform that picture.

You can dissect it, analyze it, uncover what is in it that is not true about yourself, and alter it. You can modify it without archaeological examination of the past.

But you cannot escape it. You will always act and perform—and experience appropriate results—in accordance with what you imagine to be true about yourself and your environment. This is a basic and fundamental law of mind. It is the way we are built.

When we see this law of mind graphically and dramatically demonstrated in a hypnotized subject, we are prone to think that there is something occult or supernormal at work, or to discredit it as simple stage illusion. Actually, what we are witnessing often is the normal operating processes of the human brain and nervous system.

For example, if a good hypnotic subject is told that she is at the North Pole, she will not only shiver and *appear* to be cold, her body will react just *as if she were cold*, and goose pimples will develop. The same phenomena has been demonstrated on wide awake college students by asking them to *imagine* that one hand is immersed in ice water. Thermometer readings show that the temperature drops in the "treated" hand. Tell a hypnotized subject that your finger is a red hot poker and he will not only grimace with pain at your touch, but his cardiovascular and lymphatic systems will react just as if your finger were a red hot poker and produce inflammation and perhaps a blister on the skin. In one demonstration, when college students, wide awake, have been told to *imagine* that a spot on their foreheads was hot, temperature readings documented an actual increase in skin temperature.

These are elementary experiments just one step away from the rather cruel but common children's game, the practical joke played at school—and sometimes by adults at work. In this prank, a person is secretly targeted by the group, then one person after another engages the target in conversation, asking "Aren't you feeling well, Bob?" "You look pretty white-faced." "Bob, are you feeling alright?" Soon poor Bob is in the restroom, checking himself out in the mirror. Before long Bob is feeling queasy and weak. Bob may even actually become so sick he must lie down or go home.

Your nervous system cannot tell the difference between an imagined experience and a "real" one. Your nervous system reacts appropriately to what you *think* or *imagine* to be true.

This phenomenon that can be produced as a practical joke or by a hypnotist on stage for entertainment is actually identical to, or illustrative of, the basic process that governs much of our behavior, and that can be taken ahold of and deliberately used to advantage.

How the Hypnotic Power of Negative Imagination Can Be a Fatal Disease

When I wrote my book for physicians in 1936, *New Faces—New Futures*, about the impact of plastic surgery on personality, I reprinted in it a newspaper article from a St. Louis newspaper headlined:

"Inferiority Complex" Caused by Long Nose
Drives College Student to Commit Suicide

This article reported the suicide of a 24-year-old student of Washington University, named Theodore Hofman. Ironically, the article reported that those who knew him considered him popular. Here is the text of this young man's suicide note:

To the world:

When I was a child, other children abused and mistreated me because I was weaker and uglier than they. I was a sensitive, bashful boy and was teased because of my face and long nose. The more they offended me, the more they teased. I became afraid of people. I knew that many of them hated me for things that I was not responsible for—my sentimental nature and my appearance. I was unable to speak to anyone. My confidence was gone. A teacher spelled my name with two "F's" although it has only one, yet I became so backward I was unable to correct her and therefore spelled it with two F's throughout my school career. God forgive everyone for this. I am afraid of the world but I'm not afraid to die.

At the time, a professor at the university judged this to be the most severe case of an inferiority complex ever known. Nonsense. Believe me, this young man's desperation, which first killed his self-image and then led him to take his own life, mirrors the same desperation affecting thousands and thousands of people—and missed entirely or underestimated in importance by the people around them. In fact, suicide among teenagers in recent years has reached epidemic proportions, though rarely discussed in the media.

Anorexia is a chilling demonstration of the hypnotic power of negative imagination. In *Battling the Inner Dummy*, the authors (David Weiner and Dr. Gilbert Hefter) describe an encounter with a 15-year-old girl, Ellen, shown on the CBS television program *48 Hours* in 1998. Ellen weighed only 82 pounds, and looked like a sickly child wasting away, but Ellen was firmly convinced she was fat. As a result, she avoided meals, refused to eat or would even purge herself after eating. In this child's hospital room, the television reporter interviewing her got her to stand in front of a full-length mirror and asked her if she saw how gaunt and weak she looked. "I think I look fat," Ellen insisted. The reporter then tried fact: "But you now weigh only 82 pounds. Do you think that is a person who is fat?" Ellen sensibly replied "No." But then Ellen immediately said that *she* was fat and would grow fatter if she ate. So, determined not to eat, Ellen would pull out the intravenous feeding needles if not closely supervised.

For parents, teachers, counselors, and coaches, this should be a cautionary tale, a vivid reminder of the need to be ever vigilant for some young person whose self-image is shrinking so dramatically that self-inflicted physical harm is likely to follow.

For all, it is a vivid illustration of the incredible power of imagination. A person can so magnify the importance of some flaw, and of the world's response to the flaw, with his own negative imagination that he commits suicide! A person can similarly so "color" her perceptions of her strengths and opportunities with her own positive imagination that she accomplishes the most amazing things.

The Secret of "Hypnotic Power"

In the 1950s, Dr. Theodore Xenophon Barber conducted extensive research into the phenomena of hypnosis, both when he was associated with the psychology department of American University in Washington, D.C., and also after becoming associated with the Laboratory of Social Relations at Harvard. Writing in *Science Digest*, he said:

> We found that hypnotic subjects are able to do surprising things only when *convinced* that the hypnotist's words are true statements .... When the hypnotist has guided the subject to the point where he is convinced that the hypnotist's words are *true statements*, the subject then behaves differently because he *thinks* and *believes* differently.
>
> The phenomena of hypnosis have always seemed mysterious because it has always been difficult to understand how belief can bring about such unusual behavior. It always seemed as if there must be something more, some unfathomable force or power, at work.
>
> However, the plain truth is that when a subject is convinced that he is deaf, he behaves as if he is deaf; when he is convinced that he is insensitive to pain, he can undergo surgery without anesthesia. The mysterious force or power does not exist. ("Could You Be Hypnotized?" *Science Digest*, January 1958).

Note that his comments were published in 1958. Today, hypnosis as a tool of therapy is widely accepted and used. For many, hypnosis and self-hypnosis to facilitate weight loss makes the surgical quick fix of liposuction unnecessary, a perfect analogy to my examples of emotional surgery versus actual surgery. In these cases, hypnosis is the scalpel. In dentistry, hypnosis is used to facilitate treatment of the phobic patient with virtually uncontrollable anxiety and, in many instances, proves to be a perfectly successful alternative to the problematic solution of anesthesia.

With regard to the links between childhood programming, past experiences and peer programming on one hand, and the imagination, the self-image and the servo-mechanism on the other, my conclusion is that people are literally hypnotized by their own self-images. In fact, many people virtually "sleep walk" through their entire lives under unrecognized hypnotic suggestion. In Quentin Reynolds' book *Intuition: Your Secret Power*, a hypnotist is quoted as saying: "Clients visit me hoping that I will put them in a trance and fix their lives. In fact many of them live in a trance and need a dose of reality."

If you are stuck in a dark elevator for a couple of frightening hours as a child, you may still be fearful of elevators, unable to get into an elevator forty years later, regardless of all the safety statistics, factual information, demonstration, observation of thousands using elevators, or even the daunting task of hiking up a dozen flights of stairs. You are still in the hypnotic trance from forty years ago!

Still, a little reflection will show why it is a very good thing for us that we do feel and act according to what we believe or imagine to be true. All of this does not mean the system itself is "bad"; it only requires learning how to better use the "system."

Truth Determines Action and Behavior

The human brain and nervous system are engineered to react automatically and appropriately to the problems and challenges in the environment. For example, a man does not need to stop and think that self-survival requires that he run if he meets a grizzly bear on a trail. He does not need to decide to become afraid. The fear response is both automatic and appropriate. First, it makes him want to flee. The fear then triggers bodily mechanisms that "soup up" his muscles so that he can run faster than he has ever run before. His heart beat is quickened. Adrenaline, a powerful muscle stimulant, is poured into the bloodstream. All bodily functions not necessary to running are shut down. The stomach stops working and all available blood is sent to the muscles. Breathing is much faster and the oxygen supply to the muscles is increased manyfold.

All this, of course, is nothing new. Most of us learned it in high school. What we have not been so quick to realize, however, is that the brain and nervous system that reacts automatically to environment is the same brain and nervous system that tells us what the environment is. The reactions of the man meeting the bear are commonly thought of as due to "emotion" rather than to ideas. Yet it was an *idea-information* received from the outside world and evaluated by the mind that sparked the so-called "emotional reactions." Thus, it was basically idea or belief that was the true causative agent, rather than emotion, which came as a result. In short, the man on the trail reacted to what he *thought, believed,* or *imagined* the environment to be. The messages brought to us from the environment consist of nerve impulses from the various sense organs. These nerve impulses are decoded, interpreted, and evaluated in the brain and made known to us in the form of ideas or mental images. In the final analysis, it is these mental images that we react to.

Note that I've used the terms *thought, believed,* and *imagined* as synonymous. In affecting your entire system, they are the same.

You act and feel not according to what things are really like, but according to the image your mind holds of what they are like. You have certain mental images of yourself, your world, and the people around you, and you behave as though these images were the truth, the reality, rather than the things they represent.

Suppose, for example, that the man on the trail had not met a real bear, but a movie actor dressed in a bear costume. If he thought and imagined the actor to be a bear, his emotional and nervous reactions would have been exactly the same. Or suppose he met a large shaggy dog, which his fear-ridden imagination mistook for a bear. Again, he would react automatically to what he believed to be true concerning himself and his environment.

It follows that, if our ideas and mental images concerning ourselves are distorted or unrealistic, then our reaction to our environment will likewise be inappropriate.

Can these causative factors change?

Certainly. Consider the child raised in an intentionally segregated environment by racists. The child could be a white person in a family of white supremacists who devoutly believe that blacks are "mud people," evil, and a threat to their well-being, or the child could be black in a family with comparable hatred for whites. Either way, the child is programmed with certain beliefs that will govern her behavior. In her imagination, she constructs certain truths that will be very difficult to modify as she matures. However, some people make a 180-degree change in their beliefs and behavior at some point in their lives. These days, this has even become a popular staple of the confrontation-style daytime TV talk shows. How does a person change? Through life experience broader and more diverse than her family upbringing, societal pressure, being befriended by people of the race she was programmed to hate, one way or another, *challenging what she believed to be true, discovering it is based on illusion, and replacing that truth with another truth.*

Now consider the child raised in a poor family, made up of people who profoundly believe that their unhappy circumstances are the fault of evil rich people and a corrupt government, who constantly program the child with class warfare ideas, and who insist that they just cannot get ahead no matter what they do. This truth may very well block that person's academic achievement, direct him away from college, have him blindly follow his father to work in the factory or the coal mine. (Well, I show my age with "coal mine," I suppose.) Yet even today, the basic path of accepting poverty as "fact" is prevalent in many, many people. But how does one person rise out of such a background to become a highly successful entrepreneur, for example? Through books he's exposed to, people he sees on television, the influence of a mentor, life experiences, one way or another challenging what he believed to be true, discovering it is based on illusion, and replacing that truth with another truth.

Just as the Knights Of Spanish Harlem I mentioned earlier transformed from street toughs to chess champions, from likely criminals to model citizens pursuing adult careers as doctors, lawyers, and businesspersons, you can change *from* anything *to* anything by changing your self-image, by providing it with new truth.

From fat and flabby to fit and strong. From mousy and timid to assertive and confident. From clumsy and awkward to capable and graceful. New evidence—actual, experiential evidence and/or vividly imagined, synthetic evidence and/or reinforcement from other authoritative influencers—convinces the self-image. In turn, it relays the appropriate new directives to your servo-mechanism, and a new truth exists, a new reality occurs.

Why Not Imagine Yourself Successful?

Realizing that our actions, feelings, and behavior are the result of our own images and beliefs gives us the lever that psychology has always needed for changing personality.

It opens a powerful psychological door to gaining skill, success, and happiness.

Mental pictures offer us an opportunity to practice new traits and attitudes, which otherwise we could not do. This is possible because, again, your nervous system cannot tell the difference between an actual experience and one that is vividly imagined.

If we picture ourselves performing in a certain manner, it is nearly the same as the actual performance. Mental practice is as powerful as actual practice.

When I first made this assertion, and when others began making it, it was a radical idea; that you could practice in your imagination and achieve comparable results to actual physical practice. Today, it is widely accepted, having been proved by countless trials and experiments. Athletes of every stripe routinely rely on mental or imagination practice. For example, consider Dr. Richard Coop's advice to golfers, as follows (italics are mine):

> Before you play any shot, you need to have a *mental picture* of how you want the ball to react once you deliver the clubhead to the ball. You need to have a definite, *positive visualization* of what your shot will look like. The *picture* should indicate the trajectory, the direction, the spot where you intend the ball to land, and how far you want the ball to roll when it lands ... if the flight of a shot is difficult for you to picture, try *visualizing* a strip of highway that curves in the manner that you wish your ball to travel. Your options in this *visualization* are limited only by your *imagination*. You might see the green as a pin cushion ready to accept your shot ... pick *visual images* that work for you. *Visualization* is one of the most individual aspects of golf psychology.

Jack Nicklaus has said, "I never hit a golf shot without having a sharp picture of it in my head. First I 'see' where I want the ball to finish. Then I 'see' it going there; its trajectory and landing. The next 'scene' shows me making the swing that will turn the previous images into reality." Take note of the striking similarities between The Golden Bear's description of what he actually does, Dr. Coop's instructions, and the instructions in this book.

It's important to understand that imagination practice need not be restricted to your golf or tennis swing. The same principles of mental practice apply to virtually anything, including broader behaviors, such as speaking up confidently and asserting your opinions in business meetings versus remaining intimidated and silent (and regretting it later), or directly asking prospects for orders rather than leaving sales presentations "hanging" with wimpy, vague endings. And so on.

I have developed a very specific regimen for mental or imagination practice, using what I call The Theater of the Mind, which I will get to later. Dr. Coop also goes on to describe virtually the same "mental movies technique" I first began teaching in the late 1950s and wrote about in the original version of this book. Jack Nicklaus uses the word "scene"; he is playing out his successful shot as a little mental movie, literally stepping out of actual play and into the Theater of the Mind to watch the movie, then stepping back out to experience the deja vu effect. In an article in *Golf Magazine* (July 2000), Jack Nicklaus said, "The more deeply you ingrain what I like to call my going-to-the-movies discipline, the more effective you will become at hitting the shots you want to hit." In his four-step process, in step four he even says "Select the club that the completed 'movie' *tells you* is the right one."

Remarkably, Jack Nicklaus has found his way to virtually the same mental movies techniques I prescribe, even going so far as to turn the pesky details of correct club selection over to his Automatic Success Mechanism, rather than attempting conscious choice. I say "remarkably" because, as far as I know, Mr. Nicklaus has never read this book, although he has likely been influenced by the many other golfers and golf coaches who have. However, it's really not all that remarkable, since it seems almost all peak performers find their way to this technique one way or another.

In a few moments, we'll talk more about the specifics of these mental movies. Let me first tell you about some of the scientific documentation that supports the entire idea of imagination practice. In one of the first controlled experiments I read about, psychologist R. A. Vandll proved that mental practice in throwing darts at a target, wherein the person sits for a period each day in front of the target, and imagines throwing darts at it, improves aim just as much as actually throwing darts.

Research Quarterly reported an experiment on the effects of mental practice on improving skill in sinking basketball free throws. One group of students actually practiced throwing the ball every day for 20 days, and were scored on the first and last days. A second group was scored on the first and last days, and engaged in no sort of practice in between. A third group was scored on the first day, then spent 20 minutes a day, imagining that they were throwing the ball at the goal.

When they missed they would imagine that they corrected their aim accordingly.

The first group, which actually practiced 20 minutes every day, improved in scoring 24%.

The second group, which had no sort of practice, showed no improvement.

The third group, which practiced only in their imagination, improved in scoring 23%!

This particular experiment has been widely reported and referenced, and since repeated at many universities over the years. Of course, none of this is infallible. After all, Shaq's problem with foul shots remains a mystery! However, while an inexact science, the use of imagination practice is nevertheless an effective science, a proven and practical means of improving skills or altering imbedded "truths" in order to alter behavior.

Mental Pictures Are Powerful Medicine

Kay Porter, Ph.D. and Judy Foster, authors of *The Mental Athlete: Inner Training for Peak Performance*, provided an excellent, detailed prescription for relieving pain and accelerating recovery from injury. In an article in *Tennis World Magazine*, they noted "an important element of self-healing is a mental image that projects a positive future outcome. This visualization stimulates your mind and body and creates an intention to heal ... through mental imagery, it is possible to alter the body's autonomic physiological responses. When you use imagination, mental pictures and suggestion, you can communicate with your body and make it respond."

Make no mistake: This is medical, scientific truth not mumbo-jumbo. If every hospital patient and every person entering physical rehabilitation were given a copy of Psycho-Cybernetics, they would be considerably better off. Keep this in mind if you ever have a loved one or friend in such circumstances.

This article is so revealing and useful, we've posted more extensive excerpts at the Psycho-Cybernetics Foundation's web site, www.psycho-cybernetics.com, should you care to read it or refer a friend to it. (You will also find other articles, book reviews and book excerpts directly related to this book, in a special section of this web site.)

Mental Pictures Can Help You Sell at a Higher Level

In his book, *How to Make $25,000 a Year Selling*, Charles B. Roth told how a group of salespeople in Detroit who tried a new idea increased their sales 100%. Another group in New York increased their sales by 150%. And individual salespeople, using the same idea, had increased their sales up to 400%. And what is this magic that accomplishes so much for salespeople? From Mr. Roth's book:

> It is something called role-playing, and you should know about it, because if you will let it, it may help you to double your sales.
>
> What is role-playing?
>
> Well it is simply *imagining* yourself in various sales situations, then solving them *in your mind*, until you know what to say and what to do whenever the situation comes up in real life.
>
> The reason why it accomplishes so much is that selling is simply a matter of situations.
>
> One is created every time you talk to a customer. He says something or asks a question or raises an objection. If you always know how to counter what he says or answer his question or handle the objection, you make sales …
>
> A role-playing salesman, at night when he is alone, will create these situations. He will imagine the prospect throwing the widest kind of curves at him. Then he will work out the best answer to them…
>
> No matter what the situation is, you can prepare for it before-hand by means of imagining yourself and your prospect face to face while he is raising objections and creating problems and you are handling them properly.

I suspect Mr. Roth's book is now out of print. The "$25,000" in its title telegraphs its age. But countless sales books, sales training programs, and professional sales trainers have since incorporated this idea into their methods and advice to sales professionals. In fact, if you are engaged in the field of selling, you've undoubtedly participated in actual role-playing in the classroom, in the seminar room, or at a sales meeting, and may have then practiced with a colleague or a spouse. What you may not have realized is that moving the role-playing from the seminar room to the Theater of the Mind can be just as effective, and arguably more effective because you can progress from fumbling awkwardness and uncertainty to "perfection" and success. You can then rehearse only that drama repetitively until it becomes "second nature" and your real selling experiences so closely mirror those practiced perfectly in your imagination that they are deja vu.

If you view "negotiation" as high-level selling, then this story demonstrates this well. It is a letter I received from a professional brought in by a company to represent it in a very complex and challenging negotiation with millions of dollars at stake, with the CEO of a public company, famous for being difficult. While I cannot reveal the names involved, I assure you the letter is in my possession. Here it is, excerpted in part:

Dear Dr. Maltz,

... since I had the luxury of several weeks to prepare for our first meeting that would take place behind closed doors, I immersed myself in preparation by studying everything I could obtain about this man. I read a book he had written, books and articles about him, watched video tapes of interviews with him from TV networks and programs, analyzed his biography, and ultimately produced a walking, talking replica of him in my imagination, so that I could carry on conversations with him. I did not have means to have someone else ably act as this person in actual role-play, as politicians do when preparing for debates, so instead I created an imaginary clone.

Frankly I chose not to let any of my associates know exactly what I was doing, for fear of having the men in white coats called! My client might have had second thoughts about entrusting this high-wire negotiation to a someone who had an "imaginary man" he was talking with for hours each day.

Anyway, I followed the instructions I found in your book, *Psycho-Cybernetics*, as inspiration for my approach. After constructing this imaginary person, I then spent hours in what you call "The Theater of the Mind" actually playing out the meeting and dialogue we would have, myself the scriptwriter, director, lead actor and observer, which I found difficult at first, but less difficult as I stayed with it. Soon I found my imagined clone actively raising issues, questions and arguments on his own. Once I recall sitting in my easy chair, eyes closed, immersed in this imaginary meeting, catching myself losing my temper and pounding my fist on the arm of the chair!

As this evolved into a 'mental movie' with a successful outcome, I transitioned into re-playing that identical movie repeatedly. I even went so far, after many viewings, to write it out word for word, as if a courtroom transcriptionist was there to accurately record our conversation word for word.

Here is what is remarkable: when the actual meeting took place, not only did it follow my script in order and flow, and not only did I voice things exactly as I had many times in the mental movie as you might expect, but he also performed as if working from the very same script!

In his letter, he goes on to describe a very successful outcome, the earning of a substantial fee.

By the way, I received this letter in 1974, 14 years after the first publication of my book. He made mention of noting its copyright and at first questioning how relevant and beneficial such "old" techniques might be. You may very well be reading this book 30 or 40 years after its first edition, and even after I have left the living. It will not matter. These techniques will be used by top professionals in every field of endeavor long after the bulky computer has been reduced to a device you can wear on your arm like a wristwatch.

There is now a book based on Psycho-Cybernetics specifically for professional salespeople: *Zero Resistance Selling*, published by Prentice-Hall, and available in bookstores, from online booksellers, or at www.psycho-cybernetics.com.

Use Mental Pictures to Get a Better Job

The late William Moulton Marston, well-known psychologist, recommended what he called "rehearsal practice" to men and women who came to him for help in job advancement. If you have an important interview coming up, such as making an application for a job, his advice was: plan for the interview in advance. Go over in your mind all the various questions that are likely to be asked. Think about the answers you are going to give. Then rehearse the interview in your mind. Even if none of the questions you have rehearsed come up, the rehearsal practice will still work wonders. It gives you confidence. And even though real life has no set lines to be recited like a stage play, rehearsal practice will help you to ad lib and react spontaneously to whatever situation you find yourself in, because you have practiced reacting spontaneously.

This should come as no surprise, based on everything I just had to say about mental rehearsal for sales professionals: In a job interview, you are selling yourself. You are the product and its sales representative. Like the negotiator, you may even have the luxury of time—several weeks, maybe even several months—to plan and prepare to search for a new or better position. If so, by all means use it to your advantage by using your imagination to construct and rehearse the "perfect" job interview, so that when the actual interviews take place, you'll be relaxed, confident, and comfortable.

A Concert Pianist Practices "In His Head"

Arthur Schnabel, the world famous concert pianist, took lessons for only seven years. He hated practice and seldom practiced for any length of time at the actual piano keyboard. When questioned about his small amount of practice, as compared with other concert pianists, he said, "I practice in my head."

C. G. Kop, of Holland, a recognized authority on teaching piano recommended that all pianists "practice in their heads." A new composition, he says, should be first gone over in the mind. It should be memorized and played in the mind *before* ever touching fingers to the keyboard.

"Practicing in the head" has actually become the basis for quite a bit of modern piano instruction. Composer, performer, and instructor, Patty Carlson achieved considerable fame promoting her "How to Play Piano Overnight" video program, in which she teaches people how to "feel" the music rather than learning to read sheet music and engage in tedious practice.

Imagination Practice Can Lower Your Golf Score

Golf has become an enormously popular recreation, and there's a long relationship between golf and Psycho-Cybernetics. I've already mentioned the great Jack Nicklaus' mental rehearsal as just one example.

Time Magazine reported that, when Ben Hogan was playing in a tournament, he mentally rehearsed each shot, just before making it. He made the shot perfectly in his imagination—felt the clubhead strike the ball just as it should, felt himself performing the perfect follow-through—and then stepped up to the ball, and depended on what he called "muscle memory" to carry out the shot just as he imagined it.

Ben Hogan was ahead of the curve of modern golf psychology, which has become an industry unto itself and is largely based on visualization and relaxation techniques.

Alex Morrison, perhaps the best-known golf instructor in the world at the time I was writing the first edition of this book, actually worked out a system of mental practice to improve your golf score while sitting in an easy chair and practicing mentally what he called the Seven Morrison Keys. According to Morrison, the mental side of golf represents 90% of the game, the physical side 8%, and the mechanical side 2%. In his book, *Better Golf Without Practice*, Morrison told how he taught Lew Lehr to break 90 for the first time, with no actual practice whatsoever!

Morrison had Lehr sit in an easy chair in his living room and relax while he demonstrated for him the correct swing and gave a brief lecture on the Morrison Keys. Lehr was instructed to engage in no actual practice on the links, but instead spend five minutes each day, relaxing in his easy chair, visualizing himself attending to the Keys correctly.

Morrison goes on to report how several days later, with no physical preparation whatever, Lehr joined his regular foursome, and amazed them by shooting 9 holes in an even par, 36.

The core of the Morrison system is, "You must have a clear mental picture of the correct thing before you can do it successfully." Morrison, by this method, enabled many celebrities to chop as many as 10 to 12 strokes off their scores.

Clearly See the Target, and Let Your Automatic Success Mechanism Take Care of the Details

Johnny Bulla, a well-known professional golfer, wrote an article in which he said that having a clear mental image of just where you wanted the ball to go and what you wanted it to do was more important than form in golf. Most of the pros, said Bulla, have one or more serious flaws in their form. Yet they manage to shoot good golf. It was Bulla's theory that if you picture the end result, see the ball going where you want it to go, and have the confidence to know that it was going to do what you wanted, your subconscious would take over and direct your muscles correctly. If your grip was wrong, and your stance not in the best form, your subconscious would still take care of that by directing your muscles to do whatever was necessary to compensate for the error in form.

> **This describes the payoff of mastering these
> Psycho-Cybernetics techniques: that you reach a point
> of efficiency where you can simply, quickly hand a clear
> picture of the desired outcome over to your
> servo-mechanism and let it take care of the mechanical
> details of making that outcome take place.**

Golf is such an excellent laboratory for these techniques because, unlike many other sports, it is stripped down to pure competition with yourself.

Morrison's coaching of Lehr exclusively with mental practice came many years before Tim Gallwey, author of *The Inner Game of Tennis*, accepted the challenge of an experiment—to see how much golf he could learn just by adapting the inner game (mental) skills he had developed in playing and coaching tennis. He set the goal of breaking 80 while playing only once weekly, receiving no technical instruction, and otherwise relying on practice in his imagination, in one year or less. At that time, he played only several times a year, scoring between 95 and 105. His diary of that experiment is included in his book *The Inner Game of Golf*. His book is well worth reading whether you have any interest in golf or not, as it is a thoroughly detailed case history in the triumph of mind over mechanics or technical information—actually the triumph of Psycho-Cybernetics.

Over the years, I've had the pleasure of working with many top golfers and golf instructors, although professional discretion requires me to maintain confidentiality for most of them. Some engineered improvement in their performance with only this book and no other assistance from me. Here's one that is public knowledge: In 1964, Dave Stockton was struggling to survive on the pro tour. "Overall, I was playing well but my putting was lousy," Stockton told an *L.A. Times* reporter. "My father, a retired pro, insisted my putting problems were mental, not physical, and he gave me a copy of *Psycho-Cybernetics* to read. I read it just one week before the PGA Tournament; then I went in *knowing* I was going to win." Dave Stockton beat Arnold Palmer in that event and went on to enjoy a long and successful career. In fact, he became famous for his putting! And 22 years later, Dave won the 1996 U.S. Senior Open.

The Real Secret of Mental Picturing

Successful men and women have, since the beginning of time, used mental pictures and rehearsal practice to achieve success. Napoleon, for example, practiced soldiering in his imagination, for many years before he ever went on an actual battlefield. Webb and Morgan in their book *Making the Most of Your Life*, tell us that "the notes Napoleon made from his readings during these years of study filled, when printed, four hundred pages. He imagined himself as a commander, and drew maps of the island of Corsica showing where he would place his calculations with mathematical precision."

Conrad Hilton imagined himself operating a hotel long before he ever bought one. As a boy, he used to play that he was a hotel operator. His earliest successes were in buying dilapidated, "dowager" properties and restoring their beauty, rebirthing them as first-class properties. He said that, when he spotted such a property to acquire, he ceased seeing its actual condition, instead forming a vividly detailed collection of *photographs in his mind* of the hotel as it would appear after its makeover. By seeing what would be, he saw value invisible to others.

A Strong Mental Picture Can Pull You Toward Success Even When You Have No Logical Argument for It

Jane Savoie is one of the most respected horse riding coaches in America. In 2000, she coached the U.S. Olympic equestrian team competing in Sydney. She describes an instance in which imagination power superceded probabilities:

> Take, for example, my experience at the screening trials for the North American Championships in 1989. I had a whole bunch of facts that supported the improbability of my doing well at the screening trials. I did have a top horse, Zapatero, but the other facts were: one, Zapatero was new to me and we had not had time to develop a solid relationship and real communications; two, he was a young horse and not yet strong enough to do what was required ...
>
> These facts made it difficult to imagine the perfect test. So I visualized the awards ceremony instead. Several times over the course of the day, I would find a quiet spot, close my eyes, relax and visualize leading the vic-

tory lap. In the process I stopped thinking about "the facts" and thus prevented doubts and insecurities from creeping in. When the results were posted, Zapatero and I were, in fact, there to lead the lap of honor.

It sounds incredible, and I in no way minimize the necessity for all the preparation and hard work involved. But mentally zeroing in on desired results as if they were already in existence was a significant factor in our ultimate success. It was important to focus on a positive outcome as a foregone conclusion rather than allow my rather vivid imagination to conjure up failure pictures. My mind (servo-mechanism) could then supply the means to achieve my goal by helping me to (letting me) ride skillfully and effectively.

Of course, the skeptic would want to attribute this incident to coincidence or luck. But Jane Savoi is a skilled practitioner of Psycho-Cybernetics, with many evidentiary incidents to support her convictions. In fact, she has utilized Psycho-Cybernetics for many years as an instructor and coach of champion riders, as noted, most recently with the Olympic team.

Even a single, simple, vividly imagined picture of successful achievement can be sufficient to block out doubts, fears, insecurities, and worries, and direct the Success Mechanism to the desired target. Full-scale mental rehearsal is even more powerful.

There is simply no sensible case to be made anymore against incorporating mental rehearsal into your own daily regimen, whether you are a pro or weekend athlete, sales professional, entrepreneur, executive, school teacher, doctor, whatever. The evidence mandates that you learn to use this tool and do so regularly, for a myriad of productive purposes. It is fair to insist that if you are *not* utilizing this approach, you are operating without benefit of one of the fundamental, universal, most relied-on psychological tools of success we know of. It is much like being a carpenter choosing to operate without benefit of electric power and power tools. You could, but why?

Why Mental Picturing Is So Powerful

The science of Cybernetics gives us insight into why mental picturing produces such amazing results. I find that the more people understand about why this works so well, the more likely they are to use it.

This Automatic Success Mechanism within you—a highly complex automatic goal-seeking machine that steers its way to a target or goal by use of feed-back data and stored information, automatically correcting course when necessary—can operate in only one way. It must have a target to shoot at. As the famous golf instructor Alex Morrison said, you must first clearly see a thing in your mind before you can do it. (As stated earlier, this new concept does not mean that you are a machine, but that your physical brain and body functions as a machine that you operate.)

**When you see a thing clearly in your mind,
your creative "success mechanism" within you takes over
and does the job much better than you could do it by
conscious effort or willpower.**

Instead of trying hard by conscious effort to do the thing by iron-jawed willpower, all the while worrying and picturing to yourself all the things that are likely to go wrong, you simply relax, stop trying to "do it" by strain and effort, picture the target you really want to hit, and let your creative success mechanism take over. You are not relieved thereafter from effort and work, but your efforts are used to carry you forward toward your goal, rather than in futile mental conflict which results when you want and try to do one thing, but picture to yourself something else.

Finding Your Best Self

This same creative mechanism within you can help you achieve your best possible self if you will form a picture in your imagination of the self you want to be and see yourself in the new role. This is a necessary condition to personality transformation, regardless of the method of therapy used. Somehow, before you can change, you must "see" yourself in a new role.

I myself have witnessed veritable miracles in personality transformation when an individual changes his or her self-image. However, today we are only beginning to glimpse the potential creative power that stems from the human imagination, particularly images concerning ourselves. Consider the implications, for example, in the following news release, which appeared in 1958 under an Associated Press dateline:

Just Imagine You're Sane

San Francisco. Some mental patients can improve their lot and perhaps shorten their stay in hospitals just by imagining they are normal, two psychologists with the Veterans Administration at Los Angeles reported.

Dr. Harry M. Grayson and Dr. Leonard B. Olinger told the American Psychological Assn. they tried the idea on 45 men hospitalized as neuropsychiatrics.

The patients first were given the usual personality test. Then they were asked flatly to take the test a second time and answer the questions as they would if they were 'a typical, well-adjusted person on the outside.'

Three-fourths of them turned in improved test performances and some of the changes for the better were dramatic, the psychologists reported.

In order for these patients to answer the questions "as a typical, well-adjusted person" would answer, they had to imagine how a typical well-adjusted person would act. They had to imagine themselves in the role of a well-adjusted person. And this in itself was enough to cause them to begin "acting like" and "feeling like" a well-adjusted person.

I am not certain what became of these good doctors and their innovative experiments. However, we know that today every aspect of self-image psychology, the very idea of self-image as steersman, and related techniques like "act as if" visualization are widely accepted and used in assisting the mentally ill, the handicapped, addicts, and incarcerated inmates involved with rehabilitation.

Of course, you are probably not clinically insane or addicted to chemicals, but more likely a successful individual looking to Psycho-Cybernetics to help you do even better or to improve some aspect of your life. The fact that these techniques have become part and parcel of most therapies and treatments for people with far more severe emotional and psychological difficulties than you face or can even imagine holds out for you the promise that they can be even more powerful, fast-acting, and effective from your more favorable starting point.

Discover the Truth About Yourself

The aim of self-image psychology is not to create a fictitious self that is all-powerful, arrogant, egoistic, all-important. Such an image is as inappropriate and unrealistic as the inferior image of self. Our aim is to find the real self. However, it is common knowledge among psychologists that most of us underrate ourselves, short-change ourselves, sell ourselves short. Actually, there is no such thing as a superiority complex. People who seem to have one are actually suffering from feelings of inferiority; their "superior" self is a fiction, a coverup, to hide from themselves and others their deep-down feelings of inferiority and insecurity.

How can you discover the truth about yourself? How can you make a true evaluation? It seems to me that here psychology must turn to religion. The Scriptures tell us that God created man "a little lower than the angels" and "gave him dominion"; that God created man in his own image. If we really believe in an all-wise, all-powerful, all-loving Creator, then we can draw some logical conclusions about what He has created—Man. In the first place such an all-wise and all-powerful Creator would not turn out inferior products, anymore than a master painter would paint inferior canvases. Such a Creator would not deliberately engineer the product to fail, anymore than a manufacturer would deliberately build failure into an automobile.

The Fundamentalists tell us that man's chief purpose and reason for living is to "glorify God," and the Humanists tell us that man's primary purpose is to "express himself fully."

However, if we take the premise that God is a loving Creator and has the same interest in Creation that an earthly father has in his children, then it seems to me that the Fundamentalists and the Humanists are saying the same thing. What brings more glory, pride, and satisfaction to a father than seeing his offspring do well, succeed, and express to the full their abilities and talents? Have you ever sat by the father of a football star during a game? Jesus expressed the same thought when he told us "not to hide our light under a bushel, but to let *our* light shine so that your Father may be glorified." I cannot believe that it brings any "glory" to God when his children go around with hang-dog expressions, being miserable, afraid to lift up their heads and be somebody.

Over the years following the first publication of the book, I've been invited to speak at many different kinds of churches, from evangelical Christian to Baptist to Episcopal to so-called "new thought" and "science of mind." I've had in-depth discussions about Psycho-

Cybernetics with ministers, priests, a Zen monk, agnostics, even athe-
ists. I have had no difficulty navigating these different waters, and we
have always found common ground in the basic premise of liberating
individuals from their own inner, mental, often unconscious self-sabotage, and the corollary premise of individuals being intended (if not
engineered) to succeed, not fail.

Dr. Norman Vincent Peale had kind things to say about Psycho-
Cybernetics, and he and I had several good discussions, even though I
have on occasion commented that simple "positive thinking" as most
people think of it is too often destined to disappoint, as it tries to force
the issue from the circumference of our being rather than to reprogram at the core.

I don't think you can have a legitimate religious or spiritual dis-
agreement with Psycho-Cybernetics.

The Final Word on Imagination Practice

It doesn't matter what religious, spiritual, or philosophical background
or viewpoint you come from. It doesn't matter how you describe it:
imagination practice, visualization, mental picturing, or using my ter-
minology, Theater of your Mind. What's important is that you do it!
If you will choose a target to apply this to, and give it a solid, honest
21-day trial, you will be so gratified with the results that you will certainly choose to continue using this tool for the rest of your life, and
benefit enormously by doing so, just as countless athletes, entertainers, doctors, lawyers, business leaders, and others have before you.
Here are a few exercises to get you started:

MENTAL TRAINING EXERCISE

Your present self-image was built on your own imagination pictures of
yourself in the past, which grew out of interpretations and evaluations you
placed on *experience*. Now you are to use the same method to build an adequate self-image that you previously used to build an inadequate one.

Set aside a period of 30 minutes each day where you can be alone and
undisturbed. Relax and make yourself as comfortable as possible. Now close
your eyes and exercise your imagination.

Many people find they get better results if they imagine themselves sitting before a large motion picture screen and imagine that they are seeing a motion picture of themselves. The important thing is to make these pictures as *vivid* and as *detailed* as possible. You want your mental pictures to approximate actual experience as much as possible. The way to do this is to pay attention to small details, sights, sounds, objects, in your imagined environment. *Details* of the imagined environment are all-important in this exercise because, for all practical purposes, you are creating a *practice experience*. And if the imagination is vivid enough and detailed enough, your imagination practice is equivalent to an actual experience, insofar as your nervous system is concerned.

The next important thing to remember is that during these 30 minutes you see yourself acting and reacting appropriately, successfully, ideally. It doesn't matter how you acted yesterday. You do not need to try to have faith you will act in the ideal way tomorrow. Your nervous system will take care of that in time—if you continue to practice. See yourself acting, feeling, being as you want to be. Do not say to yourself, "I am going to act this way tomorrow." Just say to yourself, "I am going to imagine myself acting this way now—for 30 minutes today." Imagine how you would feel if you were already the sort of personality you want to be. If you have been shy and timid, see yourself moving among people with ease and poise and *feeling good* because of it. If you have been fearful and anxious in certain situations, see yourself acting calmly and deliberately, acting with confidence and courage, and feeling expansive and confident because you are.

This exercise builds new "memories" or stored data into your midbrain and central nervous system. It builds a new image of self. After practicing it for a time, you will be surprised to find yourself "acting differently," more or less automatically and spontaneously, without trying. This is as it should be. You do not need to take thought, or try, or make an effort now in order to feel ineffective and act inadequately. Your present inadequate feeling and doing are automatic and spontaneous, because of the memories, real and imagined you have built into your automatic mechanism. You will find it will work just as automatically upon positive thoughts and experiences as upon negative ones.

Step One: Take pad and pen and write out a brief outline or description of the mental movie you intend to construct, experiment with, develop, and view in the Theater in the Mind.

Step Two: Set aside 30 minutes a day, preferably at the same time each day, to find a quiet, private place, relax, close your eyes, enter your Theater, and begin playing, editing, replaying your movie.

Step Three: Gradually "massage" your movie so that its "star" (you) performs exactly as you desire, and achieves the experience and results you desire. Strive to arrive at this point within the first 10 days.

Step Four: For the remaining 11 days, play and enjoy that movie repeatedly without change.

CHAPTER FOUR

How to Dehypnotize Yourself from False Beliefs

Convictions are more dangerous enemies of truth than lies.
—Friedrich Wilhelm Nietzsche

*A*question that I have been asked many times about Psycho-Cybernetics equates as-if imagination with "fake it 'til you make it" or pure fantasy. Nothing could be further from the truth. "Fake it 'til you make it" is external, superficial, and unrealistic. It is sometimes taught to salespeople, to their financial and emotional detriment.

Instead, Psycho-Cybernetics, including as-if imagination practice, is *not* about fraud but a search for hidden truth. It is about uncovering your true self by creatively challenging ideas your self-image accepts as "facts" about you, that may or may not have been valid once, but need not be valid today or tomorrow. This story from my original book illustrates this:

My friend Dr. Alfred Adler had an experience with a young boy that illustrates just how powerful belief can be on behavior and ability. He got off to a bad start in arithmetic and his teacher became *convinced* that he was "dumb in mathematics." The teacher then advised the parents of this "fact" and told them not to expect too much of him. They too were *convinced*. Adler passively accepted the evaluation they had placed on him, and his grades in arithmetic proved they had been correct. One day, however, he had a sudden flash of insight and thought he saw how to work a problem that the teacher had put on the board and that none of the other pupils could work. He announced as much to the teacher. She and the whole class laughed, whereupon he became indignant, strode to the blackboard, and worked the problem—much to their amazement. In doing so, he realized that he could understand arithmetic. He felt a new confidence in his ability and went on to become a good math student.

Dr. Adler's experience was very much like that of a patient of mine some years back, a businessperson who wanted to excel in public speaking because he had a vital message to impart about his outstanding success in a difficult field. He had a good voice and an important topic, but he was unable to get up in front of strangers and put his message over. What held him back was his belief that he could not make a good talk and that he would fail to impress his audience, simply because he did not have an imposing appearance ... he did not "look like a successful executive." This belief had burrowed so deeply into him that it threw up a road block every time he stood up before a group of people and began to talk. He mistakenly concluded that, if he could have an operation to improve his appearance, he would then gain the confidence he needed. An operation might have done the trick and it might not. My experience with other patients had shown that physical change did not always guarantee personality change. The solution in this man's case was found when he became convinced that his negative belief was preventing him from delivering the vital information he had. He succeeded in replacing the negative belief with a positive belief that he had a message of extreme importance that he alone could deliver, no matter what he looked like. In due time, he was one of the most sought-after speakers in the business world. The only change was in his belief and in his self-image.

Now the point I want to make is this: Adler had been *hypnotized* by a false belief about himself—not figuratively, but literally and actually hypnotized. Remember that we said in the last chapter that the power of hypnosis is the power of belief. Let me repeat here Dr. Barber's explanation of the power of hypnosis: "We found that hypnotic subjects are able to do surprising things only when *convinced* that the hypnotist's words are true statements ... When the hypnotist has guided the subject to the point where he is convinced that the hypnotist's words are true statements, the subject then behaves differently because he *thinks and believes* differently."

The important thing for you to remember is that it does not matter in the least how you got the idea or where it came from. You may never have met a professional hypnotist. You may have never been formally hypnotized. But if you have accepted an idea—from yourself, your teachers, your parents, friends, advertisements, or any other source—and further, if you are firmly *convinced* that idea is *true*, it has the same power over you as the hypnotist's words have over the hypnotized subject.

Scientific research has shown that Dr. Adler's experience was not one in a million, but typical of practically all students who make poor grades. In Chapter One we told of how Prescott Lecky had brought about almost miraculous improvement in the grades of school children by showing them how to change their self-image. After thousands of experiments and many years of research, Lecky concluded that poor grades in school are in almost every case due in some degree to students' self-conception and self-definition. These students had been literally hypnotized by such ideas as "I am dumb," "I am poor in arithmetic," "I am a naturally poor speller," "I do not have a mechanical type mind," etc. With such self-definitions, students had to make poor grades in order to be true to themselves. Unconsciously, making poor grades became a moral issue with them. It would be as wrong, from their viewpoint, for them to make good grades as it would be to steal if they define themselves as honest persons.

Remember that this hypnotic programming gains permanence by coming from an authoritative source, through repetition, and through intensity. Deprogramming and reprogramming requires you to provide these very same factors. Dr. Adler's childhood experience included authoritative sources—his parents and teachers, hearing it repeatedly, and having it reinforced through intensely humiliating experience. His liberation began with another intense experience and emotional reaction, which freed him and motivated him to question and challenge the belief.

The Case of the Hypnotized Salesperson

In the book, *Secrets of Successful Selling,* John D. Murphy tells how the famous sales expert Elmer Wheeler used Lecky's theory to increase the earnings of a certain salesperson:

Elmer Wheeler had been called in as a sales consultant to a certain firm. The sales manager called his attention to a very remarkable case. A certain salesman always managed to make almost exactly $5,000 per year, regardless of the territory they assigned him or the commission he was paid.

Because this salesman had done well in a rather small territory, he had been given a larger and much better one. But the next year his commission amounted to almost the same amount as that he had made in the smaller one—$5,000. The following year the company increased the commission paid to all salesmen, but this salesman still managed to make only $5,000. He was then assigned one of the company's poorest territories—and again made the usual $5,000.

Wheeler had a talk with this salesman and found that the trouble was not in the territory but in the salesman's own evaluation of himself. He thought of himself as a $5,000-per-year man and as long as he held that concept of himself, outside conditions didn't seem to matter much.

When he was assigned a poor territory, he worked hard to make that $5,000. When he was assigned a good territory, he found all sorts of excuses to coast when the $5,000 was in sight. Once, when the goal had been reached, he got sick and was unable to work any more that year, although doctors could find nothing wrong with him and he miraculously recovered by the first of the next year.

Obviously, that's an old story, dated by the $5,000 earnings number. After it appeared in the first edition of this book, I began to get letters about this story from sales manager after sales manager, each citing a similar story. They all would say that they had a person just like that in their organization, with whom they were frustrated beyond all belief. One sales manager wrote, "It is as if Howard has a pre-set income limit that he will not go past no matter the opportunities or circumstances." And that is exactly right; it is "set" deep in his self-image. Until it is reset, he will manage to avoid going past it.

How a False Belief Aged a Man 20 Years

In my previous book, *Adventures in Staying Young*, I gave a detailed case history of how Mr. Russell aged 20 years almost overnight because of a false idea, then regained his youth almost as quickly when he accepted the truth.

Briefly, the story is this: I performed a cosmetic operation on Mr. Russell's lower lip for a very modest fee, under the condition that he must tell his girlfriend that the operation had cost him his entire life-time savings. His girlfriend had no objection to his spending money on her, and she insisted that she loved him, but explained she could never marry him because of his too large lower lip. However, when he told her this and proudly exhibited his new lower lip, her reaction was just as I had expected, but not as Mr. Russell had anticipated. She became hysterically angry, called him a fool for having spent all his money, and advised him in no uncertain terms that she had never loved him and never would. She had merely played him for a sucker as long as he had money to spend on her. However, she went further than I had counted on. In her anger and disgust she also announced that she was placing a "voodoo curse" on him. Both Mr. Russell and his girl-friend had been born on an island in the West Indies where voodoo was practiced by the ignorant and superstitious. His family had been rather well-to-do. His background was one of culture and he was a college graduate.

When in the heat of anger, his girlfriend "cursed" him, he felt vaguely uncomfortable but did not think too much about it.

However, he remembered and wondered when a short time later he felt a strange small hard bump on the inside of his lip. A friend who knew of the voodoo curse, insisted that he see a Dr. Smith, who promptly assured him that the bump inside his mouth was the feared African Bug, which would slowly eat away all his vitality and strength. Mr. Russell began to worry and look for signs of waning strength. He was not long in finding them. He lost his appetite and his ability to sleep.

I learned all this from Mr. Russell when he returned to my office several weeks after I had dismissed him. My nurse didn't recognize him, and no wonder. The Mr. Russell who had first called upon me had been a very impressive individual, slightly too-large lip and all. He stood about six feet four, a large man with the physique of an athlete and the bearing and manner that bespoke an inner dignity and gave him a magnetic personality. The very pores of his skin seemed to exude an animal-like vitality.

The Mr. Russell who now sat across the desk from me had aged at least 20 years. His hands shook with the tremor of age. His eyes and cheeks were sunken. He had lost perhaps 30 pounds. The changes in his appearance were all characteristic of the process that medical science, for want of a better name, calls aging.

After a quick examination of his mouth I assured Mr. Russell I could get rid of the African Bug in less than 30 minutes, which I did. The bump which had caused all the trouble was merely a small bit of scar tissue from his operation. I removed it, held it in my hand, and showed it to him. The important thing is he saw the truth and believed it. He gave a sigh of relief, and it seemed as if there was an almost immediate change in his posture and expression.

Several weeks later, I received a nice letter from Mr. Russell, together with a photograph of him with his new bride. He had gone back to his home and married his childhood sweetheart. The man in the picture was the first Mr. Russell. Mr. Russell had grown young again overnight. A false belief had aged him 20 years. The truth had not only set him free of fear and restored his confidence, but had actually reversed the aging process.

If you could have seen Mr. Russell as I did, both before and after, you would never again entertain any doubts about the power of belief, or that an idea accepted as true from any source can be every bit as powerful as hypnosis.

Is Everyone Hypnotized?

It is no exaggeration to say that all human beings are hypnotized to some extent, either by ideas they have uncritically accepted from others, or by ideas they have repeated to themselves or convinced themselves are true. These negative ideas have exactly the same effect on our behavior as the negative ideas implanted into the mind of a hypnotized subject by a professional hypnotist. Have you ever seen a demonstration of honest-to-goodness hypnosis? If not, let me describe just a few of the more simple phenomena that result from the hypnotist's suggestion. The hypnotist tells a strong football player that his hand is stuck to the table and that he cannot lift it. It is not a question of the football player "not trying." He simply cannot. He strains and struggles until the muscles of his arm and shoulder stand out like cords. But his hand remains fully rooted to the table. He tells a championship weight lifter that he cannot lift a pencil from the desk. And although normally he can hoist a 400-pound weight overhead, he now actually cannot lift the pencil.

Strangely enough, in these instances, hypnosis does not weaken the athletes. They are potentially as strong as ever. But, *without realizing it consciously*, they are working against themselves. On the one hand they try to lift their hand or the pencil by voluntary effort, and actually contract the proper lifting muscles. But on the other hand, the idea "you cannot do it" causes contrary muscles to contract quite apart from their will. The negative idea causes them to defeat themselves; they cannot express or bring into play their actual available strength.

The gripping strength of another athlete has been tested on a dynamometer and has been found to be 100 pounds. All his effort and straining cannot budge the needle beyond the 100-pound mark. Now he is hypnotized and told, "You are very, very strong. Stronger than you have ever been in your life. Much, much stronger. You are surprised at how strong you are." Again the gripping strength of his hand is tested. This time he easily pulls the needle to the 125-pound mark.

Again, strangely enough, hypnosis has not added anything to his actual strength. What the hypnotic suggestion did was to overcome a negative idea that had previously prevented him from expressing his full strength. In other words, the athlete in his normal waking state had imposed a limitation on his strength by the negative belief that he could only grip 100 pounds. The hypnotist merely removed this mental block, and allowed him to express his true strength. The hypnosis literally "dehypnotized" him temporarily from his own self-limiting beliefs about himself.

As Dr. Barber has said, it is awfully easy to assume that the hypnotist himself must have some magical power when you see rather miraculous things happen during a hypnotic session. The stutterer talks fluently. The timid, shy, retiring Caspar Milquetoast becomes outgoing, poised, and makes a stirring speech. Another individual who is not especially good in adding figures with a pencil and paper when awake, multiplies two three-digit figures in his head. All this happens because the hypnotist tells them that they can and instructs them to go ahead and do it. To onlookers, the hypnotist's word seems to have a magical power. Such, however, is not the case. The power, the basic ability, to do these things was inherent in the subjects all the time, before they met the hypnotist. The subjects, however, were unable to use this power because they themselves did not know it was there. They had bottled it up and choked it off because of their own negative beliefs. Without realizing it, they had hypnotized themselves into believing they could not do these things. And it would be truer to say that the hypnotist had dehypnotized them than to say he had hypnotized them.

Within you, whoever you may be, is the ability and the power to do whatever you need to do to be happy and successful. Within you right now is the power to do things you never dreamed possible. This power becomes available to you just as soon as you can change your beliefs. Just as quickly as you can dehypnotize yourself from the ideas of "I can't," "I'm not worthy," "I don't deserve it," and other self-limiting ideas.

You Can Cure Your Inferiority Complex

At least 95% of the people have their lives blighted by feelings of inferiority to some extent, and to millions this same feeling of inferiority is a serious handicap to success and happiness.

Every person on the face of the earth is inferior to some other persons or person. I *know* that I cannot beat Jack Nicklaus on the links, throw a football as straight and far as any NFL pro quarterback, and the list goes on. Even though I have appeared as a speaker in front of a number of large audiences, I know there's a long list of people who are more polished and stylish and charismatic on the platform. I know this, but it does not induce feelings of inferiority within me and blight my life, simply because I do not compare myself unfavorably with them and do not feel that I am no good merely because I cannot do certain things as skillfully or as well as they. I also know that in certain areas, every person I meet, from the newsboy on the corner, to the president of the bank, is superior to me in certain respects. But neither can any of these people repair a scarred face or do any number of other things as well as I. And I am sure they do not feel inferior because of it.

Feelings of inferiority originate not so much from facts or experiences, but from our conclusions regarding facts and our evaluation of experiences. For example, the fact is that I am an inferior golfer to Jack Nicklaus or Arnold Palmer. This does not, however, make me an inferior person. Arnold Palmer's inability to perform surgery makes him an inferior surgeon, but not an inferior person. It all depends on what and whose norms we measure ourselves by.

It is not *knowledge* of actual inferiority in skill or knowledge that gives us an inferiority complex and interferes with our living. It is the *feeling* of inferiority that does this.

And this feeling of inferiority comes about for just one reason: We judge ourselves, and measure ourselves not against our own norm or par but against some other individual's norm. When we do this, we always, without exception, come out second best. But because we *think*, and *believe* and *assume* that we *should* measure up to some other person's norm, we feel miserable and second-rate, and conclude that there is something wrong with us. The next logical conclusion in this cockeyed reasoning process is to conclude that we are not "worthy," that we do not deserve success and happiness, and that it would be out of place for us to fully express our own abilities and talents, whatever they might be, without apology, or without feeling guilty about it.

All this comes about because we have allowed ourselves to be hypnotized by the entirely erroneous idea that "I should be like so-and-so" or "I should be like everybody else." The fallacy of the second idea can be readily seen through, if analyzed, for in truth there are no fixed standards common to everybody else. "Everybody else" is composed of individuals, no two of whom are alike.

Neither a New Nose or New Shoes Guarantee Success

Consider the famous advertising campaign constructed around Michael Jordan with the slogan "I Want To Be Like Mike." The blunt truth is that very few young men have the physical talent to replicate Michael Jordan's performance, even if they replicated his remarkable discipline, commitment, work ethic, and competitive spirit. If this ad campaign harmlessly sells shoes and clothing, so be it. For some, it will serve as positive stimulus and motivation to strive to achieve, and that is constructive. For others, however, sadly, it will serve only to set up an impossible ideal to compare to or, worse, send young people away from the core to the circumference of being, guaranteed disappointment when they discover that a new pair of shoes has no more magic than a new nose provided by my scalpel.

The more mature, intelligent observer of Michael and of this ad campaign can choose not to be adversely hypnotized by it, but to be motivated by it, and look past it, more thoughtfully at the characteristics and behavior (other than innate, exceptional physical talent) that have contributed most to Michael Jordan's success, that may be uncovered in oneself, strengthened, even emulated. It is even true that a basketball player less innately, physically gifted than Jordan could replicate or even surpass his success in the sport and do so, in part, thanks to Jordan as inspiration.

The person with an inferiority complex invariably compounds the error by striving for superiority. Her feelings spring from the false premise that she is inferior. From this false premise, a whole structure of "logical thought" and feeling is built. If she feels bad because she is inferior, the cure is to make herself as good as everybody else, and the way to feel really good is to make herself superior. This striving for superiority gets her into more trouble, causes more frustration, and sometimes brings about a neurosis where none existed before. She becomes more miserable than ever, and "the harder she tries," the more miserable she becomes.

Inferiority and superiority are reverse sides of the same coin. The cure lies in realizing that the coin itself is spurious.

The *truth* about you is this:

You are not "inferior."

You are not "superior."

You are simply "you."

"You" as a personality are not in competition with any other personality simply because there is not another person on the face of the earth like you or in your particular class. You are an individual. You are unique. You are not "like" any other person and can never become "like" any other person. You are not supposed to be like any other person and no other person is supposed to be like you.

God did not create a standard person and in some way label that person by saying, "This is it." He made every human being individual and unique just as He made every snowflake individual and unique.

God created short people and tall people, large people and small people, skinny people and fat people, black, yellow, red and white people. He has never indicated any preference for any one size, shape, or color. Abraham Lincoln once said, "God must have loved the common people for he made so many of them." He was wrong. There is no "common man"—no standardized, common pattern. Lincoln would have been nearer the truth had he said, "God must have loved uncommon people for he made so many of them."

An inferiority complex, and its accompanying deterioration in performance can be made to order in the psychological laboratory. All you need to do is to set up a "norm" or "average," then convince your subject he does not measure up. In my original book, I reported on a psychologist who wanted to find out how feelings of inferiority affected the ability to solve problems. He gave his students a set of routine tests. "But then he solemnly announced that the *average person* could complete the test in about one-fifth the time it would really take. When in the course of the test a bell would ring, indicating that the 'average man's' time was up, some of the brightest subjects became very jittery and incompetent indeed, thinking themselves to be morons." ("What's on Your Mind?", Science Digest, February 1952)

Imagine, if you didn't know any better, being taken to the golf course for the first time, shown the basics of the game, and told that the average new player hit 80. If you were convinced this was true, how would you feel at the conclusion of your first round of golf?

Or imagine if you didn't know better, if you were to enter the insurance business convinced that the average new agent instantly began making $20,000 a month in commissions. How would you feel at the conclusion of the first month? The second?

Consider also the dangers of measuring yourself against a very unfair apples-to-oranges standard. For example, if I were to measure my worth as an author by comparing my book's number of copies sold to novelist Tom Clancy or Stephen King, I would be comparing apples to oranges.

Stop measuring yourself against "their" standards. You are not "them" and can never measure up. Neither can "they" measure up to yours—nor should they.

As you utilize Psycho-Cybernetics to communicate with your self-image, your objective should not be to feel superior to others, nor should you continue permitting feelings of inferiority to others. Your objective is to develop your own unique personality and accomplishments.

How to Use Relaxation to Dehypnotize Yourself

Physical relaxation plays a key role in the dehypnotization process. Our currently held beliefs, whether good or bad, true or false, were formed *without effort,* with no sense of strain, and without the exercise of willpower. Our habits, whether good or bad, were formed in the same way. It follows that we must employ the same process in forming new beliefs or new habits, that is, in a relaxed condition.

Physical relaxation, when practiced daily, brings about an accompanying "mental relaxation" and a "relaxed attitude," which enables us to better consciously control our automatic mechanism. Physical relaxation also, in itself, has a powerful influence in dehypnotizing us from negative attitudes and reaction patterns.

Mental Training Exercise

(To be practiced for at least 30 minutes daily)

Seat yourself comfortably in an easy chair or lie down on your back. Consciously "let go" the various muscle groups as much as possible without making too much of an effort of it. Just consciously pay attention to the various parts of your body and let go a little. You will find that you can always voluntarily relax to a certain degree. You can stop frowning and let your forehead relax. You can ease up a little on the tension in your jaws. You can let your hands, your arms, your shoulders, your legs become a little more relaxed than they are. Spend about five minutes on this and then stop paying any attention to your muscles. This is as far as you are going to try to go by conscious control. From here on you will relax more and more by using your creative mechanism to automatically bring about a relaxed condition. In short, you are going to use "goal pictures," held in your imagination and let your automatic mechanism realize those goals for you.

Mental Picture 1

In your mind's eye see yourself lying stretched out upon the bed. Form a picture of your legs as they would look if made of concrete. See yourself lying there with two very heavy concrete legs. See these very heavy concrete legs sinking far down into the mattress from their sheer weight. Now picture your arms and hands as made of concrete. They also are very heavy and are sinking down into the bed and exerting tremendous pressure against the bed. In your mind's eye see a friend come into the room and attempt to lift your heavy concrete legs. He takes hold of your feet and attempts to lift them. But they are too heavy for him. He cannot do it. Repeat this process with your arms, neck, etc.

Mental Picture 2

Your body is a big marionette doll. Your hands are tied loosely to your wrists by strings. Your forearm is connected loosely by a string to your upper arm. Your upper arm is connected very loosely by a string to your shoulder. Your feet, calves, thighs are also connected together with a single string. Your neck consists of one very limp string. The strings that control your jaw and hold your lips together have slackened and stretched to such an extent that your chin has dropped down loosely against your chest. All the various strings connecting the various parts of your body are loose and limp, and your body is just sprawled loosely across the bed.

Mental Picture 3

Many people will find this the most relaxing of all. Just go back in memory to some relaxing and pleasant scene from your past. There is always some time in every one's life when he felt relaxed, at ease, and at peace with the world. Pick out your own relaxing picture from your past and call up detailed memory images. Yours may be a peaceful scene at a mountain lake where you went fishing. If so, pay particular attention to the little incidental things in the environment. Remember the quiet ripples on the water. What sounds were present? Did you hear the quiet rustling of the leaves? Maybe you remember sitting perfectly relaxed and somewhat drowsy before an open fireplace long ago. Did the logs crackle and spark? What other sights and sounds were present? Maybe you choose to remember relaxing in the sun on a beach. How did the sand feel against your body? Could you feel the warm relaxing sun, touching your body, almost as a physical thing? Was there a breeze blowing? Were there gulls on the beach? The more of these incidental details you can remember and picture to yourself, the more successful you will be.

Daily practice will bring these mental pictures or memories clearer and clearer. The effect of learning will also be cumulative. Practice will strengthen the tie-in between mental image and physical sensation. You will become more and more proficient in relaxation, and this in itself will be "remembered" in future practice sessions.

CHAPTER FIVE

How to Succeed with the Power of Rational Thinking

I get the facts, I study them patiently, I apply imagination.
—Bernard Baruch

M any of my patients were plainly disappointed when I prescribed something as simple as using their God-given power of reason as a method of changing negative beliefs and behavior. To some, it seemed incredibly naive and unscientific. Yet it does have one advantage: It works. And as we shall see later, it is based on sound scientific findings.

There is a widely accepted fallacy that rational, logical, conscious thinking has no power over unconscious processes or mechanisms, and that to change negative beliefs, feelings, or behavior, it is necessary to dig down and dredge up material from the "unconscious."

Your automatic mechanism is absolutely impersonal. It operates as a machine and has no will of its own. It always tries to react appropriately to your current beliefs and interpretations concerning environment. It always seeks to give you appropriate feelings, and to accomplish the goals that you consciously determine upon. It works only on the data that you feed it in the form of ideas, beliefs, interpretations, opinions.

It is conscious thinking that is the "control knob" of your unconscious machine. It was by conscious thought, though perhaps irrational and unrealistic, that the unconscious machine developed its negative and inappropriate reaction patterns, and it is by conscious rational thought that the automatic reaction patterns can be changed.

You Can Get Positive Results Now!

In movies and television programs, "therapy" is usually portrayed as a psychiatrist guiding a patient into an archeological dig of distant childhood memories. As a result, it is a popular notion that, once in therapy, you stay in therapy.

I recall an executive telling me that he had many issues he would like to work on and behavior he would like to change, but that he would never agree to go to a psychiatrist's office week after week, dredging up and endlessly discussing matters from his childhood. With all due respect to psychiatrists, theirs is not the only path to a healthy self-image and, to be fair, this idea of psychiatry is not accurately representative of all doctors' methods.

In any case, I asked him if he would seriously like to make some changes, if he could do it without ever having to revisit his childhood. When he said yes, I talked with him about the ideas in this chapter, the use of *current* rational thought in concert with the imagination to modify the self-image.

If you remember the formula we looked at earlier, we will simply add a precursor to it, so that it becomes:

You as Creator of Your Own Life Experiences

Rational Thinking Leads To (1) Conscious Mind Decision +
(2) Imagination Communicates Goal/Target
to (3) Self-Image
= (4) "Work Order" Instructions to
Servo-Mechanism

In simple terms, sticking to the guided missile analogy central to Psycho-Cybernetics, we use deliberate, rational conscious thought to choose the "target," then we use the imagination to communicate the "target" to the self-image in a manner that it will be accepted and acted upon.

How Testing Self-Imposed Limits with Rational Thinking Can Surprise You

Consider a very simple situation: likes and dislikes of food. I once had a friend who refused to ever eat green beans and bacon, a side dish I enjoyed immensely, often with a good steak. Many times I tried to get him to try some, but he insisted that he hated beans. Finally I wore him down and one evening, in a restaurant where we were sharing a meal, he grudgingly agreed to taste "your damned beans," as he put it, "just to get you off my back."

After his first bite, he murmured, "Hmmm." He tried a second bite. And a third. He said, "These are quite tasty."

Some months later, when we again dined together, he ordered green beans with bacon!

Now, there was some reason he believed it to be fact that he did not like the taste of green beans. I don't know the reason, and I don't know if he did either. I'd suppose not, since he never enunciated it. But he didn't need to ferret through his childhood experiences, holding all manner of youthful experiences up to the light, contemplating overheard adult conversations while hiding on the stairs, in order to challenge his belief and test it in his adult life, in the current moment.

Admittedly, few psychologic issues are as innocuous as a like or dislike for green beans and bacon. But many ways in which you might desire to improve or to feel more at peace with yourself are actually not all that much more complex than your taste for beans either.

I maintain, acknowledging that members of the psychiatric profession may differ, that most people can, in fact, resolve most of the self-sabotage plaguing them with Psycho-Cybernetics and possibly other, related self-improvement modalities, without in-depth analysis of all prior life events.

It May Be Perfectly Okay to Let Sleeping Dogs Lie

The fact that buried in the unconscious are memories of past failures, along with unpleasant and painful experiences, does not mean that these must be "dug out," exposed or examined, in order to effect personality changes. As we have pointed out earlier, all skill learning is accomplished by trial and error, by making a trial, missing the mark, consciously remembering the degree of error, and making correction on the next trial—until finally a "hit," or successful attempt is accomplished. The successful reaction pattern is then remembered, or recalled, and "imitated" on future trials. This is true for a man learning to pitch horseshoes, throw darts, sing, drive a car, play golf, get along socially with other human beings, or any other skill. Thus, all servo-mechanisms, by their very nature, contain "memories" of past errors, failures, painful and negative experiences. These negative experiences do not inhibit, but *contribute* to the learning process, as long as they are used properly as negative feedback data, and are seen as deviations from the positive goal desired.

However, as soon as the error has been recognized as such, and correction of course made, it is equally important that the *error be consciously forgotten*, and that the successful attempt remembered and dwelt upon.

These memories of past failures do no harm as long as our conscious thought and attention is focused on the positive goal to be accomplished. Therefore, it is best to let these sleeping dogs lie.

Our errors, mistakes, failures, and sometimes even our humiliations were necessary steps in the learning process. However, they were meant to be means to an end, not an end in themselves. When they have served their purpose, they should be *forgotten*. If we consciously dwell on the error or consciously feel guilty about the error and keep berating ourselves because of it, then—unwittingly—we make the error or failure itself the "goal" that is consciously held in imagination and memory. The unhappiest of mortals are those who insist on reliving the past, over and over in their imagination, continually criticizing themselves for past mistakes, continually condemning themselves for past sins.

The new term for taking control of your emotions and self-image without probing your past for root causes is Solution-Oriented Therapy, and if you are interested in a current book on this subject, I recommend *Do One Thing Different*, by Bill O'Hanlon.

The Power of "Forgetfulness"

When asked to name the most important characteristic of a truly great pass receiver in football, the great quarterback of the Cleveland

Browns, Otto Graham, said, "A damned short memory." Players and coaches have explained that to me, and echoed it year after year in media interviews. What is meant is that the most important skill the receiver possesses is the ability to instantly forget about the catchable pass he just embarrassingly dropped so as to focus on the "target"— successfully catching the next one thrown in his direction.

I have many times watched a football game on television, seen the field goal kicker hook a kick badly and miss a short 20- or 30-yard field goal, only to return later in the game, even with the entire game on the line, and make a much longer, more difficult field goal. The kicker's ability to forget and refocus was every bit as important as his physical strength and kicking mechanics.

Continually criticizing yourself for past mistakes and errors— whether from years ago or minutes ago—does not help matters, but on the other hand tends to perpetuate the very behavior you would change. Memories of past failures can adversely affect present performance, if we dwell on them and foolishly conclude: "I failed yesterday; therefore I will fail again today." However, this does not "prove" that unconscious reaction patterns have any power in themselves to repeat and perpetuate themselves or that all buried memories of failure must be eradicated before behavior can be changed. If we are victimized, it is by our conscious, thinking mind and not by the unconscious. For it is with the thinking part of our personality that we draw conclusions and select the goal images that we shall concentrate on. The minute that we *change our minds* and stop giving power to the past, the past with its mistakes loses its power over us.

Ignore Past Failures and Forge Ahead

When a shy, timid, wallflower is told in hypnosis, and *believes* or *thinks* that he is a bold, self-confident orator, his reaction patterns are changed instantly. He currently acts as he currently believes. His attention is given over completely to the positive desired goal, and no thought or consideration whatsoever is given to past failures.

Dorothea Brande tells in her charming book, *Wake Up and Live*, how this one idea enabled her to become more productive and successful as a writer, and to draw upon talents and abilities she never knew she had. She had been both curious and amazed after witnessing a demonstration in hypnosis. Then she happened to read one sentence written by psychologist F. M. H. Myers, which she says changed her whole life. The sentence by Myers explained that the talents and abilities displayed by hypnotic subjects were due to a "purgation of memory" of past failures, while in the hypnotic state. If this were possible under hypnosis, Dorothea Brande asked herself—if ordinary people carried around within themselves talents, abilities, powers, that were held in check and not used merely because of memories of past failures—why couldn't a person in the wakeful state use these same powers by ignoring past failures and "acting as if it were impossible to fail"? She determined to try it. She would act on the assumption that the powers and abilities were there and that she could use them, if only she would go ahead and *act as if*, instead of in a tentative half-hearted way. Within a year her production as a writer had increased many times. So had her sales. A rather surprising result was that she discovered a talent for public speaking, became much in demand as a lecturer and enjoyed it, whereas previously she had not only shown no talent for lecturing, but disliked it intensely.

With Psycho-Cybernetics exercises like those described in many chapters in this book, as well as even more extensive and sophisticated mental training exercises provided in my twelve-week course on Psycho-Cybernetics, one of the things I strive for is equipping you with ways to "act as if" within your own imagination and to encourage your doing so repetitively and creatively.

Bertrand Russell's Method

In his book *The Conquest of Happiness*, Bertrand Russell wrote:

> I was not born happy. As a child, my favorite hymn was: 'Weary of earth and laden with my sin.' ... In adolescence, I hated life and was continually on the verge of suicide, from which, however, I was restrained by the desire to know more mathematics. Now, on the contrary, I enjoy life; I might almost say that with every year that passes I enjoy it more ... very largely it is due to a diminishing preoccupation with myself. Like others who had a Puritan education, I had the habit of meditating on my sins, follies, and shortcomings. I seemed to myself—no doubt justly—a miserable specimen. Gradually I learned to be indifferent to myself and my

deficiencies; I came to center my attention increasingly upon external objects: the state of the world, various branches of knowledge, individuals for whom I felt affection.

In the same book, he describes his method for changing automatic reaction patterns based on false beliefs:

It is quite possible to overcome infantile suggestions of the unconscious, and even to change the contents of the unconscious, by employing the right kind of technique. Whenever you begin to feel remorse for an act which your reason tells you is not wicked, examine the causes of your feeling of remorse, and convince yourself in detail of their absurdity. Let your conscious beliefs be so vivid and emphatic that they make an impression upon your unconscious strong enough to cope with the impressions made by your nurse or your mother when you were an infant. Do not be content with an alternation between moments of rationality and moments of irrationality. Look into the irrationality closely with a determination not to respect it and not to let it dominate you. Whenever it thrusts foolish thoughts or feelings into your consciousness, pull them up by the roots, examine them, and reject them. Do not allow yourself to remain a vacillating creature, swayed half by reason and half by infantile folly ...

But if the rebellion is to be successful in bringing individual happiness and in enabling a man to live consistently by one standard, not to vacillate between two, it is necessary that he should think and feel deeply about what his reason tells him. Most men, when they have thrown off superficially the superstitions of their childhood, think that there is no more to be done. They do not realize that these superstitions are still lurking underground. When a rational conviction has been arrived at, it is necessary to dwell upon it, to follow out its consequences, to search out in oneself whatever beliefs inconsistent with the new conviction might otherwise survive ...

What I suggest is that a man should make up his mind with emphasis as to what he rationally believes, and should never allow contrary irrational beliefs to pass unchallenged or obtain a hold over him, however brief. This is a question of reasoning with himself in those moments in which he is tempted to become infantile, but the reasoning, if it is sufficiently emphatic, may be very brief.

Ideas Are Changed Not by "Will," but by Other Ideas

It can be seen that Bertrand Russell's technique of searching out ideas that are inconsistent with some deeply felt conviction, is essentially the same as the method tested clinically with such amazing success by

Prescott Lecky. Lecky's method consisted of getting subjects to "see" that some negative concept of theirs was *inconsistent* with some other deeply held belief. Lecky believed that it was inherent in the very nature of "mind" itself, that all ideas and concepts making up the total content of "personality" must *seem to be* consistent with each other. If the inconsistency of a given idea is consciously recognized, it *must be rejected.*

In my original book, I told of my encounter with a salesperson in which I employed this technique of shining the spotlight on two conflicting beliefs, to get rid of the unproductive one.

One of my patients was a salesperson who was "scared to death" when calling on "big shots." His fear and nervousness were overcome in just one counseling session, during which I asked him, "Would you physically get down on all fours and crawl into the man's office, prostrating yourself before a superior personage?"

"I should say not!" he bristled.

"Then why do you mentally cringe and crawl?"

Another question: "Would you go into a man's office with your hand out like a beggar, and beg for a dime for a cup of coffee?"

"Certainly not."

"Can't you see that you are doing essentially the same thing, when you go in overly concerned with whether or not he will approve of you? Can't you see that you have your hand out, literally begging for his approval and acceptance of you as a person?"

Two Psychologic Levers You Can Use to Remove Any "Mountain" in Your Way

Lecky found that there were two powerful levers for changing beliefs and concepts. There are *standard* convictions, which are strongly held by nearly everyone. These are (1) the feeling or belief that you are capable of doing your share, holding up your end of the log, exerting a certain amount of independence, and (2) the belief that there is "something" inside you that should not be allowed to suffer indignities.

Interestingly, NLP (neuro-linguistic programming), which is based on extensive work by Drs. Grindler and Bandler and has been popularized by Tony Robbins, offers a tool-kit of two items: pain and accomplishment.

I do not think it coincidental that pain and the deep-seated belief that you should not suffer great indignities are the triggers that most quickly or easily and definitively motivate people to action. Knowing this, you can use it to motivate yourself to constructive action.

Let me tell you of a person just so motivated. Today, one of the members of The Psycho-Cybernetics Foundation's Board of Directors and a coauthor of the Psycho-Cybernetics book *Zero Resistance Selling*, Jeff Paul, was once a Certified Financial Planner with some significant success, but horribly unhappy in his work. He disliked the commute to the office, wearing a suit and tie, selling on the telephone and in person, and the repetitive nature of the work. One day, he had the flash of rational thought that he need not continue making his living doing something he intensely disliked doing. He correctly, consciously acknowledged there must be any number of other ways he could meet his financial goals.

You know, a great many people never take that simple realization seriously.

Jeff then set about doing what we now call *backwards goal-setting*. He mentally prepared a list of things he did not want to do at all. His list included having to wear a suit and tie; having to manage a staff; some dozen or so items in total. Then he utilized his imagination to "shop around" for ideas about other careers and businesses that he might have some affinity for, but that would never require him to do the things on his I Never Want to Do These Things Again List.

After considerable thought, he decided upon the mail-order business. He recognized that a great many financial planners could benefit from the methods he had perfected for successfully attracting clients. He envisioned a business in which he would publish that information in the form of books, manuals, and recordings, then sell the products to members of his profession by advertising and direct-mail. He could operate from an office in his home and have functions like order-taking, printing and shipping done for him by outside contractors. He convinced his self-image he could do this by focusing on his strengths, such as his intimate knowledge of the desires and frustrations of his peers, his possession of useful knowledge to sell, his evolving avid interest in mail order and willingness to learn. While his earliest attempts were markedly unsuccessful, he "course corrected" by a number of means and ultimately achieved extraordinary success I will briefly enumerate here:

First, Jeff built a mail-order publishing business selling to financial planners and insurance agents that provided an income of more than $100,000 a month, from a small home office. Second, Jeff created a home study course, seminar, and other materials to teach his mail-order business model to others, and he has thus inspired many others to create such businesses. A book he wrote about his experiences, to promote his course, *How To Make $4,000.00 A Day Sitting At Your Kitchen Table In Your Underwear*, has sold well over 100,000 copies. Third, he developed such a high level of marketing and sales letter copywriting skills that he has become a much sought after, highly paid consultant. Maybe most importantly, he has developed his businesses and significant wealth without conflict with his I Never Want to Do These Things Again List.

Jeff credits the use of Psycho-Cybernetics techniques, but also emphasizes what he calls "Accurate Thinking," what I have called "rational thought," as the all-important starting point.

Examine and Reevaluate Your Beliefs

One of the reasons that the power of rational thinking goes unrecognized is that it is so seldom used.

Trace down the belief about yourself, about the world, or about other people that is behind your negative behavior. Does something always happen to cause you to miss out just when success seems within your grasp? Perhaps you secretly feel unworthy of success, or that you do not deserve it. Are you ill at ease around other people? Perhaps you believe you are inferior to them, or that other people per se are hostile and unfriendly. Do you become anxious and fearful for no good reason in a situation that is relatively safe? Perhaps you believe that the world you live in is a hostile, unfriendly, dangerous place, or that you deserve punishment.

How many people do you suppose would love to have a perfect lifestyle business like Jeff's, but, if asked about it, would quickly produce a laundry list of reasons why they cannot do what he has done. These "reasons" are not reasons based on current rational thought at all. They are just beliefs, subject to change.

Remember that both behavior and feeling spring from belief. To root out the belief responsible for your feeling and behavior, ask yourself why? Is there some task you would like to do, some channel in which you would like to express yourself, but you hang back feeling that "I can't"? Ask yourself *why*?

"Why do I believe that I can't?"

Then ask yourself, "Is this belief based on an actual fact or on an assumption—or a false conclusion?"

Then ask yourself these four questions:

1. Is there any rational reason for such a belief?
2. Could it be that I am mistaken in this belief?
3. Would I come to the same conclusion about some other person in a similar situation?
4. Why should I continue to act and feel as if this were true if there is no good reason to believe it?

Don't just pass these questions by casually. Wrestle with them. Think *hard* on them. Get emotional about them. Can you see that you have cheated yourself and sold yourself short, not because of a "fact," but only because of an irrational and erroneous belief? If so, try to arouse some indignation or even anger. Indignation and anger can sometimes act as liberators from false ideas. Alfred Adler "got mad" at himself and at his teacher, and was enabled to throw off a negative definition of himself. This experience is not uncommon.

An old farmer said he quit tobacco for good one day when he discovered he had left his tobacco home and started to walk the two miles for it. On the way, he saw that he was being "used" in a humiliating way by a habit. He got mad, turned around, went back to the field, and never smoked again.

Clarence Darrow, the famous attorney, said his success started the day that he got mad when he attempted to secure a mortgage for $2,000 to buy a house. Just as the transaction was about to be completed, the lender's wife spoke up and said, "Don't be a fool. He will never make enough money to pay it off." Darrow himself had had serious doubts about the same thing. But "something happened" when he heard her remark. He became indignant, both at the woman and at himself, and determined he would be a success.

Walt Disney said that he went from exploring ideas to being determined to make a success of them, when a group of amusement park owners criticized and laughed at his plans for Disneyland.

A businessman friend of mine had a very similar experience. A failure at 40, he continually worried about how things would come out, about his own inadequacies, and whether or not he would be able to complete each business venture. Fearful and anxious, he was attempting to purchase machinery on credit, when the man's wife objected. She did not believe he would ever be able to pay for it. At first his hopes were dashed. But then he became indignant. Who was he to be pushed around like that? Who was he to skulk through the world, continually fearful of failure? The experience awakened "something" within him—some "new self"—and at once he saw that this woman's remark, as well as his own opinions of himself, were an affront to this "something." He had no money, no credit, and no way to accomplish what he wanted. But he found a way, and within three years was more successful than he had ever dreamed of being—not in one business, but in three.

The Power of Deep Desire

Rational thought, to be effective in changing belief and behavior, must be accompanied with deep feeling and desire.

Picture to yourself what you would like to be and have, and assume for the moment that such things might be possible. Arouse a deep desire for these things. Become enthusiastic about them. Dwell on them, and keep going over them in your mind. Your present negative beliefs were formed by thought plus feelings. Generate enough emotion or deep feeling, and your new thoughts and ideas will cancel them out.

If you will analyze this, you will see that you are using a process you have often used before: worry! The only difference is that you change your goals from negative to positive. When you worry, you first picture an undesirable future outcome or goal very vividly in your imagination. You use no effort or willpower. But you keep dwelling on the end result. You keep thinking about it—dwelling on it—picturing it to yourself as a possibility. You play with the idea that it might happen.

This constant repetition, and thinking in terms of possibilities, makes the end result appear more and more real to you. After a time, appropriate emotions are automatically generated—fear, anxiety, discouragement—all appropriate to the undesirable end result you are worrying about. Now change the goal picture,—and you can as easily generate "good" emotions. Constantly picturing to yourself and dwelling on a desirable end result will also make the possibility seem more real, and again appropriate emotions of enthusiasm, cheerfulness, encouragement, and happiness will automatically be generated.

What Rational Thought Can and Cannot Do

Remember that your automatic mechanism can as easily function as a Failure Mechanism as a Success Mechanism, depending on the data you give it to process and the goals you set for it. It is basically a goal-striving mechanism. The goals it works on are up to you. Many of us unconsciously and unwittingly, by holding negative attitudes and habitually picturing failure to ourselves in our imagination, set up goals of failure.

Also remember that your automatic mechanism does not reason about, or question the data you feed it. It merely processes it and reacts appropriately to it.

The stage fright experienced by people called upon to speak in public is interesting. It is, according to many surveys, one of the top three or four fears shared by all adults. It can be paralyzing. Yet, rationally, you can understand that no one has been hanged for giving a poor public speech in quite a long time, at least in this country. In most situations, there is no dire consequence of appearing a bit nervous, forgetting a few points, or telling a joke that falls flat. The fear felt is excessive in relationship to the possible penalty for making mistakes.

It is very important that the automatic mechanism be given true facts concerning the environment. This is the job of conscious rational thought: to know the truth, to form correct evaluations, estimations, opinions. In this connection most of us are prone to underestimate ourselves and overestimate the nature of the difficulty facing us.

"I have made extensive experiments to discover the common causes of that conscious effort which freezes the thinking mind," wrote psychologist Daniel W. Josselyn. "Practically always it seems to be due to the tendency to exaggerate the difficulty and importance of your mental labors, to take them too seriously and fear they will find you incapable." (Daniel W. Josselyn, *Why Be Tired?*)

It's Just a Game

In his book *Golf's Mental Hazards: Overcome Them and Put an End to the Self Destructive Round*, Dr. Alan Shapiro enumerates six mental hazards, the first four of which are directly relevant to this discussion, and have application far beyond the game of golf. Here are his descriptions, in abbreviated form:

> **Hazard 1: The Fear of Fear.** Golfers who fall prey to this experience anticipatory anxiety before a round, have first-tee jitters, and "choke" during critical moments.

> **Hazard 2: Losing Your Cool.** This is the golfer who slams the club into the ground, throws it into a water hazard, or wraps it around a tree.

> **Hazard 3: Getting Too Up or Too Down.** These golfers are quick to get down on themselves. Their emotions can range from euphoria after making a difficult par to utter despair after knocking a tee shot out of bounds on the very next hole. On the basis of performance on any given day, these golfers can remain elated or depressed for days after a round of golf.

> **Hazard 4: Worry What Others Think.** These individuals dread embarrassment on the golf course, are prone to feelings of inferiority, sensitive to ridicule, and feel that others are always closely watching and judging.

Any of these is obviously sufficient to jam the servo-mechanism. On analysis, they are, of course, irrational. Hazard 3 is classic overreaction to individual incidents in life, most of which are never as important days or weeks after their occurrence as they seemed at the immediate moment. Persons cursed with the habit of overreaction are one step short of manic-depressive, will be profoundly and unnecessarily miserable at least half of their lifetime, will gradually convince their self-image that they have no self-control, and will cause others to avoid relationships with them. And Hazard 3 worsens the others.

There's a classic golf story about the weekend duffer returning home horribly depressed, sulking and moping about the house until, finally, his wife says "Honey, remember it's just a game." He angrily snaps back, "You don't know the first damned thing about golf!"

But it *is* just a game. And today is just today. A mistake is just a mistake. We must use rational thinking to achieve perspective, to rise above these paralyzing mental hazards. However, rational thought expressed as willpower—I will not lose my cool, I will not overreact—is a losing proposition. Rational thought used creatively to develop entirely new mental pictures in the imagination, feeding the self-image dynamic new evidence, transmitting a new target to the servo-mechanism is a winning process.

It Ain't Necessarily So!

It is the job of rational, conscious thought to examine and analyze incoming messages, to accept those that are true and reject those that are untrue. Many people are bowled over by the chance remark of a friend: "You do not look so well this morning." If they are rejected or snubbed by someone, they blindly swallow the fact that this means they are an inferior person. Most of us are subjected to negative suggestions every day. If our conscious mind is working and on the job, we do not have to accept them blindly. "It ain't necessarily so," is a good motto.

In the book *Battling the Inner Dummy*, the author describes this as "limbic hijacking," a sort of abrupt uprising of the Automatic Failure Mechanism that is always lurking about, waiting to wrest control away from both your rational thinking and your Automatic Success Mechanism. After all, the Automatic Failure Mechanism and Automatic Success Mechanism are two sides of the same coin, separated only by the thinnest edge. He wrote: "… one of my tennis partners said to me, 'Boy, are you putting on weight.' Within hours, captured by an irrational fear of looking fat, I was on a crash diet. The scale showed I had put on only three pounds, but it was the perception of looking fat rather than reality that created the fear. Today, when somebody tells me something like that, I go into the bathroom, close the door and scream at my Inner Dummy: 'Don't pay attention to that insensitive remark. Don't get upset. Do you hear me, inside there? So okay, tonight, we'll lay off the mashed potatoes and gravy, but that's it.'"

Taking time out for a "rational thought coaching session" with yourself can be effective, and is a precursor to installing rational thought-based mental pictures that can be recalled at a moment's notice, to accomplish the same interruption of overreaction.

The Problem That Can't Be Solved Won't Be Solved

It is the job of the conscious rational mind to form logical and correct conclusions. "I failed once in the past, so I will probably fail in the future" is neither logical nor rational. To conclude "I can't" in advance, without trying, and in the absence of any evidence to the contrary, is not rational. We should be more like the man who was asked if he could play the piano. "I don't know," he said. "What do you mean you don't know?" He said, "I have never tried."

Michael Vance, the former Dean of Disney University, author of the book *Think Outside The Box*, and an authority on creative thinking, tells of the corporate executive he queried about the company's biggest problem. After listening to the problem described in all its magnitude and severity, Vance asked "Who's working on solving it?" "No one," replied the executive. "Why not?" Vance asked. "Because it cannot be solved," replied the executive.

I imagine that executive saying "because it cannot be solved" to Mr. Vance in an exasperated, impatient tone, thinking Vance the dolt for not grasping this simple and obvious truth.

Too many people live their entire lives just like this executive, believing that their circumstances cannot be improved, their problems cannot be solved, even that somehow they are incapable of achieving the career success or prosperity or happiness that they see others achieving routinely. As a result, they are as vulnerable to "mental hazards" unleashing the Automatic Failure Mechanism as a hemophiliac is to paper cuts proving fatal.

Decide What You Want—Not What You Don't Want

It is the job of conscious rational thought to decide what you want, select the goals you wish to achieve, and concentrate on these rather than on what you do not want. Once you have arrived at an understanding of what you want, spending time and effort concentrating on what you do *not* want is not rational. When President Eisenhower was General Eisenhower in World War II, he was asked what would have been the effect on the allied cause if the invasion troops had been thrown back into the sea from the beaches of Italy? "It would have been very bad," he said, "but I never allow my mind to think in that way."

How do *you* let your mind think?

Most people go about their daily business exercising no control whatsoever over what pops into—or is popped into—their minds. Television, radio, the newspaper, casual conversation, overheard conversation, any critical remark, even an advertising billboard takes control. A cumbersome but illuminating exercise is to carry a pad or bound notebook with you all day and jot down every thought that occurs to you. Take a look at this diary at the end of the day, and see for yourself how little of what you thought you chose to think! We are too often like the couch potato whose TV remote control battery goes dead, and too lazy to go and install a new battery, he simply sits there all evening watching whatever comes on the station he is stuck on!

Can't you do better than this?

Keep Your Eye on the Ball

It is the job of your conscious mind to pay strict attention to the task at hand, to what you are doing and what is going on around you, so that these incoming sensory messages can keep your automatic mechanism currently advised of the environment and allow it to respond spontaneously. In baseball parlance, you must "keep your eye on the ball."

It is *not* the job of your conscious rational mind, however, to create or to do the job at hand. We get into trouble when we either neglect to use conscious thinking in the way that it is meant to be used, or when we attempt to use it in a way that it was never meant to be used. We cannot squeeze creative thought out of the Creative Mechanism by making a conscious effort. We cannot do the job to be done by making strained conscious efforts. And because we try and cannot, we become concerned, anxious, frustrated. The automatic mechanism is unconscious. We cannot see the wheels turning. We cannot know what is taking place beneath the surface. And because it works spontaneously in reacting to present and current needs, we can have no intimation or certified guarantee in advance that it will come up with the answer. We are forced into a position of trust. And only by trusting and acting do we receive signs and wonders. In short, conscious rational thought selects the goal, gathers information, concludes, evaluates, estimates and starts the wheels in motion. It is not, however, responsible for results. We must learn to do our work, act on the best assumptions available, and *leave the results to take care of themselves.*

MENTAL TRAINING EXERCISES:

1. Have a heart-to-heart talk with yourself and honestly assess whether you have any problems you're no longer attempting to resolve only because you have accepted as "fact" that they cannot be solved, whether you are living out circumstances in your life that are unfulfilling or even demeaning to you because you have accepted as fact that you cannot alter them. Reconsider! Apply current rational thought to challenge these beliefs and then use your imagination to "shop around" and try out new and different possibilities.

Consider the questions I suggested in this chapter about each of these "facts" you uncover in your heart-to-heart:

"Why do I believe that I can't?"

Then ask yourself, "Is this belief based on an actual fact or on an assumption or false conclusion?"

"Is there any rational reason for such a belief?"

"Could it be that I am mistaken in this belief?"

"Would I come to the same conclusion about some other person in a similar situation?"

"Why should I continue to act and feel as if this were true if there is no good reason to believe it?"

2. Out of all this rational thought, you may identify a new target (goal) to assign to your Automatic Success Mechanism. If so, review the exercises provided at the end of each of the prior chapters as means of getting started.

Summary Checklist of The Uses of Rational Thought

1. It is the job of rational, conscious thought to examine and analyze incoming messages, to accept those that are true and reject those that are untrue.

2. It is the job of the conscious rational mind to form logical and correct conclusions.

3. It is the job of conscious rational thought to decide what you want, select the goals you wish to achieve, and concentrate on these rather than on what you do not want.

4. It is the job of your conscious mind to pay strict attention to the task at hand, to what you are doing and what is going on around you, so that these incoming sensory messages can keep your automatic mechanism currently advised of the environment and allow it to respond spontaneously.

CHAPTER SIX

How to Relax and Let Your Automatic Success Mechanism Work for You

Determine that the thing can and shall be done,
and then we shall find the way.

—Abraham Lincoln

"Stress has recently become a popular word in our language. We speak of this as the age of stress. Worry, anxiety, insomnia, stomach ulcers have become accepted as a necessary part of the world in which we live." I wrote that in 1960.

In 1960, we didn't know what stress was!

We did not have the incessant cacophony of cellular phones, beepers, e-mail, and other technologies keeping us constantly accessible, constantly communicating, constantly under pressure to respond to everyone instantly. We could never have foreseen the collapse of middle management in most corporate cultures, forcing each person to do the work of three. We did not even yet have the two-career household as a norm.

Today, the typical person has less leisure time, much less private "recovery" time, longer and more congested commutes, and a much greater and faster flow of information and a more complex environment to deal with.

It is far more critical today to conquer stress and anxiety, and to exert control over your life, than it was when I first began talking about Psycho-Cybernetics as stress management.

I remain convinced that life need not be relentless pressure and stress.

We could relieve ourselves of a vast load of care, anxiety, and worry, if we could but recognize the simple truth, that our Creator made ample provisions for us to live successfully in this or any other age by providing us with a built-in Creative Mechanism. Changes in society or technology can easily be handled by our infinitely capable servo-mechanism. In fact, it does not understand the meaning of being overworked or stressed out, because its capacity is unlimited.

Our trouble is that we ignore the automatic creative mechanism and try to do everything and solve all our problems by conscious thought or willpower. It is the job of the conscious mind to pose problems and to identify them, but by its very nature it was never engineered to solve problems itself. You pile on stress by striving to do it all; you relieve stress by learning to assign "problems" to your Automatic Success Mechanism, then letting go of them.

Don't Be Too Careful

The example I used early in this book had Dr. Weiner showing us that man cannot even perform such a simple operation as picking up a pencil from a table by conscious thought or will.

When a person depends almost entirely upon conscious thought and willpower, he becomes too careful, too anxious, and too fearful of results, and the advice of Jesus to "take no thought for the morrow" or of St. Paul to be "careful in nothing" is regarded as impractical nonsense.

Yet this is precisely the advice that William James, dean of American psychologists, gave us years ago, if we would but have listened to him. In his little essay "The Gospel of Relaxation," he said that modern man was too tense, too concerned for results, too anxious (this was in 1899), and that there was a better and easier way. "*When once a decision is reached and execution is the order of the day, dismiss absolutely all responsibility and care about the outcome.* Unclamp, in a word, your intellectual and practical machinery, and let it run free; and the service it will do you will be twice as good."

Incidentally, this is different from simple intuition. I am well aware that a great many people rebel at the thought of entrusting important decisions and responsibilities to something as ethereal as intuition. What we are talking about, I remind you, is a practical formula beginning with conscious, rational thought, but then delegating via the imagination in concert with the self-image, to an amazingly powerful "search engine" and servo-mechanism that will work for you toward the resolution of any problem entirely free of stress.

The Secret of Creative Thinking and Creative Doing

Proof of the fact that what we have been saying is true can be seen in the experience of writers, inventors, and other creative workers. Invariably, they tell us that creative ideas are not consciously thought out by conscious thinking, but come automatically, spontaneously, and somewhat like a bolt out of the blue, when the conscious mind has let go of the problem and is engaged in thinking of something else. These creative ideas do not come willy-nilly without some preliminary conscious thought about the problem. All the evidence points to the conclusion that in order to receive an "inspiration" or a "hunch," the person must first of all be intensely interested in solving a particular problem or securing an answer. He or she must think about it consciously, gather all the information available on the subject, consider all the possible courses of action. And above all, there must be a burning desire to solve the problem. But, having defined the problem, having seen in the imagination the desired end result, having secured all the information and facts, then additional struggling, fretting and worrying over it does not help, but seems to hinder the solution.

In his classic, best-selling book *Think and Grow Rich*, Napoleon Hill tells of being put under pressure by his publisher to come up with an appropriate title for his book in just 24 hours. Such a title idea had been eluding Hill for months, while he completed and submitted his manuscript. At "D-day," his editor told him he had only 24 hours to come up with a good idea, or the book would go to press with the editor's best idea, a title of *Use Your Noodle to Get the Boodle*. Hill protested the outrageous hype and tabloid nature of the title, saying it would ruin him, that he'd never be taken seriously. "24 hours," his publisher said.

That is stress! Briefly, Hill tried to consciously create the title, but soon gave up, as he had been trying for months with no success. He decided instead to turn the whole matter over to his subconscious and let whatever would be, be. Then, he awoke from a nap with the title. On close examination, we can easily see that all his Automatic Success Mechanism did was rewrite the "bad" title. "Noodle" is "Think"; "Boodle" is "Rich."

I believe every author has had this kind of experience. Some of us have gone out of our way to have it deliberately and repeatedly, often letting whole chapters or lectures be written for us by our servo-mechanisms while we nap or play with our grandchildren or sit in a boat, fish pole in hand. The editor of this book, the President of The Psycho-Cybernetics Foundation, Dan Kennedy, has written nine books and numerous articles, writes a monthly newsletter, creates dozens of audio cassette programs, and is a busy advertising copy-writer as well. He has made a point of mastering the application of Psycho-Cybernetics for this purpose, so that he can go to sleep at night, then awake and instantly sit at his computer keyboard and "pour out" the writing work that has been done "for him" as he slept. While others tell of writing being enormously stressful and difficult, for him it is virtually free of stress.

Dan Kennedy says he was first inspired to attempt this by my writing about Bertrand Russell's experience in the original edition of this book. Bertrand Russell said:

> I have found, for example, that, if I have to write upon some rather diffi-cult topic, the best plan is to think about it with very great intensity—the greatest intensity of which I am capable—for a few hours or days, and at the end of that time give orders, so to speak, that the work is to proceed underground. After some months I return consciously to the topic and find that the work has been done. Before I had discovered this technique, I used to spend the intervening months worrying because I was making no progress; I arrived at the solution none the sooner for this worry, and the intervening months were wasted, whereas now I can devote them to other pursuits." (Bertrand Russell, *The Conquest of Happiness*)

What works for writers can work for you. The delegation of cre-ation, i.e., problem solving (they are one and the same), to the servo-mechanism is a universally applicable process.

Lenox Riley Lohr, once president of National Broadcasting Company, once wrote an article telling how ideas that had helped him in business came to him. "Ideas, I find, come most readily when you are doing something that keeps the mind alert without putting too much strain upon it. Shaving, driving a car, sawing a plank, or fishing or hunting, for instance. Or engaging with some friend in stimulating conversation. Some of my best ideas came from information picked up casually and entirely unrelated to my work." (Anyone Can Be an Idea Man," *American Magazine*, March 1940)

C. G. Suits, once Chief of Research at General Electric, said that nearly all the discoveries in research laboratories came as hunches during a period of relaxation, following a period of intensive thinking and fact-gathering.

In other words, when the stress of trying to force the answer through conscious thought is turned off, the servo-mechanism is liberated to function as an Automatic Success Mechanism, and often does just that.

You Are a "Creative Worker"

The mistake we make is assuming that this process of "unconscious cerebration" is reserved for authors, artists, inventors, and other so-called "creative workers." We are all creative workers, whether we are cooks working in a kitchen, school teachers, students, sales professionals, or entrepreneurs. We all have the same success mechanism within us, and it will work in solving personal problems, running a business, or selling goods, just as it will in writing a story or inventing a product. Bertrand Russell recommended that the same method he used in his writing be employed by his readers in solving their mundane personal problems. Dr. J. B. Rhine of Duke University said that he was inclined to think that what we call "genius" is a process—a natural way in which the human mind works to solve any problem—but that we mistakenly apply the term "genius" only when the process is used to write a book or paint a picture.

Michael J. Gelb's fascinating book, *How to Think Like Leonardo da Vinci*, is based on the premise that genius is a process more so than genetic gift.

In effect, each of us has genius within, in most cases waiting to be awakened, liberated, energized, and utilized. Right now, being a genius might not be part of your self-image, but soon I hope it will be, based on this expanded idea of what genius really is and how it works.

The Secret of "Natural" Behavior and Skill

The Success Mechanism within you can work in the same way to produce creative *doing* as it does to produce creative ideas.

Skill in any performance, whether it be in sports, in playing the piano, in conversation, or in selling merchandise, consists not in painfully and consciously thinking out each action as it is performed, but in relaxing and letting the job do itself through you. Creative performance is spontaneous and natural, as opposed to self-conscious and studied. The most skilled pianist in the world could never play a simple composition if she tried to consciously think out just which finger should strike which key while she was playing. She has given conscious thought to this matter previously (while learning) and has practiced until her actions become automatic and habit-like. She was able to become a magnificent performer only when she reached the point where she could cease conscious effort and turn the matter of playing over to the unconscious habit mechanism that is a part of the Success Mechanism.

You may have read elsewhere about this in the context of four steps or levels of learning:

1. Unconscious Incompetence
2. Conscious Incompetence
3. Conscious Competence
4. Unconscious Competence

In the first, you don't even know what you don't know. As you move to the second level, you are painfully aware of what is difficult for you. In the third level, you become able to do the thing, but you are still doing it the hard way, relying on conscious thought, possibly willpower as well. Rising to the fourth level, what was difficult becomes automatic. This is a reasonably accurate depiction of each learning experience, whether it is tying a shoelace as a child or operating a computer as an adult.

What is very important and exciting is how much you can accelerate the movement up this four-rung ladder, and how much stress you can surgically remove from it, through Psycho-Cybernetics, most notably by using Theater in Your Mind techniques in place of or in supplement to actual, physical fumbling.

Don't Jam Your Creative Machinery

Conscious effort inhibits and jams the Automatic Creative Mechanism. The reason some people are self-conscious and awkward in social situations is simply that they are too consciously concerned, too anxious to do the right thing, and too fearful of saying or doing the wrong thing. They are painfully conscious of every move they make. Every action is thought out. Every word spoken is calculated for its effect. We speak of such persons as inhibited, and rightly so. But it would be more true were we to say that the "person" is not inhibited, but that the person has "inhibited" the creative mechanism. If these people could let go, stop trying, not care, and give no thought to the matter of their behavior, they could act creatively, spontaneously, and "be themselves."

In sports, it's said, "You can't win by playing not to lose." In life, even in everyday situations, we might say the same. In fact, playing not to lose only serves to manufacture and magnify stress, thus increasing the likelihood of making mistakes, not vice versa.

Five Prescriptions for Freeing Your Creative Machinery

1. Once a decision is made, focus on supporting it, not second-guessing it.

In the original book, I told of the business executive with a penchant for gambling on roulette, who gave me the idea: *"Do your worrying before you place your bet, not after the wheel starts turning."*

I happened to quote to him the advice of William James, mentioned earlier, to the effect that emotions of anxiety have their place in planning and deciding on a course of action, but that, "When once a decision is reached and execution is the order of the day, dismiss absolutely all responsibility and care about the outcome. Unclamp, in a word, your intellectual and practical machinery, and let it run free."

Several weeks later he burst into my office to report, "It hit me all of a sudden," he said, "during a visit to Las Vegas. I've been trying it and it works."

"What hit you and what works?" I asked.

That advice of William James. It didn't make too much of an impression when you told me, but while I was playing roulette it came back to me. I noticed any number of people who appeared not to worry at all before placing their bets. Apparently odds meant nothing to them. But once the wheel started turning, they froze up, and began to worry whether their number would come up or not. How silly, I thought. If they want to worry or be concerned or figure odds, the time to do that is *before* the decision is made to place a bet. There is something you can do about it then, by thinking about it. You can figure out the best odds possible, or decide not to take the risk at all. But after the bets are placed and the wheel starts turning, you might as well relax and enjoy it. Thinking about it is not going to do one bit of good, and is wasted energy.

Then I got to thinking that I myself had been doing exactly the same thing in my business and in my personal life. I often made decisions or embarked on courses of action, without adequate preparation, without considering all the risks involved and the best possible alternative. But after I had set the wheels in motion, so to speak, I continually worried over how it would come out, whether I had done the right thing. I made a decision right then that in the future I would do all my worrying, all my conscious thinking, *before* a decision was made, and that after making a decision, and setting the wheels in motion, I would "dismiss absolutely all care or responsibility about the outcome." Believe it or not, it works. I not only feel better, sleep better, and work better, but my business is running much smoother.

I also discovered that the same principle works in a hundred different little personal ways. For example, I used to worry and fume about having to go to the dentist and other unpleasant tasks. Then I said to myself, "This is silly. You know the unpleasantness involved before you make the decision to go. If the unpleasantness is all that important to cause so much concern, and not worth the worry involved, you can simply decide not to go. But, if the decision is that the trip is worth a little unpleasantness, and a definite decision is made to go—then forget about it. Consider the risk before the wheel starts turning." I used to worry the night before I had to make a speech at a board meeting. Then I said to myself, "I'm either going to make the speech or I'm not. If the decision is to make it, then there's no need in considering not making it—or trying to mentally run away from it." I have discovered that much nervousness and anxiety is caused by mentally trying to escape or run away from something that you have decided to go through with physically. If the decision is made to go through with it—not to run away physically—why mentally keep considering or hoping for escape. I used to detest social gatherings and go along only to please my wife, or for business reasons. I went, but mentally I resisted it, and was usually pretty grumpy and uncommunicative. Then I decided that if the decision was to go along physically, I might as well go along mentally—and dismiss all thoughts of resistance. Last night I not only went to what I would formerly have called a stupid social gathering, but I was surprised to find myself thoroughly enjoying it.

One of the many conversations I had with business leaders after the publication of Psycho-Cybernetics focused on this story. I was conducting a seminar for the giant insurance corporation, Metropolitan

Life, and on a break, one of the top executives mentioned the story of the man who worried too much after his decisions to me, and he said something I believe to be profoundly liberating:

"Dr. Maltz, the truth is that there are few inherently right decisions or wrong decisions. Instead, we make decisions, then make them right. That's what leadership is all about."

The chairman of the world's largest ad agency, McCann-Erickson, Nina DiSesa, was named by *Fortune Magazine* (in 2000) as one of the 50 most powerful women in American business. "You can always correct a poor decision, but if you do nothing, you can never get the time back," she says.

PRESCRIPTION

Strive for greater decisiveness and finality in small matters, to build the evidence shown to your self-image that you are the kind of person who makes a firm decision, then ceases to worry over it. If in a restaurant with friends, do not be the person who agonizes over choices, even changes his mind after ordering. Pick something and close the menu. If shopping, pick and buy.

MENTAL TRAINING EXERCISE

Consider creating a useful little mental picture or mental movie to use, immediately after reaching a decision, whether an important business or personal decision, choosing the golf club to use, or picking a tie to wear with your tan sports jacket. In the 2000 Presidential elections, in a different context, Vice-President Al Gore became so famous for overusing the word "lock box" that television comedy programs and imitators had weeks of fun with it. "Lock box" is a good visualization for this: As soon as you make a decision, see yourself taking all the information, concerns, and pros and cons you sifted through to make it in a big pile into a storage room, putting it all into a large box or container of some kind and locking it shut. Then see yourself taking a sheet of paper on which the decision is written, sealing it in an envelope, marking "Done" with today's date and time, then putting the envelope in the "Done" file cabinet drawer and locking it away as well. Finally, see yourself brushing your hands off like a man does after doing some kind of satisfying manual labor, turning out the light in the storage room, and walking out of the dark room into sunlight, like the ship sailing from dark into light in the painting given to me by Salvador Dali. After viewing this movie a few times, for the sake of speed, you can cut it up into stills or slides and view them quickly—click, click, click, click.

2. The secret of focusing only on the here and now.

There is a need to consciously consider goals, evaluate progress, and construct plans, but such thinking needs to occur at appropriate times and places, set just for such purposes. The rest of the time, consciously practice the habit of "taking no anxious thought for tomorrow" by *giving all your attention to the present moment.* Your creative mechanism cannot function or work tomorrow—or even a minute from now. Only right now. It can only function in the present—today, the present moment. Make plans for tomorrow. But don't try to *live* in tomorrow or in the past. Creative living means *responding* and *reacting* to environment spontaneously. Your creative mechanism can respond appropriately and successfully to present environment only if you have your full attention upon present environment and give it information concerning what is happening now. Plan all you want to for the future. Prepare for it. But don't worry about how you will react tomorrow or even five minutes from now. Your creative mechanism will react appropriately in the now if you pay attention to what is happening now. It will do the same tomorrow. It cannot react successfully to what *may* happen, only to what is happening.

I once dined with a president of a large corporation in a very pricey gourmet restaurant. He wolfed his dinner down quickly and still had a plate full of food. When I asked him about it he said, "I never taste food. I'm too busy thinking about other, more important things." Well, he might as well get his nutrients from a pill. Someday I imagine it may come to that. But there are two troubling things about Mr. Dynamo's approach: First, he is denying himself the great pleasure of a fine dining experience, of sipping the wine, tasting each morsel, relishing how perfectly prepared is the cut of meat, how crisp and fresh the tomato. One can assume he misses out on many other sensual enjoyments of life as well. Second, his preoccupation is a conceit, not a genuine display of superior commitment, executive discipline, entrepreneurial zeal, or time efficiency. People cannot function at their best if moving at the fastest possible speed all the time, without relief or recovery. It is a safe wager that he rarely is in the moment, fully focused and involved with only one thing or one person, and while that may impress others with his busy-ness, it will not lead to maximum utilization of his wisdom and capability. The following morning, based on my diagnosis, I called my broker and sold the shares of stock I held in the company captained by this fellow.

You will have a far more enjoyable life and be a far more effective individual if you learn to mentally s-l-o-w yourself down enough to savor your experiences.

MENTAL TRAINING EXERCISE

After you have left a place, such as a restaurant or shop, stop and see how much of it you can recall and describe in copious, exacting detail. In order to sharpen your powers of observation for this challenge, you will automatically slow yourself down and be more "there" (wherever you are).

If you have read the accounts of the fictional (yet fact-based) detective Sherlock Holmes, you know that he demonstrated remarkable observatory powers, recalling and analyzing the minutest details. In one of these stories, the author, Arthur Conan Doyle, has the Dr. Watson character say to Holmes: "It seems obvious your faculty of observation and your peculiar facility for deduction are due to your own systematic training." Doyle knew that the person he modeled Holmes after, his pathology professor at Edinburgh University, was well-known for his extraordinary powers of observation and had taken great pains to train his mind to capture all the minute detail of a scene, an experience, or a person.

---

3. Try to do only one thing at a time.

Another cause of confusion, as well as the resulting feelings of nervousness, hurry, and anxiety, is the absurd habit of trying to do many things at one time. The student studies and watches TV simultaneously. The businessperson, instead of concentrating on and only trying to "do" the one letter that he is presently dictating, is thinking in the back of his mind of all the things he *should* accomplish today, or perhaps this week, and unconsciously trying mentally to accomplish them all at once.

The habit is particularly insidious because it is seldom recognized for what it is. When we feel jittery, worried, or anxious in thinking of the great amount of work that lies before us, the jittery feelings are not caused by the work, but by our mental attitude, which is, "I ought to be able to do this all at once." We become nervous because we are trying to do the impossible, and thereby making futility and frustration inevitable. The truth is that we can only do one thing at a time. Realizing this, fully convincing ourselves of this simple and obvious truth, enables us to mentally stop trying to do the things that lie next and to concentrate all our awareness, all our responsiveness, on this one thing we are doing now. When we work with this attitude, we are relaxed, we are free from the feelings of hurry and anxiety, and we are *able to concentrate* and think at our best.

If you watch much football on television, you have seen receivers drop balls that pass right through their hands, and hear the commentators explain that "he was running before he caught the ball" or "he must have heard footsteps." In other words, instead of being totally focused on catching and securing the ball, he was worrying about other players converging on him, where he would go once he had the ball, even prematurely moving his body away from the ball.

There's a relatively new word for this in the occupational world—"multitasking"—and for most people, most of the time, it is an empty conceit. Be careful whom you emulate, the herd or the leader. Top performers stick with focus rather than multitasking. While many run-of-the-mill sales professionals talk with their clients on their cell phones while driving through traffic or even walking down a busy, noisy street, you will not catch the top sales pro doing that; you will find that when she has to make such a call, she does so in a place and at a time where she can give it 100% of her attention. While many run-of-the-mill executives permit continuous interruptions by phone, intercom, or walk-ins while they are meeting with someone or reviewing important information, the most successful executives I know tolerate no such chaos.

The Lesson of the Hourglass

Dr. James Gordon Gilkey preached a sermon in 1944 called "Gaining Emotional Poise," which was reprinted in *Reader's Digest* and became a classic almost overnight. He had found, through many years of counseling, that one of the main causes of breakdown, worry, and all sorts of other personal problems was the bad mental habit of feeling that you should be doing many things now. Looking at the hourglass on his desk, he had an inspiration. Just as only one grain of sand could pass through the hourglass at a time, so could we only do one thing at a time. It is not the job, but the way we insist on thinking of the job that causes the trouble.

Most of us feel hurried and harried, said Dr. Gilkey, because we form a false mental picture of our duties, obligations, and responsibilities. There seem to be a dozen different things pressing in on us at any given moment; a dozen different things to do; a dozen different problems to solve; a dozen different strains to endure. No matter how hurried or harried our existence may be, said Dr. Gilkey, this mental picture is entirely false. Even on the busiest day the crowded hours come to us one moment at a time; no matter how many problems, tasks, or strains we face, they always come to us in *single file*, which is the only way they can come. To get a true mental picture, he suggested visualizing an hourglass, with the many grains of sand dropping *one by one*. This mental picture will bring emotional poise, just as the false mental picture will bring emotional unrest.

Another similar mental device that I have found very helpful to my patients is telling them:

> Your success mechanism can help you do any job, perform any task, solve any problem. Think of yourself as "feeding" jobs and problems to your success mechanism as a scientist "feeds" a problem to an electronic brain. The "hopper" to your success mechanism can handle only one job at a time. Just as an electronic brain cannot give the right answer if three different problems are mixed up and fed in at the same time, neither can your own success mechanism. Ease off on the pressure. Stop trying to cram into the machinery more than one job at a time.

PRESCRIPTION

Purchase an hourglass and place it where you work most of the time, where it will catch your eye often. Place a small placard on it or next to it, on which you have written "One Grain at a Time."

---

4. Sleep on it.

If you have been wrestling with a problem all day without making any apparent progress, try dismissing it from your mind and putting off making a decision until you've had a chance to "sleep on it." Remember that your creative mechanism works best when there is not too much interference from your conscious "I." In sleep, the creative mechanism has an ideal opportunity to work independently of conscious interference, if you have previously started the wheels turning.

Remember the fairy story about the Shoemaker and the Elves? The shoemaker found that if he cut out the leather, and laid out the patterns before retiring, little elves came and actually put the shoes together for him while he was sleeping.

Many creative workers have used a very similar technique. Mrs. Thomas A. Edison has said that each evening her husband would go over in his mind those things which he hoped to accomplish the next day. Sometimes, he would make a list of the jobs he wanted to do and problems he hoped to solve.

Edison's well-known "cat-naps" were far more than mere respites from fatigue. Joseph Rossman, in the *Psychology of Invention*, says, "When stumped by something, he would stretch out in his Menlo workshop and, half-dozing, get an idea from his dream mind to help him around the difficulty."

Henry Ward Beecher once preached every day for 18 months. His method? He kept a number of ideas "hatching" and each night before retiring would select an "incubating idea" and "stir it up" by thinking intensely about it. The next morning it would have fitted itself together for a sermon.

5. Relax while you work.

MENTAL TRAINING EXERCISE

In Chapter Four you learned how to induce physical and mental relaxation while resting. Continue with the daily practice in relaxation, and you will become more and more proficient. In the meantime, you can induce something of that relaxed feeling and the relaxed attitude, while going about your daily activities, if you will form the habit of mentally *remembering* the nice relaxed feeling that you induced. Stop occasionally during the day—it need only take a moment—and *remember in detail* the sensations of relaxation. Remember how your arms felt, your legs, back, neck, face. Sometimes forming a mental picture of yourself lying in bed or sitting relaxed and limp in an easy chair helps to recall the relaxed sensations. Mentally repeating to yourself several times, "I feel more and more relaxed" also helps. Practice this remembering faithfully several times each day. You will be surprised at how much it reduces fatigue and how much better you are able to handle situations. By relaxing and maintaining a relaxed attitude, you remove those excessive states of concern, tension, and anxiety, which interfere with the efficient operation of your creative mechanism. In time, your relaxed attitude will become a habit, and you will no longer need to consciously practice it.

Stressless Success

Success without stress is, in one sense, as foolish an idea as weight loss without deprivation. However, the popular axiom "no pain, no gain" is just as foolish an idea. You were not intended to suffer and struggle mightily as if pushing a giant boulder up the side of a steep mountain for every accomplishment or satisfaction in life. Believing that to be true fact or moral imperative is a severely limiting belief, an opinion that guarantees you much misery.

Throughout this chapter, and elsewhere in this book, I have used the terms "creative mechanism," "automatic creative mechanism," and "servo-mechanism" interchangeably, and I want to take a moment to clarify things. This mechanism has the ability to do much of the work you struggle to do through furrowed-brow conscious thought, worry, and calculation and teeth-gritted willpower. And it can do so with zero stress for you. You must learn to direct it and trust it, to delegate to it, and then let go.

General George S. Patton said, "Never tell people how to do things. Tell them what to do and they will surprise you with their ingenuity." The identical leadership principle applies to your relationship with your creative mechanism. Tell it what to do; let it pleasantly surprise you with its ingenuity!

Think of this in terms of two executive styles: macromanagement and micromanagement. The executives I have seen age on the job are the micromanagers; even though they have armies of competent people at their beck and call, they cannot delegate even a trivial task like purchasing office supplies without micromanaging every detail of the endeavor and second-guessing the person charged with the task. Executives who can carry great responsibility without quickly becoming gray-haired and stooped over (physically, mentally, and emotionally) learn to delegate and let go, striving to most accurately express their intentions and objectives, then relying on a well-selected associate to carry out their vision or directive. The micromanager often inhibits the growth and prosperity of the organization; the macromanager often liberates it.

Similarly, you are well advised not to micromanage your servomechanism. Such fussing over every detail is not necessary and often even counterproductive. Your job is to most accurately communicate your target; that communication determines whether your servomechanism operates as an Automatic Success or Failure Mechanism. By all means, let it do its work. There's no good reason for both of you hiking the very same trail.

My wife Anne had the, to me, odd habit of cleaning the house before the cleaning-person arrived on Wednesdays. I'm told Anne shares this habit with a great many women. The reason I say it is odd is that we have two people doing the same work. I wouldn't hire a driver to chauffeur me through the congested streets of Manhattan, then have him sit in the passenger seat while I drive myself. Why would you clean your house, then hire a cleaning person to clean what you've just cleaned? I urge you, don't "hire" your servo-mechanism to act on an imperative, then run around getting in its way trying to do its work before, during, and after it does.

CHAPTER SEVEN

You Can Acquire the
Habit of Happiness

Most people are quiet in the world,
and live in it tentatively, as if it were not their own.
—E.L. Doctorow

"*I* just want to be happy" is a common answer, when people are asked about their goals in life. Mostly, this is just an excuse for not having given goals serious thought! They seek to escape into the vague and indefinable rather than confront the specific and measurable. However, there is a practical approach to happiness.

In this chapter I will discuss the subject of happiness not from a philosophical, but from a medical standpoint. Dr. John A. Schindler's definition of happiness is, "A state of mind in which our thinking is pleasant a good share of the time." From a medical standpoint, and also from an ethical standpoint, I do not believe that simple definition can be improved on. It is what we are talking about in this chapter.

Happiness Is Good Medicine

Happiness is native to the human mind and its physical machine. We think better, perform better, feel better, and are healthier when we are happy. Even our physical sense organs work better. Russian psychologist K. Kekcheyev tested people when they were thinking pleasant and unpleasant thoughts. He found that when thinking pleasant thoughts, they could see, taste, smell, and hear better, and they could detect finer differences in touch. Dr. William Bates proved that eyesight improves immediately when the individual is thinking pleasant thoughts or visualizing pleasant scenes. Psychosomatic medicine has proved that our stomachs, liver, heart, and all our internal organs function better when we are happy.

Medical traditionalists previously resistant to admitting direct connection between improving state of mind and curing illness were swayed by the publisher of the *Saturday Evening Post*, Norman Cousins' now famous battle with cancer, in which he made use of "humor therapy sessions," including viewing video tapes of The Three Stooges and Buster Keaton in his hospital room. Mr. Cousins' remarkable and instructive experiences are detailed in his book, *Anatomy of an Illness*. Dr. Bernie Siegel has done outstanding work in the area of happiness therapy, and I suggest reading his books or hearing him lecture, if the opportunity arises.

Dr. Schindler has said that unhappiness is the sole cause of all psychosomatic ills and that happiness is the only cure. The very word "disease" means a state of unhappiness—"dis-ease."

Common Misconceptions About Happiness

Happiness is not something that is earned or deserved. Happiness is not a moral issue, anymore than the circulation of the blood is a moral issue. Both are necessary to health and well-being. Happiness is simply a "state of mind in which our thinking is pleasant a good share of the time." If you wait until you "deserve" to think pleasant thoughts, you are likely to think unpleasant thoughts concerning your own unworthiness. "Happiness is not the reward of virtue," said Spinoza, "but virtue itself; nor do we delight in happiness because we restrain our lusts; but, on the contrary, because we delight in it, therefore are we able to restrain them."

The Pursuit of Happiness Is Not Selfish

Many sincere people are deterred from seeking happiness because they feel that it would be "selfish" or "wrong." Unselfishness does make for happiness, for it not only gets our minds directed outward away from ourselves and our introspection, our faults, sins, troubles (unpleasant thoughts), or pride in our "goodness," but it also enables us to express ourselves creatively and fulfill ourselves in helping others. One of the most pleasant thoughts to any human being is the thought that he is needed, that he is important enough and competent enough to help and add to the happiness of some other human being. However, if we make a moral issue out of happiness and conceive of it as something to be earned as a sort of reward for being unselfish, we are very apt to feel guilty about wanting happiness. Happiness comes from being and acting unselfishly, as a natural accompaniment to the being and acting, not as a "payoff" or prize. If we are rewarded for being unselfish, the next logical step is to assume that the more self-abnegating and miserable we make ourselves, the more happy we will be. The premise leads to the absurd conclusion that the way to be happy is to be unhappy.

There is a line: *The best way I know to help the poor is not be one of them.* Whether or not that is the best way, it is difficult to see how you help those in poverty by reducing your own success or standard of living, unless you erroneously believe in a universe of compensating balances rather than unlimited abundance. Similarly, you cannot possibly help the unhappy by being one of them.

A woman once told me, "My co-workers are both so miserable and frustrated in their jobs, so visibly unhappy at work, I feel bad about enjoying being there and doing my work, and fight my tendency to go about doing things cheerily so as not to annoy them or make them feel worse."

Happiness is not meted out in compensating balances. By being happy, she does not consume such an unfair and selfish quantity of finite available happiness that her co-workers are deprived of their share. By consciously suppressing and reducing her happiness, she does not make available a new supply of happiness that is automatically transferred to them. Happiness (or prosperity) is not a commodity like the last candy bar on a deserted island populated by three castaways or the last hour of oxygen in a sealed vault in which several people have been locked up.

Happiness Lies in the Present, Not in the Future

"We are never living, but only hoping to live; and, looking forward always to being happy, it is inevitable that we never are so," said philosopher Pascal.

I have found that one of the most common causes of unhappiness among my patients is that they are attempting to live their lives on the deferred payment plan. They do not live, nor do they enjoy life now, but wait for some future event or occurrence. They will be happy when they get married, when they get a better job, when they get the house paid for, when they get the children through college, when they have completed some task or won some victory. Invariably, they are disappointed. Happiness is a mental habit, a mental attitude, and if it is not learned and practiced in the present it is never experienced. It cannot be made contingent on solving some external problem. When one problem is solved, another appears to take its place. Life is a series of problems. If you are to be happy at all, you must be happy— period!—not happy "because of."

Happiness Is a Mental Habit Which Can Be Cultivated and Developed

"Most people are about as happy as they make up their minds to be," said Abraham Lincoln.

"Happiness is purely internal," says psychologist Dr. Matthew N. Chappell. "It is produced, not by objects, but by ideas, thoughts, and attitudes which can be developed and constructed by the individual's own activities, irrespective of the environment."

No one, other than a saint, can be 100% happy all the time. And, as George Bernard Shaw quipped, we would probably be miserable if we were. But we can, by taking thought and making a simple decision, be happy and think pleasant thoughts a large share of the time, regarding that multitude of little events and circumstances of daily living that now makes us unhappy. To a large extent we react to petty annoyances, frustrations, and the like with grumpiness, dissatisfaction, resentment, and irritability, purely out of habit. We have *practiced* reacting that way so long, it has become habitual. Much of this habitual unhappiness reaction originated because of some event that we *interpreted* as a blow to our self-esteem. A driver honks at us unnecessarily; someone interrupts and doesn't pay attention while we're talking; someone doesn't come through for us as we think she should. Even impersonal events can be interpreted and reacted to as affronts to our self-esteem. The bus we wanted to catch had to be late; it had to go and rain when we had planned to play golf; traffic had to get into a snarl just when we needed to catch the plane. We react with anger, resentment, self-pity, or, in other words, *unhappiness.*

A chief cause of unhappiness is taking things personally that are not personal at all.

Stop Letting Things Push You Around

The best cure I have found for this sort of thing is to use unhappiness' own weapon—self-esteem. "Have you ever been to a TV show and seen the master of ceremonies manipulate the audience?" I asked a patient. "He brings out a sign that says 'applause' and everyone applauds. He brings out another that says 'laughter' and everyone laughs. They act like sheep, as if they were slaves, and meekly react as they are told to react. You are acting the same way. You are letting outward events and other people dictate to you how you shall feel and how you shall react. You are acting as an obedient slave and reacting when circumstance signals to you: 'Be angry.' 'Get upset.' 'Now is the time to feel unhappy.'"

Learning the happiness habit, you become a master instead of a slave, or, as Robert Louis Stevenson said, "The habit of being happy enables one to be freed, or largely freed, from the domination of outward conditions."

Your Opinion Can Add to Unhappy Events

Even in regard to tragic conditions, and the most adverse environment, we can usually manage to be happier, if not completely happy, by not adding to the misfortune our own feelings of self-pity, resentment, and our own adverse opinions.

"How can I be happy?" the woman of an alcoholic husband asked me. "I don't know," I said, "but you can be happier by resolving not to add resentment and self-pity to your misfortune."

"How can I possibly be happy?" asked a businessman, "I have just lost $200,000 on the stock market. I am ruined and disgraced."

"You can be happier," I said, "by not adding your own opinion to the facts. It is a fact that you lost $200,000. It is your opinion that you are ruined and disgraced."

I then suggested that he memorize a saying of Epictetus, which has always been a favorite of mine: "Men are disturbed," said the sage, "not by the things that happen, but by their opinion of the things that happen."

Happiness versus Unhappiness = Facts versus Opinions

When I announced that I wanted to be a doctor, I was told that this could not be because my folks had no money. It was a fact that my mother had no money. It was only an opinion that I could never be a doctor. Later, I was told I could never take postgraduate courses in Germany and that it was impossible for a young plastic surgeon to hang out his own shingle and go into business for himself in New York. I did all these things, and one of the things that helped me was that I kept reminding myself that all these "impossibles" were opinions, not facts. I not only managed to reach my goals, but I was happy in the process, even when I had to pawn my overcoat to buy medical books and do without lunch in order to purchase cadavers. I was in love with a beautiful girl. She married someone else. These were facts. But I kept reminding myself that it was merely my opinion that this was a "catastrophe" and that life was not worth living. I not only got over it, but it turned out it was one of the luckiest things that ever happened to me.

In the years that have passed since first writing the original Psycho-Cybernetics book, I have often been asked by interviewers or audience members if I could boil Psycho-Cybernetics down to one idea or one statement or one skill that is *the* "make it or break it" factor in successful versus unsuccessful living. When first asked this, I caught myself taking it personally and becoming a bit annoyed; how dare they trivialize all my work by suggesting it might be summarized on the head of a pin? Of course, that was me falsely interpreting peoples' understandable desire to simplify the complex, not any disrespect to me personally or to my work, and, fortunately, I practiced what I preach, used rational thought, and prevented this from being a blood-drawing needle stuck into my self-image. Which, not coincidentally, brings me to the answer to the "one big thing" question:

The essence of Psycho-Cybernetics is the accurate, calm, and ultimately automatic separation of fact from fiction, fact from opinion, actual circumstance from magnified obstacle, so that our actions and reactions are solidly based on truth, not our own or others' opinions.

The Attitude That Makes for Happiness

It has been pointed out earlier that since humans are goal-striving beings, they function naturally and normally when oriented toward a positive goal and striving toward a desirable goal. Happiness is a symptom of normal, natural functioning and when humans are functioning as goal-strivers, they tend to feel fairly happy, regardless of circumstances. My young business executive friend was very unhappy because he had lost $200,000. Thomas A. Edison lost a laboratory worth millions in a fire with no insurance. "What in the world will you do?" someone asked. "We will start rebuilding tomorrow morning," said Edison. He maintained an aggressive attitude, he was still goal-oriented despite his misfortune. And because he did maintain an aggressive goal-striving attitude, it is a good bet that he was never very unhappy about his loss.

Looking back on my own life, I can see that some of the happiest years were those when I was a struggling medical student living from hand to mouth in my early days of practice. Many times I was hungry. I was cold and ill-clad. I worked hard a minimum of about 12 hours a day. Many times I did not know from month to month where the money was coming from to pay my rent. But I did have a goal. I had a consuming desire to reach it and a determined persistence that kept me working toward it.

I related all this to the young business executive and suggested that the real cause of his unhappy feeling was not that he had lost $200,000, but that he had lost his goal; he had lost his aggressive attitude, and was yielding passively rather than reacting aggressively.

"I must have been crazy," he told me later, "to let you convince me that losing the money was not what was making me unhappy, but I'm awfully glad that you did." He stopped moaning about his misfortune, faced about, got himself another goal, and started working toward it. Within five years he not only had more money than ever before in his life, but for the first time he was in a business that he enjoyed.

PRESCRIPTION

Form the habit of reacting aggressively and positively toward threats and problems. Form the habit of keeping goal-oriented all the time, regardless of what happens. Do this by practicing a positive aggressive attitude, both in actual everyday situations and in your imagination. See yourself in your imagination taking positive, intelligent action toward solving a problem or reaching a goal. See yourself reacting to threats not by running away or evading them, but by meeting them, dealing with them, grappling with them in an aggressive and intelligent manner. "Most people are brave only in the dangers to which they accustom themselves, either in imagination or practice," said Bulwer-Lytton, the English novelist.

Take Responsibility for Your Own Happiness

The idea that happiness, or keeping one's thoughts pleasant most of the time, can be deliberately and systematically cultivated by practicing in a more or less cold-blooded manner, strikes many of my patients as rather incredible, if not ludicrous, when I first suggest it. Yet experience has shown not only that this can be done, but that it is about the only way that the habit of happiness can be cultivated. In the first place happiness isn't something that happens to you. It is something you yourself do and determine. If you wait for happiness to catch up with you, just happen, or be brought to you by others, you are likely to have a long wait. No one can decide what your thoughts shall be but yourself. If you wait until circumstances justify your thinking pleasant thoughts, you are also likely to wait forever. Every day is a mixture of good and evil; no day or circumstance is completely 100% "good." The elements and facts in the world and in our personal lives at all times can justify either a pessimistic and grumpy outlook or an optimistic and happy outlook, depending on our choice. It is largely a matter of selection, attention, and decision. Nor is it a matter of being intellectually honest or dishonest. Good is as "real" as evil. It is merely a matter of what we choose to give primary attention to—and what thoughts we hold in the mind.

In the charming David Mamet film, *State and Main*, released in early 2001, a young woman with a happy outlook is engaged in conversation with a writer from the big city, somewhat bemused by her small town life. "You make your own fun?" he asks. "It is only fun if you make it," she patiently explains. "If someone else does it for you, it is entertainment." Similarly, we can make our own happiness because we can choose our own thoughts and even choose our own self-image, and we are well advised to do so rather than depending on someone else to do it for us.

A Salesman Who Needed Surgery on His Thoughts Rather Than His Nose

In my book for my medical colleagues, *New Faces—New Futures*, published back in 1936, I included a case history about a salesman named Arthur Williams who was involved in an automobile accident while traveling in his New England sales territory. A country doctor took care of him, and patched up his severely broken nose. When the bandages were removed, his nose had reset in a very distorted manner. It was humped above, depressed in the middle and twisted to one side. When Mr. Williams resumed work, he soon became conscious of buyers seeming to focus their gaze on his disfigurement, to his and their embarrassment. They seemed eager to rush through meetings with him. His sales volume declined rapidly. After several months of this, Mr. Williams determined he needed to correct this problem, and I operated on his nose, successfully completing plastic surgery that restored his preaccident appearance. It should come as no surprise that his self-confidence returned, and a natural upturn in his sales followed as day to night.

Arthur Williams had a legitimate physical disfigurement, not exaggerated by his own negative imagination, and he accurately assessed others' reactions to it, and, in my opinion, acted accordingly in seeking reconstructive and cosmetic surgery.

However, for every Arthur Williams, there are a hundred men and women who suffer similarly, not because of others' actual reactions to them, but because of their own negative imaginings. Robert Benjamin gave himself Arthur William's problem, not in an auto accident, but inside his own self-image.

A young salesman, Mr. Benjamin, had made up his mind to quit his job when he consulted me about an operation on his nose. His nose was slightly larger than normal, but certainly not "repulsive," as he insisted. He felt that prospects were secretly laughing at his nose or repulsed because of it. It was a fact that he had a large nose. It was a fact that three customers had called in to complain of his rude and hostile behavior. It was a fact that his boss had placed him on probation and that he hadn't made a sale in two weeks. Instead of an operation on his nose, I suggested he perform surgery on his own thinking. For 21 days he was to cut out all these negative thoughts. He was to completely ignore all the negative and unpleasant facts in his situation, and deliberately focus his attention upon pleasant thoughts. We agreed on some specific visualizations and affirmations.

Quite honestly, I know that he agreed to the experiment with little belief it would alter anything; he was pacifying me in order to schedule the surgery he wanted. It is interesting that a person does not necessarily have to believe in the efficacy of Psycho-Cybernetics in order to test its concepts and find them useful. At the end of twenty-one days Mr. Benjamin not only felt better, but he found that prospects and customers had become much more friendly, his sales were steadily increasing, and his boss had publicly congratulated him in a sales meeting. He decided to "postpone" his surgery.

Pattern Interrupt

In her book *Success Is An Inside Job*, motivational speaker Lee Milteer describes this interesting technique:

> When your actions or performance does not meet your expectations, don't belittle yourself with negative self-talk ... You must replace those images of yourself that do not create value in your life and which you do not want to continue.
>
> As an example, how many times have you caught yourself saying—*I am always late*. Now think about what you are programming yourself to be— late!
>
> "In the future, instead of reinforcing the unwanted habit, say to yourself: Cancel. That's not like me. Next time I'll ... .
>
> Then you want to follow-up immediately with statements to imprint a new program. In this case: That's not like me to be late. I always leave ten minutes early and I am always on time.

Lee points out this is not an instant "fix." However, we do need to catch and cancel the reoccurring, habitual affirmation of unwanted or unproductive behavior, to interrupt unhelpful patterns of thought, just as I cajoled and led Mr. Benjamin into doing. If you cancel the particular reoccurring piece of programming often and repetitively enough, the Automatic Failure Mechanism will stop going to all the trouble of sending it up to the surface. Your self-image will get the message: *No point in giving out this information anymore if all she's going to do every time is yell "Cancel!" at us. Let's try something else.* You see, we are always engaged in an undercurrent of running dialogue with our self-image. Through the use of the pattern-interrupt technique and emphatic, positive affirmation repeated each time, you become your own authoritative source repetitively programming the self-image. (Remember: Authoritative source, repetition, and intensity are the keys to this programming.)

If happiness is, ultimately, the product of our collection of habits of thought, then the skill of altering a particular habit is extremely useful. Lee Milteer has appeared as a guest expert on hundreds of radio talk shows to talk about "habit busting," and has her own Psycho-Cybernetics-based audio cassette program on this subject, which you may want to avail yourself of.

An Exercise for Canceling Negative Thoughts

Martial arts movie star Bruce Lee had an exercise for ridding himself of negative thoughts: He visualized himself writing them down on a piece of paper, crumpling up the paper, lighting it on fire, and burning it to ashes.

Actor and entrepreneur Chuck Norris, a close friend of the late Bruce Lee, takes Lee's exercise even further. In his book *The Secret Power Within You*, Norris wrote, "I actually write down on a scrap of paper whatever negative thoughts I have and then burn them. When I dispose of the ashes, the thoughts, too, are removed from my mind."

I would point out that these people—Lee Milteer, a successful businesswoman; Chuck Norris, a martial arts practitioner and very successful actor, producer, and businessman—are not "heads in the clouds" type people, not childish or foolish at all. They are pragmatists of the highest order, who have found simple, practical things to do, to take control of their thoughts in a purposeful manner.

To Be Happy, We Must Make a Sacrifice

A sacrifice? Yes, you may need to sacrifice skepticism, cynicism, old habits and beliefs, which, even though they do not serve you well, are "comfortable."

In Daniel Defoe's classic novel *Robinson Crusoe*, when Crusoe is shipwrecked on the deserted island, he makes his camp near the place where he washed ashore. But as he began exploring the entire island, he soon recognized that, for all practical purposes, he had camped on the wrong side of the island. The opposite side offered a better supply of food, it was easier to create shelter there, and so forth. But even though Crusoe saw this to be true, he was still reluctant to move!

We cannot let "our reluctance to move" imprison our self-image and servo-mechanism! When our rational thought tells us something is not working for us, we have to move forward to try something else. A popular axiom defines "insanity" as the insistence on doing the same thing over and over while hoping for different results. My friend, you are *not* a tree, deeply rooted in any one psychological or behavioral place, unable to move to a sunnier spot. Like Crusoe, you may be reluctant to uproot yourself, but you *can*!

A Scientist Tests the Theory of Happiness and Uproots Himself from Unhappiness

Dr. Elwood Worcester, in his book *Body, Mind and Spirit*, relates the testimony of a world-famous scientist:

> Up to my fiftieth year I was an unhappy, ineffective man. None of the works on which my reputation rests were published ... I lived in a constant sense of gloom and failure. Perhaps my most painful symptom was a blinding headache which recurred usually two days of the week, during which I could do nothing.
>
> I had read some of the literature of New Thought, which at the time appeared to be buncombe, and some statement of William James on the directing of attention to what is good and useful and ignoring the rest. One saying of his stuck in my mind, "We might have to give up our philosophy of evil, but what is that in comparison with gaining a life of goodness?", or words to that effect. Hitherto these doctrines had seemed to me only mystical theories, but realizing that my soul was sick and growing worse and that my life was intolerable, I determined to put them to the proof ... I decided to limit the period of conscious effort to one month, as I thought this time long enough to prove its value or its worthlessness to me. During this month I resolved to impose certain restrictions on my thoughts. If I thought of the past, I would try to let my mind dwell only on its happy, pleasing incidents, the bright days of my childhood, the inspiration of my teachers and the slow revelation of my lifework. In thinking of the present, I would deliberately turn my attention to its desirable elements, my home, the opportunities my solitude gave me to work, and so on, and I resolved to make the utmost use of these opportunities and to ignore the fact that they seemed to lead to nothing. In thinking of the future I determined to regard every worthy and possible ambition as within my grasp. Ridiculous as this seemed at the time, in view of what has come to me since, I see that the only defect of my plan was that it aimed too low and did not include enough.

He then tells how his headaches ceased within one week and how he felt happier and better than ever before in his life. But he adds:

> The outward changes of my life, resulting from my change of thought have surprised me more than the inward changes, yet they spring from the latter. There were certain eminent men, for example, whose recognition I deeply craved. The foremost of those wrote me, out of a clear sky, and invited me to become his assistant. My works have all been published, and a foundation has been created to publish all that I may write in the future. The men with whom I have worked have been helpful and cooperative toward me chiefly on account of my changed disposition.

Formerly they would not have endured me… As I look back over all these changes, it seems to me that in some blind way I stumbled on a path of life and set forces to working for me which before were against me.

I'm certain Dr. Worcester's book is long out of print. His story is only still significant because of the heavy skepticism he held for the ideas he experimented with, which ultimately set him free. While still in practice, I have many times given someone a Psycho-Cybernetics prescription, a psychologic experiment to try for just thirty days, with the promise that if they still wanted the cosmetic surgery performed after doing the experiment, I would do so. In these cases, these people often followed my instructions as best they could grudgingly and skeptically, initially merely with the intent of pacifying me so that they could get what they wanted; some physical deformity, magnified in their imagination to epic proportions, removed or altered.

Even with skepticism in the way, these techniques performed noticeable results, and many times the discoveries they made about themselves and their thinking were as clear to them as to Worcester, or to the aforementioned Benjamin, and after thirty days, they no longer wanted surgery.

How an Inventor Used "Happy-Thoughts"

Professor Elmer Gates of the Smithsonian Institution was one of the most successful inventors this country has ever known and a recognized genius. He made a daily practice of "calling up pleasant ideas and memories" and believed that this helped him in his work. If a person wants to improve himself, he said, "Let him summon those finer feelings of benevolence and usefulness, which are called up only now and then. Let him make this a regular exercise like swinging dumbbells. Let him gradually increase the time devoted to these psychological gymnastics, and at the end of a month he will find the change in himself surprising. The alteration will be apparent in his actions and thoughts. Morally speaking, the man will be a great improvement of his former self."

Gates' use of the term "psychological gymnastics" led to identifying the various exercises and techniques presented in the original book, this book, my other books, and my twelve-week home study course as "mental training exercises." While the analogy of self-image to muscle is not precisely correct, the deliberate daily practice of certain techniques—such as the construction and playing of positive mental movies in The Theater of Your Mind, relaxation, and so forth—does strengthen your self-image and does ultimately lead to truly automatic Psycho-Cybernetic responses to situations.

The present-day rule for adequate physical exercise is thirty-minute sessions, at least three days a week. I can assure you: Give that same minimum investment to Psycho-Cybernetics "gymnastics" and you will quite literally change your life.

How to "Install" the Happiness Habit

Our self-image and our habits tend to go together. Change one and you automatically change the other. The word "habit" originally meant a garment or clothing. We still speak of riding habits and habiliments. This gives us an insight into the true nature of habit. Our habits are literally garments worn by our personalities. They are not accidental or happenstance. We have them because *they fit us.* They are consistent with our self-image and our entire personality pattern. When we consciously and deliberately develop new and better habits, our self-image tends to outgrow the old habits and grow into the new pattern.

I can see many patients cringe when I mention changing habitual action patterns or acting out new behavior patterns until they become automatic. They confuse "habit" with "addiction." An addiction is something you feel compelled to, something that causes severe withdrawal symptoms. Treatment of addiction is beyond the scope of this book. If you do suffer from a physical, chemical, or even emotional addiction, the most important things that I can say to you relative to your self-image is that the decision and action to seek help is not an admission of weakness but a special, courageous kind of strength.

Habits, on the other hand, are merely reactions and responses that we have learned to perform automatically without having to think or decide. They are performed by our servo-mechanism.

Fully 95% of our behavior, feeling, and response is habitual. The pianist does not "decide" which keys to strike. The dancer does not "decide" which foot to move where. The reaction is automatic and unthinking.

In much the same way our attitudes, emotions, and beliefs tend to become habitual. In the past we "learned" that certain attitudes and ways of feeling and thinking were "appropriate" to certain situations. Now, we tend to think, feel, and act the same way whenever we encounter what we interpret as the same sort of situation.

Arguments between longtime spouses or business partners become habitual. You say this to me, I say this to you, and back and forth, reenacting the identical script, responding in exactly the same way to the same stimulus.

What we need to understand is that these habits, unlike addictions, can be modified, changed, or reversed, simply by taking the trouble to make a *conscious decision*, and then by practicing or acting out the new response or behavior. The pianist can consciously decide to strike a different key, if he chooses. The dancer can consciously "decide" to learn a new step—and there is no agony about it. The partner can decide to break the pattern and imaginatively engineer a different outcome to a familiar argument. It does require constant watchfulness and practice until the new behavior pattern is thoroughly learned, but it most assuredly can be accomplished.

MENTAL TRAINING EXERCISE

Habitually, you put on either your right shoe first or your left shoe. Habitually, you tie your shoes by either passing the right-hand lace around the left-hand lace, or vice versa. Tomorrow morning determine which shoe you put on first and how you tie your shoes. Now, consciously decide that for the next thirty days you are going to form a new habit by putting on the other shoe first and tying your laces in a different way. Now, each morning as you decide to put on your shoes in a certain manner, let this simple act serve as a reminder to change other habitual ways of thinking, acting, and feeling throughout that one day. Say to yourself as you tie your shoes, "I am beginning the day in a new and better way." Then consciously decide that throughout the day:

1. I will be as cheerful as possible.

2. I will act a little more friendly toward other people.

3. I am going to be a little less critical and a little more tolerant of other people, their faults, failings, and mistakes. I will place the best possible interpretation on their actions.

4. Insofar as possible, I am going to act as if success were inevitable, and I already am the sort of personality I want to be. I will practice acting like and feeling like this new personality.

5. I will not let my own opinion color facts in a pessimistic or negative way.

6. I will practice smiling at least three times during the day.

7. Regardless of what happens, I will react as calmly and as intelligently as possible.

8. I will ignore completely and close my mind to all those pessimistic and negative "facts" that I can do nothing to change.

Simple? Yes. But each of these habitual ways of acting, feeling, and thinking has beneficial and constructive influence on your self-image. Act them out for thirty days. Experience them, and see if worry, guilt, hostility have not been diminished and if confidence has not been increased.

CHAPTER EIGHT

Ingredients of the "Success-Type" Personality and How to Acquire Them

You are today where your thoughts have brought you.
You will be tomorrow where your thoughts take you.

—James Allen

*D*iagnosis: Destined for success! Just as a doctor learns to diagnose disease from certain symptoms, failure and success can also be diagnosed. The reason is that people do not simply find success or come to failure. They carry the seeds around in their personality and character; they plant them with their habits of thought and action.

I have found one of the most effective means of helping people achieve an adequate or "successful" personality is to first give them a graphic picture of what the successful personality looks like. Remember, the creative guidance mechanism within you is a goal-striving mechanism, and the first requisite for using it is to have a clear-cut goal or target. A great many people want to improve themselves and long for a better personality, but they have no clear-cut idea of the direction in which improvement lies, nor what constitutes a good personality. A good personality is one that enables you to deal effectively and appropriately with environment and reality, and to gain satisfaction from reaching the goals that are important to you.

Time and again, I have seen confused and unhappy people straighten themselves out when they were given a goal to shoot for and a straight course to follow. There was the advertising man in his early forties, for example, who felt strangely insecure and dissatisfied with himself just after receiving an important promotion.

New Roles Require New Self-Images

"It doesn't make sense," he said. "I've worked for this, and dreamed about it. It's just what I've always wanted. I know I can do the work. And yet, for some reason, my self-confidence is shaken. I suddenly wake up, as if from a dream, and ask myself, 'What in the world is a small potato like me doing in a job like this?'" He had become super-sensitive to his appearance and thought perhaps that his "weak chin" might be the cause of his discomfort. "I don't look like a business executive," he said. He felt plastic surgery might be the answer to his problem.

There was the wife and mother whose children were "running her crazy" and whose husband irritated her so much that she engaged in a shouting tirade at him at least once a week for little cause. "What is the matter with me?" she asked. "My children are really nice kids I should be proud of. My husband is really a nice guy, and I'm always ashamed of myself afterwards." She felt that a face lift might give her more confidence, and cause her family to "appreciate her more."

The trouble with these people, and many more like them, is not their physical appearance but their self-image. They find themselves in a new role and are not sure what kind of a person they are supposed to be in order to live up to that role. Or they have never developed a clear-cut self-image of themselves in any role.

The Picture of Success

In this chapter I am going to give you the same "prescription" that I would give you should you come to my office. I have found that an easy-to-remember picture of the successful personality is contained in the letters of the word "Success" itself. The "Success-type" personality is composed of:

> **S**ense of direction
> **U**nderstanding
> **C**ourage
> **C**harity (compassion)
> **E**steem
> **S**elf-confidence
> **S**elf-acceptance

Sense of Direction

The advertising executive straightened himself out and regained his confidence within a short time, once he saw clearly that for several years he had been motivated by strong personal goals that he wanted to attain, including securing his present position. These goals, which were important to him, kept him on the track. However, once he got the promotion, he ceased to think in terms of what he wanted, but in terms of what others expected of him, or whether he was living up to other people's goals and standards. He was like a mountain climber who, as long as he looked upward to the peak he wished to scale, felt and acted courageously and boldly. But when he got to the top, he began to look down and became afraid. He was now on the defensive, defending his present position, rather than acting like a goal striver and going on the offensive to attain his goal. He regained control when he set himself new goals and began to think in terms of, "What do I want out of this job? What do I want to achieve? Where do I want to go?"

In a television program about Psycho-Cybernetics, we put the host on a bicycle and instructed him to put both feet up on the pedals and stay stationary, in one place. Try it yourself; it can't be done. Functionally, a person is somewhat like a bicycle. A bicycle maintains its poise and equilibrium only as long as it is going forward toward something. Similarly, we are engineered as goal-seeking mechanisms. We are built to conquer environment, solve problems, achieve goals, and we find no real satisfaction or happiness in life without obstacles to conquer and goals to achieve. People who say that life is not worthwhile are really saying that they themselves have no worthwhile personal goals.

> ## PRESCRIPTION
>
> Earlier in this book we covered a number of ways to put your imagination to work, to come up with a new or more clearly defined target or targets for you to focus on, and assign your Automatic Success Mechanism. This is a good time to do so. Get yourself a goal worth working for. Better still, get yourself a project. Decide what you want out of a situation. Always have something ahead of you to look forward to—to work for and hope for. Look forward, not backward. Develop a "nostalgia for the future" instead of for the past. The nostalgia for the future can keep you youthful. Even your body doesn't function well when you stop being a goal striver and have nothing to look forward to. This is the reason that very often a person dies shortly after retirement. When you're not goal-striving, not looking forward, you're not really living. In addition to your purely personal goals, have at least one impersonal goal or cause, which you can identify yourself with. Get interested in some project to help your fellow man, not out of a sense of duty, but because you want to.

Understanding

Understanding depends on good communication. Communication is vital to any guidance system or computer. You cannot react appropriately if the information you act on is faulty or misunderstood. Many doctors believe that "confusion" is the basic element in neurosis. To deal effectively with a problem, you must have some understanding of its true nature. Most of our failures in human relations are due to misunderstandings.

We expect other people to react and respond and come to the same conclusions as we do from a given set of facts or circumstances. We should remember what we said in an earlier chapter: People react to their own mental images, not to things as they are. Most of the time others' reactions or positions are not taken to make us suffer, to be hard-headed or malicious, but because they "understand" and interpret the situation differently from us. They are merely responding appropriately to what—to them—seems to be the truth about the situation. To give others credit for being sincere, if mistaken, rather than willful and malicious, can do much to smooth out human relations and bring about better understanding between people. Ask yourself, "How does this appear to him?" "How does she interpret this situation?" "How does he feel about it?" Try to understand why he might act the way he does.

Fact versus Opinion. Many times, we create confusion when we add our own opinion to facts and come up with the wrong conclusion. Fact: A husband cracks his knuckles. Opinion: The wife concludes, "He does that because he thinks it will annoy me." Fact: The husband sucks his teeth after eating. Opinion: The wife concludes, "If he had any regard for me, he would improve his manners." Fact: Two friends are whispering when you walk up. Suddenly they stop talking and look somewhat embarrassed. Opinion: They must have been gossiping about me.

The wife, if able to understand that her husband's annoying mannerisms were not deliberate and willful acts on his part for the purpose of annoying her, if able to stop reacting *as if* she had been personally insulted, is able to pause, analyze the situation, and select an appropriate, even productive response.

Be Willing to See the Truth. Often we color incoming sensory data by our own fears, anxieties, or desires. But to deal effectively with environment, we must be willing to acknowledge the truth about it. Only when we understand what it is can we respond appropriately. We must be able to see the truth and accept it, good or bad. Bertrand Russell said one reason Hitler lost World War II was that he did not fully understand the situation. Bearers of bad news were punished. Soon no one dared tell him the truth. Not knowing the truth, he could not act appropriately. We can be glad this occurred.

The shoot-the-messenger mentality has doomed any number of military leaders, business leaders, coaches, parents. It's been widely reported that Saddam Hussein practices this, with much the same result as Hitler's. Literally shooting bearers of bad news is horrific enough, but the crime of shooting ourselves rather than rationally dealing with accurate information is arguably worse!

We do not like to admit to ourselves our errors, mistakes, or shortcomings; nor do we like to admit we have been in the wrong. We do not like to acknowledge that a situation is other than we would like it to be. So we kid ourselves. And because we will not see the truth, we cannot act appropriately. Someone has said that it is a good exercise to daily admit one painful fact about ourselves to ourselves. The Success-type personality not only does not cheat and lie to other people, he learns to be honest with himself. What we call "sincerity" is itself based on self-understanding and self-honesty. For you cannot be sincere when you lie to yourself by rationalizing or telling yourself "rational-lies."

You can do this if you accept yet another fundamental premise of Psycho-Cybernetics, to safeguard and strengthen your self-image: You are not your mistakes. Your tortured backswing and wicked slice does not make you a "disgrace to the game of golf," let alone a bad, inept, or unsuccessful person; it is only a mechanical and mental mistake that can be corrected.

A top corporate CEO once told me, "I've become somewhat famous thanks to several very notable astute decisions. But I've made a number of incredibly bad ones too. I am neither my best or my worst decision. I am a successful, capable executive who makes his fair share of blunders, and that's all there is to it."

When you thoroughly accept that you are not your mistakes, you are freed to acknowledge them, learn from them, set them aside, and move on from them without being mired in them.

PRESCRIPTION

Look for and seek out true information concerning yourself, your problems, other people, or the situation, whether it is good news or bad news. Adopt the motto, "It doesn't matter who's right, but what's right." An automatic guidance system corrects its course from negative feedback data. It acknowledges errors in order to correct them and stay on course. So must you. Admit your mistakes and errors but don't cry over them. Correct them and go forward. In dealing with other people, try to see the situation from their point of view as well as your own.

Courage

Having a goal and understanding the situation are not enough. You must have the courage to act, for only by actions can goals, desires, and beliefs be translated into realities.

Admiral William F. Halsey's personal motto was a quotation from Nelson, "No Captain can do very wrong if he places his Ship alongside that of an Enemy." "'The best defense is a strong offense,' is a military principle," said Halsey, "but its application is wider than war. All problems, personal, national, or combat, become smaller if you don't dodge them, but confront them."

How can *you* live more courageously? That's a question ably answered by Psycho-Cybernetics. When you systematically strengthen your self-image, and understand that you are not your mistakes, you find it infinitely easier to take risks without undue worry over what others will think or temporarily appearing foolish if you stumble. How can you be more assertive and forceful in advocating your ideas in the workplace? How can you more clearly and assertively ask for the order at the conclusion of a sales presentation? How can you take to the dance floor even if you've too long believed "you have two left feet?"*+ How can you embark on an entirely new career or avocation late in life when axiomatically "it's tough for an old dog to learn new tricks?" How do you bounce back from severe adversity? These are all examples of living courageously, and they all require a bulletproof self-image that can stand up under pressure.

Why Not Bet on Yourself?

Nothing in this world is ever absolutely certain or guaranteed. Often the difference between a successful person and a failure is not one's better abilities nor ideas, but the courage that one has to bet on ideas, to take a calculated risk, and to act.

We often think of courage in terms of heroic deeds on the battlefield, in a shipwreck, or during a crisis. But everyday living requires courage too.

Standing still—failure to act—causes people who are faced with a problem to become nervous, to feel stymied or trapped, and it can bring on a host of physical symptoms.

I tell such people:

> Study the situation thoroughly, go over in your imagination the various courses of action possible to you and the consequences that can and may follow from each course. Pick out the course that gives the most promise—and go ahead. If we wait until we are absolutely certain and sure before we act, we will never do anything. Any time you act, you can be wrong. Any decision you make can turn out to be the wrong one. But we

must not let this deter us from going after the goal we want. You must daily have the courage to risk making mistakes, risk failure, risk being humiliated. A step in the wrong direction is better than staying "on the spot" all your life. Once you're moving forward, you can correct your course as you go. Your automatic guidance system cannot guide you when you're stalled, standing still.

Lee Iacocca has said that decisiveness is the number-one characteristic he looked for in key people to surround himself with and depend on. General Norman Schwarzkopf has said that leadership requires making decisions.

Most leaders agree that success comes from decisiveness and course correction, not long delays and procrastination to attempt making only flawless choices. Few successes are achieved via a straight line, from point A to point B, from idea to fruition. Most successes are achieved in a zig-zag manner.

PRESCRIPTION

Be willing to make a few mistakes, to suffer a little pain to get what you want. Don't sell yourself short. "Most people," said General R. E. Chambers, once Chief of the Army's Psychiatry and Neurology Consultant Division, "don't know how brave they really are. In fact, many potential heroes, both men and women, live out their lives in self-doubt. If they only knew they had these deep resources, it would help give them the self-reliance to meet most problems, even a big crisis." You've got the resources. But you never know you've got them until you act—and give them a chance to work for you.

Another helpful suggestion is to practice acting boldly and with courage in regard to "little things." Do not wait until you can be a big hero in some dire crisis. Daily living also requires courage. By practicing courage in little things, we develop the power and talent to act courageously in more important matters.

Charity

For a time I gave a lecture titled "How to Have Self-Respect in a Disrespectful World." Just as the world of accelerating stress that I observed in the late 1950s and 1960s was a kindergarten compared to today's frenetic pace, the growing lack of civility and respect I noticed in the 1960s and 1970s was only a modest preview of today's world. Daily living is a virtual assault on self-respect, as the companies we deal with treat us as numbers in the computer; individual tradespeople, store clerks, waiters, and the like are too often rushed, harried, rude, unhappy in their jobs and taking it out on the customer; often we cannot even get through to a human being by telephone! Everywhere, as the pace has quickened, civility has been sacrificed.

All this makes my original comments all the more important. In my lecture I said that the disrespectful world is made better or worse minute by minute for each individual participant in it, in a mirror reflection of two things: the person's own self-image and respect for others.

Successful personalities have interest in and regard for other people. They have a respect for others' problems and needs. They respect the dignity of human personality and deal with other people as if they were human beings, rather than as pawns in their own game. They recognize that every person is a child of God and is a unique individuality that deserves some dignity and respect.

It is a psychologic fact that our feelings about ourselves tend to correspond to our feelings about other people. When a person begins to feel more charitably about others, he invariably begins to feel more charitably toward himself. Persons who feel that people are not very important cannot have very much deep-down respect and regard for themselves. One of the best known methods of getting over a feeling of guilt is to stop condemning other people in your own mind—stop judging them, stop blaming them, and stop hating them for their mistakes. You will develop a better and more adequate self-image when you begin to feel that other people are more worthy.

Another reason that charity toward other people is symptomatic of the successful personality is that it means the person is dealing with reality. People *are* important. People cannot for long be treated like animals or machines or as pawns to secure personal ends.

Treating everyone with respect is charity because it is not always, instantly, individually reciprocated. You cannot view it as transactional, instead you must see the big picture and act in this manner as a means of strengthening your own self-image, and as your contribution to society in general.

> ## PRESCRIPTION
>
> The prescription for charity is three-fold: (1) Try to develop a genuine appreciation for people by realizing the truth about them; they are children of God, unique personalities, creative beings. (2) Take the trouble to stop and think of the other person's feelings, viewpoints, desires, and needs. Think more of what the other fellow wants, and how he must feel. A friend of mine kids his wife by telling her, whenever she asks him, "Do you love me?" "Yes, whenever I stop and think about it." There is a lot of truth in this. We cannot feel anything about other people unless we "stop and think" about them. (3) Act as if other people are important and treat them accordingly.

Esteem

Many years ago I wrote a contribution to the "Words to Live By" feature of *This Week Magazine* on the words of Carlyle, "Alas! the fearful Unbelief is unbelief in yourself." At that time I said: "Of all the traps and pitfalls in life, self-disesteem is the deadliest, and the hardest to overcome; for it is a pit designed and dug by our own hands, summed up in the phrase, 'It's no use—I can't do it.' "

The penalty of succumbing to it is heavy, both for the individual in terms of material rewards lost and for society in gains and progress unachieved.

As a doctor I might also point out that defeatism has still another aspect, a curious one, which is seldom recognized. It is more than possible that the words quoted above are Carlyle's own confession of the secret that lay behind his own craggy assertiveness, his thunderous temper and waspish voice, and his appalling domestic tyranny.

Carlyle, of course, was an extreme case. But isn't it on those days when we are most subject to the "fearful Unbelief," when we most doubt ourselves and feel inadequate to our task, isn't it precisely then that we are most difficult to get along with?

We simply must get it through our heads that holding a low opinion of ourselves is not a virtue, but a vice. Jealousy, for example, which is the scourge of many a marriage, is nearly always caused by self-doubt. Persons with adequate self-esteem don't feel hostile toward others; they aren't out to prove anything. They can see facts more clearly and aren't as demanding in their claims on other people.

Self-doubt is insidious, and gnaws away at the self-image as cancer eats away at the body's organs.

Beware the Thief of Happiness, the Critic Within. In her outstanding book *Liberating Everyday Genius*, Dr. Mary-Elaine Jacobsen writes, "The false self is a powerful adversary, one whose sharp-tongued admonitions can be heard in every situation of self-doubt, a foe that keeps us from our true selves and sometimes distances us from others." She also wrote, "Magically, when there is no enemy within, there are far fewer without." If there was ever a great sales pitch written for investing time and energy working with Psycho-Cybernetics and yourself, that statement is it!

In coming chapters I'll again discuss controlling The Critic Within, who is, in fact, the thief of happiness, self-acceptance, self-esteem, and peace of mind, far more influential than any critics we encounter around us.

Just as the astute corporate president learns she must listen to others' opinions in order to move forward, she also learns she must exercise caution and discretion about whose opinions she listens to and on what foundation they are based. We must listen to our inner voices, but we must exercise caution!

When The Critic Within begins to harp and belittle us, we should not hesitate to yell "Stop!" and send it back to its dark corner, properly chastised for doubting us.

I was once asked in a radio interview if, at age 65, when I set out to write, have published, and popularize the original edition of this book, I hadn't thought: What makes you think people will care about the thoughts of an elderly plastic surgeon in the twilight of his career, on the workings of the human mind? I replied that it had honestly not occurred to me, not out of ego, but because this was not an impulsive upstart for me but rather the next progressive step in an entire process. I had accomplished the next steps in my imagination many times before proceeding in actuality. But I said that, if my Inner Critic had dared raise such a preposterously negative question, I would have sat down across from him and read him the riot act.

The poor interviewer undoubtedly went home wondering if he was in the right line of work, stuck late at night interviewing a doddering fool who had imaginary characters, and argued with them. It might have helped if he had read the book, but as any author who gives interviews knows all too well, that's frequently not in the cards. In any case, I'm not at all abashed to have such conversations with myself and you shouldn't be either. I believe it is a useful imagination exercise to "personalize" these enemy-thoughts as a "critic" who sits across from you and puts you on the spot, whom you can vanquish with a presentation of your reasons why you will succeed.

PRESCRIPTION

Stop carrying around a mental picture of yourself as a person less capable than others, by making unfair apples-to-oranges comparisons. Celebrate your victories small or large, recognize and build on your strengths, and continually remind yourself that you are not your mistakes.

The word "esteem" literally means to appreciate the worth of. Why do men stand in awe of the stars, the moon, the immensity of the sea, the beauty of a flower or a sunset, and at the same time downgrade themselves? Did not the same Creator make us? Is not the human being the most marvelous creation of all? This appreciation of your own worth is not egotism unless you assume that you made yourself and should take some of the credit. Do not downgrade the product merely because you haven't used it correctly. Don't childishly blame the product for your own errors like the schoolboy who said, "This typewriter can't spell."

But the biggest secret of self-esteem is this: Begin to appreciate other people more; show respect for *any* human being merely because he or she is a child of God and therefore a thing of value. Stop and think when you're dealing with people. You're dealing with unique, individual creations of the Creator of all. Practice treating other people as if they had value, and, surprisingly, your own self-esteem will go up. For real self-esteem is not derived from the great things you've done, the things you own, the mark you've made, but from an appreciation of yourself for what you are—a child of God. When you come to this realization, however, you must necessarily conclude that all other people are to be appreciated for the same reason.

Self-Confidence

Confidence is built on an experience of success. When we first begin any undertaking, we are likely to have little confidence because we have not learned from experience that we can succeed. This is true of learning to ride a bicycle, speak in public, or perform surgery. It is literally true that success breeds success. Even a small success can be used as a stepping stone to a greater one. Managers of boxers are very careful to match them so they can have a graduated series of successful experiences. We can use the same technique, starting gradually, and experiencing success at first on a small scale.

Another important technique is to form the habit of remembering past successes and forgetting failures. This is the way both an electronic computer and the human brain are supposed to operate. Practice improves skill and success in basketball, golf, horseshoe pitching, or salesmanship, but not because repetition has any value in itself. If it did, we would learn our errors instead of our hits. A person learning to pitch horseshoes, for example, will miss the stake many more times than he will hit it. If mere repetition were the answer to improved skill, his practice should make him more expert at missing since that is what he has practiced most. However, although his misses may outnumber hits ten to one, through practice his misses gradually diminish and his hits come more and more frequently. This is because the computer in his brain remembers and reinforces his successful attempts, and forgets the misses.

This is the way that both an electronic computer and our own success mechanisms learn to succeed.

Yet what do most of us do? We destroy our self-confidence by remembering past failures and forgetting all about past successes. We not only remember failures, we impress them on our minds with emotion. We condemn ourselves. We flay ourselves with shame and remorse (both are highly egotistical, self-centered emotions). And self-confidence disappears.

It doesn't matter how many times you have failed in the past. What matters is the successful attempt, which should be remembered, reinforced, and dwelt on. The great inventor and industrialist Charles Kettering said that any man who wants to be a scientist must be willing to fail 99 times before he succeeds once and *suffer no esteem damage because of it*. This could be said of just about any field of endeavor. That does not mean you must actually operate at that ratio, by the way, but you must be willing to if need be and, as he suggested, suffer no self-image damage by doing so.

When we observe others' successes, we often never see or take note of the many zig-zags they took to arrive. When the famous Hollywood actress takes the Oscar in hand and delivers her acceptance speech, we forget all about the string of clinker movies she appeared in that were ridiculed by critics and quickly rejected by the public. When the best-selling author's book is the talk of the airwaves and selling like hotcakes, we never contemplate the shoebox full of rejection slips stored in his home or the mountains of torn-up paper from unsatisfactory drafts, rewrites, drafts, and more rewrites that preceded this book now on the shelf. Almost every bright and shining success has in its shadow a long list of disappointments, frustrations, and humiliations. Why should you expect otherwise? The success personality takes such things in stride.

PRESCRIPTION

Use errors and mistakes as a way to learning; then dismiss them from your mind. Deliberately remember and picture to yourself past successes. Everyone has succeeded sometime at something. Especially when beginning a new task, call up the *feelings* you experienced in some past success, however small it might have been.

Self-Acceptance

In the book made into the popular movie *The Talented Mr. Ripley*, the main character is a tortured and inferiority complex-laden young man, so unhappy with himself, so unwilling to accept himself, and so envious of others that he murders another man of greater financial means and attempts to take over his life, even to step into his relationships with the dead man's girlfriend and family. Fortunately, few people act on their lack of self-acceptance in such a violent and antisocial manner. More typical, such a person murders himself, slowly rather than suddenly, sometimes with alcohol or drug abuse, sometimes with less obvious forms of gradual self-destruction. Many, to quote Thoreau, live out their lives in "quiet desperation."

No real success or genuine happiness is possible until a person gains some degree of self-acceptance. The most miserable and tortured people in the world are those who are continually straining and striving to convince themselves and others that they are something other than what they basically are. And there is no relief and satisfaction like what comes when you finally give up the shams and pretenses and are willing to be yourself. Success, which comes from self-expression, often eludes you when you strive and strain to "be somebody" and often comes, almost of its own accord, when you become willing to relax and be yourself.

Changing your self-image does not mean changing your self, but changing your own mental picture, your own estimation, conception, and realization of that self. The amazing results that follow from developing an adequate and realistic self-image come about not as a result of self-transformation, but from self-realization and self-revelation. Your self, right now, is what it has always been, and all that it can ever be. You did not create it. You cannot change it. You can, however, realize it, and make the most of what already is by gaining a true mental picture of your actual self. There is no use straining to be somebody. You are what you are now. You are somebody, not because you've made a million dollars, or drive the biggest car in your block, or win at bridge, but because God created you in His own image.

Most of us are better, wiser, stronger, more competent right now than we realize. Creating a better self-image does not *create* new abilities, talents, powers; it releases and utilizes them.

We can change our personality, but not our basic self. Personality is a tool, an outlet, a focal point of the self that we use in dealing with the world. It is the sum total of our habits, attitudes, and learned skills, which we use as a method of expressing ourselves.

You Are Not Your Mistakes. Self-acceptance means accepting and coming to terms with ourselves now, just as we are, with all our faults, weaknesses, shortcomings, errors, as well as our assets and strengths. Self-acceptance is easier, however, if we realize that these negatives *belong* to us; they are not us. Many people shy away from healthy self-acceptance because they insist on identifying themselves with their mistakes. You may have made a mistake, but this does not mean that you are a mistake. You may not be expressing yourself properly and fully, but this does not mean you yourself are "no good."

We must recognize our mistakes and shortcomings before we can correct them.

The first step toward acquiring knowledge is the recognition of areas where you are ignorant. The first step toward becoming stronger is the recognition that you are weak. And all religions teach that the first step toward salvation is the self-confession that you are a sinner. In the journey toward the goal of ideal self-expression, we must use negative feedback data to correct course, as in any other goal-striving situation.

This requires admitting to ourselves—and accepting the fact—that our personality, our "expressed self," or what some psychologists call our "actual self" is always imperfect and short of the mark.

No one ever succeeds during a lifetime in fully expressing or bringing into actuality all the potentialities of the Real Self. In our Actual, Expressed Self, we never exhaust all the possibilities and powers of the Real Self. We can always learn more, perform better, behave better. The Actual Self is necessarily imperfect. Throughout life it is always *moving toward* an ideal goal, but never arriving. The Actual Self is not a static but a dynamic thing. It is never completed and final, but always in a state of growth.

It is important that we learn to accept this Actual Self, with all its imperfections, because it is the only vehicle we have. Neurotics reject the Actual Self and hate it because it is imperfect. In its place they try to create a fictitious ideal self that is already perfect, has already "arrived." Trying to maintain the sham and fiction is not only a terrific mental strain, but it continually leads to disappointment and frustration when people try to operate in a real world with a fictitious self.

PRESCRIPTION

Accept yourself as you are and start from there. Learn to emotionally tolerate imperfection in yourself. It is necessary to intellectually recognize our shortcomings, but disastrous to hate ourselves because of them. Differentiate between your self and your behavior. You are not ruined or worthless because you made a mistake or got off course, anymore than a computer is worthless because it makes an error, or a violin because it sounds a sour note. Don't hate yourself because you're not perfect. You have a lots of company in imperfection. No one else is perfect and those who try to pretend they are become imprisoned in misery.

Self-Acceptance versus Self-Rejection

Many people admit that they can't stand rejection from others. Otherwise capable sales professionals, for example, will be stymied in their careers by the inability to emotionally handle the inherent truth about most selling situations; you get more no's than yes's, more rejection than acceptance. Authors, playwrights, actors, athletes, coaches have all crumbled under the weight of criticism and rejection from the public or the media. But this kind of rejection is almost insignificant in impact compared to the awesome destructive power of Self-Rejection.

People reject and demean themselves in many ways. Women frequently reject themselves because they do not conform to the current fashion or standard for physical proportions. In the 1920s many women felt ashamed of themselves because they had breasts. The boyish figure was in vogue and large breasts were taboo. Then the fashion trends reverse directions, and now many young women develop anxieties because they do not have 40-inch busts. In the 1920s women used to come to me and in effect say, "Make me somebody by reducing the size of my breasts." In the 1960s, the plea was, "Make me somebody by increasing the size of my breasts." This seeking to be "somebody" is universal, but we make a mistake when we seek it in conformity or in the approval of other people. This mistake can have very serious consequences. The thin ideal, for example, has led women to anorexia, and even to death by anorexia, as in the celebrated case of the talented singer Karen Carpenter.

This is just one example. People reject and demean themselves by comparing themselves to any number of artificial standards. They go deeply, irreversibly into debt attempting to hurriedly keep up with a colleague, relative, or neighbor. Many people say in effect to themselves, "Because I am skinny, fat, short, too tall, etc., I am nothing." Or, "Because I am not as thin or rich as she, I am a zero." I think it was the Duchess of York who once said, "You can never be too thin or too rich." But those who suffer anorexia, a physical disease manifested by the self-image, would differ!

Instead of Self-Rejection, you must strive for Self-Acceptance. This means acknowledging that you are a unique, one-of-a-kind composite of strengths, weaknesses, knowledge and ignorance, experience and naiveté, accomplishment and unrealized potential, and so is every other individual on the planet. Carefully peel back the layers of the life of any person you might envy and view yourself as inferior to, and you will find a set of flaws and frustrations different from your own but guaranteed to rival your own. Donald Trump has the Midas touch in real estate but, to date, cannot seem to sustain a personal relationship. The current golden boy of your favorite sport may be basking in the spotlight at the moment, but may also find it impossible to adjust to a career that ends while he is still in his thirties, while yours may be just taking off. We all must strive for Self-Acceptance in our own way, even if only a minority achieve it.

Accept yourself. By all means, engage in self-directed, legitimate self-improvement. But also be yourself. You cannot realize the potentialities and possibilities inherent in that unique and special something that is you if you keep turning your back on it, feeling ashamed of it, hating it, unfairly comparing it to false idols, and refusing to recognize it as your greatest asset and ally.

The Secret of AQ—Adversity Quotient

For many years, IQ was the focus of academia and thought to virtually predetermine how far a person might go in life. We now know conclusively that it is not IQ that defines the area of the possible for a person, but self-image. (We also know that IQ can be improved long into adulthood.)

There is what I call a part of the self-image or representation of the self-image that may be scientifically measured. Since 1967, a management consultant named Dr. Paul Stoltz has been studying how people respond to adversity. Through his in-depth work with over 100 companies, he has evaluated what he calls the Adversity Quotient of more than 100,000 people. Adversity Quotient is a measurement of how people perceive challenges and how well they deal with them.

Dr. Stoltz says that having a high AQ is increasingly important as the world gets more difficult to operate in. He routinely surveys his clients regarding the number of adverse events they confront each day—whether a delayed or cancelled airline flight or a key client defecting to a competitor. He says that ten years back, the average number was 7; five years ago, 13, nearly doubled; in 1999, 23.

Dr. Stoltz defines people with high AQs three ways:

1. They do not blame others for the adversities or setbacks they confront.
2. They do not blame themselves either; they do not see setbacks that occur as reflecting poorly on themselves.
3. They believe the problems they face are limited in size and duration, and can be dealt with.

If you compare these characteristics with what we've just discussed in terms of the Success Personality as a trigger for the Automatic Success Mechanism, you will see the compatibility of my ideas and Dr. Stoltz' findings.

Can you raise your AQ? Absolutely. Dr. Stoltz' entire business at the corporate level is in providing training programs that help entire organizations of people raise their AQs. His approach includes unburdening people of low-AQ assumptions, such as helplessness, self-doubt, insurmountability of problems, and blame or guilt. This is much the same as modifying or strengthening the self-image. "Unburdening" or "liberating" is "strengthening." You do not necessarily need to add to strengthen; you can strengthen by subtraction.

This, not coincidentally, is in total harmony with everything I've observed regarding people diagnosed with very serious diseases. Some people easily accept that their problem is of such overwhelming magnitude they are helpless, they feel shame and guilt, and they blame themselves for being weak, and they blame others, God or destiny for their condition. Other people, confronted with the very same debilitating disease, conform to the three high-AQ characteristics and are very aggressive in taking on their condition in every way, from active research, self-education and involvement in their medical care, to finding ways to continue meaningful and fulfilling activity. I would observe, for example, that Elizabeth Taylor and Christopher Reeve are high AQs. Elizabeth Taylor has had several brushes with death, a number of medical operations including hip replacement surgeries, undergone addiction rehabilitation at the Betty Ford Clinic twice before making it stick. Yet she has fought resiliently to keep her beauty, grace, and sense of humor. She has remained active in the entertainment industry (making a TV movie as recently as 2000), in business (with a successful perfume line), and in charitable work (founding the first major fundraising effort for AIDS research).

Christopher Reeve, paralyzed by spinal cord injury in a horse-riding accident, has continued with a successful and meaningful life as loving husband and father, author, professional speaker, and director of movies, while just getting out of bed and dressed requires massive effort, hours of time, and assistance from caregivers.

The Fishing Trip from Hell

I was having lunch with several friends who had just returned from a fishing trip together. When I asked about the trip, they all chimed in describing a trip marred by one catastrophe after another—bad weather, their cooler full of provisions floating off in a river, one man's bout of stomach sickness, and on and on. "And how would you rate the trip?" I asked.

"Best trip yet," one man said. "We had a ball."

On this trip, they acted in a high-AQ mode and made a success of a series of adverse events. If they could approach everyday life as they did their fishing trip, they'd all be happier and more successful 365 days a year rather than 5. So would we all. Of course, everyday matters may be more important than a comedy of errors weekend in the woods. Certainly, tragedies of life such as serious injury or illness, loss of love, etc. are far more important. Still, much of success has to do with expectation and response. If we are burdened with unreasonable expectations of ourselves from unfair comparison to others or insistence on perfection, or with unreasonable expectations of life itself to somehow be smooth sailing or wholly unsatisfactory, "black and white" responses to everything, these self-made burdens will crush us under their own weight.

A Fable of Unburdening

I will end this chapter with a fable or parable I have heard told several different ways. Think about how it relates to the liberation of your success personality.

The story is told of an obviously weary traveler, walking down a dusty road, with a large boulder hoisted on one shoulder, a knapsack full of bricks on his back, a huge pumpkin precariously balanced on his head, and a nest of sturdy weeds and vines wound around his legs so that he could only take short, hobbling steps. As you might imagine, this human packhorse was hobbling along, uncomfortably stooped over, his progress slow and tedious, his physical struggle great.

A person sitting by the roadside called his hello and asked, "Say, traveler, why do you burden yourself with that big, heavy rock on your shoulder?"

Incredibly the traveler said, "Hmm. You know, I never noticed just how heavy it was before and, until you mentioned it, I hadn't given much thought to my reasons for taking it with me." After a few moments' pondering, the traveler set the boulder down, left it by the side of the road, and walked on, a bit straighter, a bit quicker.

A little further along, he encountered another bystander who queried him about the knapsack full of bricks. "Hmm. I'm glad you made mention of it," said the traveler, "I really hadn't paid any attention to what was in the knapsack." He took out all the bricks, left them at the roadside, and walked on.

A little further along, a curious child playing by the road called out to him. "Hey mister, why do you have all those weeds wrapped around your legs?"

The traveler took out his pocket knife and sliced away the weeds.

One by one, the bystanders made the traveler aware of his needless burdens. So, one by one, he accepted the new awareness, rejected the old burdens and abandoned them by the side of the road. Finally, he was a truly free man, and walked straight and tall like such a man.

Were his problems the boulder, the bricks, the weeds? No, not at all. The one problem was his lack of awareness of them.

MENTAL TRAINING EXERCISE

Make a short list of the bricks and rocks you are carrying around. Get actual bricks and with a marking pen, write one emotional burden on each brick. Put all the bricks in a knapsack or duffel bag and put it in the back seat of your automobile. When you leave your home each morning, take the bag out and heft it a few times, and say to yourself, "Today I'm leaving my bricks in the car. I will go about my day without carrying these heavy bricks around with me." When you arrive home in the evening, get your briefcase or belongings out of your car, but leave the bag of bricks there, and say to yourself, "I will relax and enjoy my evening by leaving my bricks behind."

CHAPTER NINE

How to Avoid Accidentally Activating Your Automatic Failure Mechanism

A person who doubts himself is like a man who would enlist in the ranks of his enemies and bear arms against himself.
—Alexander Dumas

*H*umans have boiling points. In my day, many businesses and factories were heated with steam boilers, which were actually one step away from being bombs. Properly regulated, they provided necessary heat economically. But they also had destructive potential. Such boilers had pressure gauges to show when the pressure was reaching the danger point. By recognizing the potential danger, corrective action could be taken and safety assured. Today, similarly, we have nuclear power plants, carefully monitored and regulated by computers and humans, to prevent the kind of "boiling point" accident that occurred in Chernobyl.

I am told that one of the worst nuclear power plant disasters that almost happened but was averted in the nick of time—the Three Mile Island event—was begun by a worker spilling a cup of coffee.

Always, power incorporates danger. The servo-mechanism you possess is powerful far beyond your past experience would lead you to believe. The more you learn about it and experiment with it, the more amazed you'll be at its capabilities. However, this power, used constructively and productively as your Automatic Success Mechanism (ASM), has a destructive potential, expressed as the Automatic Failure Mechanism (AFM). We must regulate this power in ourselves, always vigilant and alert for the red marker on its gauge slipping over into AFM territory.

Negative emotions are alarms. Frustration, rage, overwhelming anxiety, unshakable depression, jealousy and resentment, sloth and the demanding of something for nothing, intolerance and disrespect, and, of course, self-rejection are all signs that the servo-mechanism's gauge is in the red zone.

The human body has its own red light signals and danger signs, which doctors refer to as symptoms or syndromes. Patients are prone to regard symptoms as malevolent; a fever, a pain, or the like is "bad." Actually, these negative signals function *for* patients and for their benefit, *if* they recognize them for what they are and take corrective action. Symptoms or syndromes are the pressure gauges and red lights that help maintain the body in health. The pain of appendicitis may seem bad to the patient, but actually it operates for the patient's survival. If he felt no pain, he would take no action to have the appendix removed.

The AFM, accidentally awakened and activated, also has its symptoms. We need to be able to recognize these symptoms in ourselves so that we can do something about them. When we learn to recognize certain personality traits as signposts to failure, these symptoms then act automatically as negative feedback and guide us down the road to creative accomplishment. However, we not only need to become aware of them. Everyone "feels" them. We need to recognize them as undesirables, as things we do not want, and most important of all we must convince ourselves deeply and sincerely that these things do not bring happiness.

No one is immune to these negative feelings and attitudes. Even the most successful personalities experience them at times. The important thing is to recognize them for what they are, and take positive action to correct course.

The Picture of Failure

Again, I have found that patients can remember these negative feedback signals, or what I call the Failure Mechanism, when they associate them with the letters that make up the word "failure." They are:

> **F**rustration, hopelessness, futility
> **A**ggressiveness (misdirected)
> **I**nsecurity
> **L**oneliness (lack of "oneness')
> **U**ncertainty
> **R**esentment
> **E**mptiness

No one sits down and deliberately, with malice aforethought, decides to develop these negative traits just to be perverse. The traits do not just happen. Nor are they an indication of the imperfection of human nature. Each of these negatives was originally adopted as a way to solve a difficulty or a problem. We adopt them because we mistakenly see them as a way out of a difficulty. They have *meaning* and *purpose*, although based on a mistaken premise. They constitute a way of life for us. Remember, one of the strongest urges in human nature is to react appropriately. We can cure these failure symptoms not by willpower, but by understanding, by being able to see that they do not work and that they are inappropriate.

The truth can set us free from them. And when we can see the truth, then the same instinctive forces that caused us to adopt them in the first place will work in our behalf in eradicating them.

For example, consider the martyr complex or victim complex. You undoubtedly know someone who is constantly presenting himself or herself as a victim of an unhappy childhood, dysfunctional family, inadequate education, unjust employers, scheming co-workers, cheating lovers, all manner of illnesses, and financial misfortunes. This person insists that all of life is a conspiracy against her. Further, this person whines and sighs and moans as a martyr all too often—"No, no, you go ahead and go to the play tonight and have a good time. Don't worry about me not feeling up to it. Don't give me a second thought. I'm used to being left behind." Looking at this from the outside, like looking at a fish in a fish bowl, we are either incredulous or angry at this person's behavior, so unreasonably determined to make herself and everybody around her miserable. But make no mistake, this person has not developed these habits by deliberate strategy to cause herself and others maximum misery. Not at all! Instead, this is the way she has latched onto, to solve certain frustrations, for example, to get the attention and compassion she craves or to get the recognition she feels unable to merit otherwise.

It is quite difficult to re-engineer all this working from the outside in, assisting some other person in your life. But you can take charge of your own self-image and re-engineer your self-image, thus altering your own behavior.

So let's consider the warning signs of the Automatic Failure Mechanism exerting control.

Frustration

Frustration is an emotional feeling that develops whenever some important goal cannot be realized or when some strong desire is thwarted. All of us must necessarily suffer some frustration by the very fact of being human and therefore imperfect, incomplete, unfinished. As we grow older we should learn that all desires cannot be satisfied immediately. We also learn that our "doing" can never be as good as our intentions. We also learn to accept the fact that perfection is neither necessary nor required, and that approximations are good enough for all practical purposes. We learn to tolerate a certain amount of frustration without becoming upset about it.

It is only when a frustrating experience brings excessive emotional feelings of deep dissatisfaction and futility that it becomes a symptom of failure.

Chronic frustration usually means that the goals we have set for ourselves are unrealistic, or that the image we have of ourselves is inadequate, or both.

Practical Goals versus Perfectionistic Goals. To his friends, Jim S. was a successful man. He had risen from stock clerk to vice-president of his company. His golf score was in the low eighties. He had a beautiful wife and two children who loved him. Nevertheless, he felt chronically frustrated because none of these measured up to his unrealistic goals. He himself was not perfect in every particular, but he should be. He should be chairman of the board by now. He should be shooting in the low seventies. He should be such a perfect husband and father that his wife would never find cause to disagree with him and his children never misbehave. Hitting the bull's-eye was not good enough. He had to hit the infinitesimal speck in the center of the bull's-eye. "You should use the same technique in all your affairs that pro golfer Jackie Burke recommends in putting," I told him. "That is not to feel that you have to pinpoint the ball right to the cup itself on a long putt, but to aim at an area the size of a washtub. This takes off the strain, relaxes you, enables you to perform better. If it's good enough for the professionals, it should be good enough for you."

His Self-Fulfilling Prophecy Made Failure Certain. Harry N. was somewhat different. He had won none of the external symbols of success. Yet he had had many opportunities, all of which he muffed. Three times he had been on the verge of landing the job he wanted and each time "something happened"; something was always defeating him just when success seemed within his grasp. Twice he had been disappointed in love affairs.

His self-image was that of an unworthy, incompetent, inferior person who had no right to succeed or to enjoy the better things in life, and unwittingly he tried to be true to that role. He felt he was not the sort of person to be successful and always managed to do something to make this self-fulfilling prophecy come true.

Frustration as a Way of Solving Problems Does Not Work. Feelings of frustration, discontent, dissatisfaction are ways of solving problems that we all learned as infants. A hungry infant expresses discontent by crying. A warm, tender hand then appears magically out of nowhere and brings milk. If he is uncomfortable, he again expresses his dissatisfaction with the status quo, and the same warm hands appear magically again and solve his problem by making him comfortable. Many children continue to get their way and have their problems solved by overindulgent parents, merely by expressing their feelings of frustration. All they have to do is feel frustrated and dissatisfied and the problem is solved. This way of life "works" for the infant and for some small children. It does not work in adult life. Yet many of us continue to try it, by feeling discontented and expressing our grievances against life, apparently in the hope that life itself will take pity—rush in and solve our problem for us—if only we feel badly enough.

Jim S. was unconsciously using this childish technique in the hope that some magic would bring him the perfection he craved. Harry N.

had "practiced" feeling frustrated and defeated so much that feelings of defeat became habitual with him. He projected them into the future and expected to fail. His habitual defeatist feelings helped create a picture of himself as a defeated person. Thoughts and feelings go together. Feelings are the soil that thoughts and ideas grow in. This is the reason that you have been advised throughout this book to imagine how you would *feel* if you succeeded—and then feel that way now.

Infant behavior is inappropriate for adult life, and you must rise above it by setting goals and working toward them. When you zig or zag off course in any way, you dare not lie there in the weeds crying like a baby demanding and waiting for some warm hands to come along, gently brush you off, and put you back on your path, headed in the right direction. You must exhibit strength of self-image, and determine to pick yourself up, replot your course, and restart your travel toward your chosen goals. You must exhibit Self-Acceptance, so that you can acknowledge having made mistakes—having zigged when you should have zagged—rather than Self-Rejection, which requires the masquerade of placing blame. You must not permit a fog bank passing through to obliterate the beacon light of your goals.

Aggressiveness

Excessive and misdirected aggressiveness follows frustration as night follows day.

One of the most horrifying diseases of the day is Alzheimer's, in which a person may retain sound physical health, but lose memory and identity, in ever increasing episodic debilitation. It is common for victims of this disease to occasionally, without warning, turn violent toward their caregivers or loved ones. I am convinced such aggressiveness is the direct product of the unimaginable frustration these people must feel at having their very identity disappear from their memory.

When people unafflicted with Alzheimer's turn violent or vicious toward others, it is often the direct product of having their true self beaten on, tortured, and imprisoned in the form of an unhealthy self-image.

A long-time friend of my wife Anne's, a successful career woman, married a somewhat younger, much less accomplished man. She seemed quite content with being the breadwinner, earning virtually all of the household income, and supporting him generously. At first so did he. But others' tacit disapproval, his friends' making jokes at his expense, her family's criticism all built up as a weight of frustration. He attempted several business ventures he was ill-equipped for, invested without due diligence, and began a pattern leading only to greater frustration. At the same pace, she was being put upon by friends and family, so that she became dissatisfied, then critical. When all of his frustration hit a boiling point in this overheated environment, an argument turned violent and he hit her a number of times, ultimately leading to a 911 call and police cars arriving, lights on, sirens blazing. The incident did not just go away, as these sort of things rarely do; it was the beginning of the end of the marriage.

There is absolutely no acceptable excuse for a man striking a woman, or vice versa. But it is easily explained as the predictable result as unchecked frustration begets aggression.

Still, with such unpleasant examples noted, aggressiveness itself is not an abnormal behavior pattern, as some psychiatrists once believed. Aggressiveness and emotional steam are very necessary in reaching a goal. We must go out after what we want in an aggressive rather than in a defensive or tentative manner. We must grapple with problems aggressively. The mere fact of having an important goal is enough to create emotional steam in our boiler and bring aggressive tendencies into play. However, trouble ensues when we are blocked or frustrated in achieving our goal. The emotional steam is then dammed up, seeking an outlet. Misdirected or unused, it becomes a destructive force. The worker who wants to punch his boss in the nose but doesn't dare goes home and snaps at his wife and kids or kicks the cat. Or he may turn his aggressiveness on himself in much the same way that a certain scorpion in South America will sting itself and die of its own poison, when angered.

Don't Lash Out Blindly—Concentrate Your Fire. The Automatic Failure Mechanism does not direct aggressiveness toward the accomplishment of a worthwhile goal. Instead it is used in such self-destructive channels as ulcers, high-blood pressure, worry, excessive drinking, or compulsive overwork; or it may be turned on other persons in the form of irritability, rudeness, gossip, nagging, fault-finding, or even violence.

The answer to aggression is not to eradicate it but to understand it, and to provide proper and appropriate channels for its expression.

When we recognize aggressiveness rearing its head, we want to turn it around on the frustration that birthed it, to use all this energy in taking productive action to resolve the frustration itself.

Knowledge Gives You Power. Merely understanding the mechanism involved helps a person handle the frustration-aggression cycle. Misdirected aggression is an attempt to hit *one* target (the original goal) by lashing out at *any* target. It doesn't work. Recall the children's cartoon of Elmer Fudd trying to hunt the wily rabbit. After shooting at him and missing several times, Fudd blasts wildly away in a dozen different directions. I suspect human duck and geese hunters sometimes succumb to the same temptation!

You don't solve one problem by creating another. If you feel like snapping at someone, stop and ask yourself, "Is this merely my own frustration at work? What has frustrated me?" "Am I just shooting in a dozen different directions?" When you see that your response is inappropriate, you have gone a long way toward controlling it. It also takes much of the sting away when someone is rude to you, if you realize that it is probably not a willful act, but an automatic mechanism at work. The other fellow is letting off steam that he could not use in achieving some goal.

Many automobile accidents are caused by the frustration-aggression mechanism. Today, it's been given the name road rage. There's also airline passenger rage. These names simply label the outcome of unchecked frustration building to aggression. The next time someone is rude to you in traffic, try this: Instead of becoming aggressive and thus a menace yourself, say to yourself, "The poor fellow has nothing against me personally. Maybe his wife burned the toast this morning, he can't pay the rent, or his boss chewed him out."

Safety Valves for Emotional Steam. When you are blocked in achieving an important goal, you are somewhat like a steam locomotive with a full head of steam with nowhere to go. You need a safety valve for your excess of emotional steam. All types of physical exercise are excellent for draining off aggression. Long brisk walks, push-ups, dumbbell exercises are good. Especially good are those games where you hit or smash something—golf, tennis, bowling, punching the bag. Another good device is to vent your spleen in writing. Write a letter to the person who has frustrated or angered you. Pull out all the stops. Leave nothing to the imagination. *Then burn the letter.*

The best channel of all for aggression is to use it up as it was intended to be used—in working toward some goal. Work remains one of the best therapies and one of the best tranquilizers for a troubled spirit.

Insecurity

The feeling of insecurity is based on a concept or belief of inner inadequacy. If you feel that you do not measure up to what is required, you feel insecure. A great deal of insecurity is due not to the fact that our inner resources are actually inadequate, but to the fact that we use a false measuring stick. We compare our actual abilities to an imagined ideal, perfect, or absolute self. Thinking of yourself in terms of absolutes induces insecurity.

The insecure person feels that he should be good—period. He should be successful—period. He should be happy, competent, poised—period. These are all worthy goals. But they should be thought of, at least in their absolute sense, as goals to be achieved, as something to reach for, rather than as "shoulds."

A friend of mine who heads up a large management consulting firm talked with me once about a popular business book entitled *The Peter Principle*, espousing the theory that business bureaucracies always err in eventually promoting people to their level of incompetence, with disastrous results. I have seen this occur many times myself: The good, effective doctor happy in his work, once promoted by the hospital to head of a department, turns out to be a miserable manager. The hospital loses a great doctor and gains an incompetent administrator. My friend differed with this as an absolute. "There is no doubt the so-called Peter Principle explains or at least provides a convenient, shorthand label for such situations," he said, "but then it fails to explain the exact same situation with a much different outcome. What about the person who gets promoted far beyond his level of experience, knowledge, preparation or confidence, and is even expected to fail by those around him, who rises to the occasion and succeeds?" As we discussed this further, I realized this was much like the earliest observations and questions that led me to Psycho-Cybernetics. Two unhappy people, with nearly identical physical flaws magnified in importance by their own imaginations, get virtually the same cosmetic surgery; one behaves as you and I would anticipate but the other retains all the same negative feelings about herself as if the scar still existed. Why?

In both these scenarios, the surgeries and the promotions, the difference in outcomes is hidden in the individuals' self-images. It cannot be seen on their faces or on their resumes.

The person who is already insecure, who is harboring a weak self-image, and who is by willpower forcing himself to the very edges of performance it will permit, if promoted responds to the promotion as "the straw that broke the camel's back," not as golden opportunity.

The Magic Power of Recalibration. There are many approaches to ridding yourself of insecurities so that you may rise to whatever occasion presents itself. One is to think rationally about the situation, the other people involved, and about yourself. Another is self-image reassurance and strengthening, including role-playing what now needs to be done competently in the Theater of Your Mind and sending your Automatic Success Mechanism on new search missions to provide ideas and answers required. Another is the immediate resetting of your sights on appropriate new targets.

Here's why recalibration is so important.

A famous New York sportswriter once gave me this example:

> Consider two very successful college football coaches who get head coaching jobs in the NFL, in essence promoted to a whole new level of competition. We sports writers immediately begin questioning their ability to succeed at this level, in effect pasting that Peter Principle thing on their foreheads. Ultimately, one of these coaches goes back to college coaching, a whipped puppy, tail between his legs, but the other takes his team to the Super Bowl.

> Certainly, there are variables, in talent, toughness of divisional opponents, schedule and so on. But the biggest variable is the actual reaction of the two coaches to their new posts. Both have hoped for just such a move up to the NFL. But one views it as having finally arrived. And he sets about behaving as a newly crowned king, hiding his own insecurities and self-doubt with autocratic, even bombastic behavior. He quickly develops adversarial relationships with us in the media, players, other coaches. His players read the papers, sense he's skating on thin ice, and do not respond. Soon he is horribly frustrated. His insecurities turn to fear of failure, his frustration turns to aggression, and he is unable to use whatever skills he did bring with him. The other newly promoted coach takes a very different approach. To him, his step up to this coaching job

is yet one more move forward on a lifeline of intended accomplishment. He is immediately focused on a whole new set of goals, from organizing a world class staff to improving team morale, to uncovering hidden talent within the team, to getting to the Super Bowl in two seasons. All of his energy is assumptively and productively focused. His goals are like lighthouses that keep him from running aground. People respond to him differently, he gets different results.

My sportswriter friend had analyzed these situations Psycho-Cybernetically! Since human beings are goal-striving mechanisms, the self realizes itself fully only when individuals are moving forward towards something. Remember our comparison with the bicycle in a previous chapter? People maintain their balance, poise, and sense of security only as they move forward or seek. When you think of yourself as having *attained* the goal, you become static, and you lose the security and equilibrium you had when you were moving towards something. If you are convinced that you are good in the absolute sense, you not only have no incentive to do better, but you feel insecure because you must defend the sham and pretense. "The man who thinks that he has 'arrived' has about used up his usefulness to us," the president of a large business said to me recently. When someone called Jesus good he admonished him, "Why callest thou me good? There is but one good and that is the Father." St. Paul is generally regarded as a good man, yet his own attitude was, "I count myself not to have *achieved* … but I press on toward the goal."

Keep Your Feet on Solid Ground. Trying to stand on the top of a pinnacle is insecure. Mentally, get down off your high horse and you will feel more secure.

This has very practical applications. It explains the underdog psychology in sports. When a championship team begins to think of itself as the champions, they no longer have something to fight for, but a status to defend. The champions are defending something, trying to prove something. The underdogs are fighting to do something and often bring about an upset.

I used to know a boxer who fought well until he won the championship. In his next fight he lost the championship and looked bad doing so. After losing the title, he fought well again and regained the championship. A wise manager said to him, "You can fight as well as a champion as when you're the contender if you'll remember one thing.

When you step into that ring you *aren't defending* the championship—you're *fighting* for it. You haven't got it—you've laid it on the line when you crawl through the ropes."

The mental attitude that engenders insecurity is a way. It is a way of substituting sham and pretense for reality. It is a way of proving to yourself and others your superiority. But it is self-defeating. If you are perfect and superior now, then there is no need to fight, grapple, and try. In fact, if you are caught trying real hard, it may be considered evidence that you are not superior. So you don't try. You lose your fight—your will to win.

In business, secure leaders attempt surrounding themselves with a team of individuals wiser, more capable, and often older and more experienced than they are. Insecure leaders surround themselves with yes-men and syncophants. Why? Because the secure leader is engaged in striving to move forward and more concerned with doing what is required than with anything else. The insecure leader is more concerned with appearances and fears showing any signs of weakness or incompetence.

If you catch yourself behaving as if your Automatic Failure Mechanism has immersed you in a swamp of insecurities and pulled you out covered in its slime and stench, you must acknowledge that "something smells and it is my own behavior!" Then do the things necessary to shower and emerge cleansed. A good soap for your shower is recalibration, goal-setting.

Loneliness

All of us are lonely at times. Again, it is a natural penalty we pay for being human and individual. But it is the extreme and chronic feeling of loneliness—of being cut off and alienated from other people—that is the work of the Automatic Failure Mechanism.

This type of loneliness is caused by an alienation from life. It is a loneliness from your real self. Those who are alienated from their real self have cut themselves off from the basic and fundamental contact with life. Lonely persons often set up a vicious cycle. Because of the feeling of alienation from self, human contacts are not very satisfying, and they become social recluses. In doing so, they cut themselves off from one of the pathways to finding themselves, which is to lose themselves in social activities with other people. Doing things and enjoying things with other people helps us to forget ourselves. In stimulating conversation, in dancing, in playing together, or in working together for a common goal, we become interested in something other than maintaining our own shams and pretenses. As we get to know the other fellow, we feel less need for pretense. We unthaw and become more natural. The more we do this, the more we feel we can afford to dispense with the sham and pretense and feel more comfortable just being ourselves.

Loneliness Is a Way That Doesn't Work. Loneliness is a way of self-protection. Lines of communication with other people—and especially any emotional ties—are cut down. It is a way to protect our idealized self against exposure, hurt, humiliation. The lonely personality is *afraid* of other people. Lonely persons often complain that they have no friends, and there are no people to mix with. In most cases, they unwittingly arrange things in this manner because of their passive attitude, that it is up to other people to come to them, to make the first move, to see that they are entertained. It never occurs to them that they should contribute something to any social situation.

Regardless of your feelings, force yourself to mix and mingle with other people. After the first cold plunge, you will find yourself warming up and enjoying it if you persist. Develop a social skill that will add to the happiness of other people: dancing, bridge, playing the piano, tennis, conversation. It is an old psychological axiom that constant exposure to the object of fear immunizes against the fear. As lonely persons continue to force themselves into social relations with other human beings—not in a passive way, but as active contributors— they gradually find that most people are friendly and that they are accepted. Their shyness and timidity begin to disappear. They feel more comfortable in the presence of other people and with themselves. The experience of their acceptance enables them to accept themselves.

The top executive who allows herself to become isolated in her ivory tower will soon inevitably find herself with the personal belongings from her office in the trunk of her car, her final check in hand, outside looking in. The high and mighty topple through isolation. The man who insulates himself from the riskiness of relationships in work alone will one day awaken to the shocking fact that he has no reason *to* work!

Isolation and loneliness are forces that destroy kings and presidents as well as "mere mortals." It was said of President Nixon's White House, as the Watergate scandal unfolded, that a "bunker mentality" consumed him. He sought security through ever increasing isolation. Compare his behavior to, say, that of Lee Iacocca at the helm of Chrysler, his ship full of holes, in eminent danger of financial capsizing. Instead of retreating into isolation, living with only his mounting crisis in a dark room, alone, he marched into the public eye as never before, cajoling, negotiating, selling and organizing Wall Street, Washington, and the buying public, and leading a dramatic corporate turnaround.

When you are tempted by aloneness, you must substitute aliveness. Think of the wonderful painting given to me as a gift by Salvador Dali, in which he depicted Psycho-Cybernetics as a steadfast ship choosing to sail toward the light rather than remain in a dark but arguably safer harbor. While you cannot stub your toe standing still in the dark, you cannot escape a burning building, get the refreshing drink in the refrigerator, or otherwise achieve anything by standing safe and still in the dark either. We must rise above loneliness by engagement, move out of isolation toward involvement, even risk criticism and confrontation to seek opportunity and improvement.

Uncertainty

Philosopher Elbert Hubbard said, "The greatest mistake a man can make is to be afraid of making one."

Uncertainty is a way of avoiding mistakes and responsibility. It is based on the fallacious premise that if no decision is made, nothing can go wrong. Being wrong holds untold horrors to the person who tries to conceive of himself as perfect. He is never wrong and always perfect in all things. If he were ever wrong, his picture of a perfect, all-powerful self would crumble. Therefore, decision making becomes a life-or-death matter.

One way is to avoid as many decisions as possible, and prolong them as much as possible. Another way is to have a handy scapegoat to blame. This type of person makes decisions, but she makes them hastily, prematurely, and is well-known for going off half-cocked. Making decisions offers her no problem at all. She is perfect. It is impossible for her to be wrong in any case. Therefore, why consider facts or consequences? She is able to maintain this fiction when her decisions back-fire, simply by convincing herself it was someone else's fault.

It is easy to see why both types fail. One is continually in hot water from impulsive and ill-considered actions; the other is stymied because he will not act at all. In other words, the "uncertainty way" of being right doesn't work.

Nobody Is Right All the Time. Realize that it is not required that a person be 100% right at all times. It is in the nature of things that we progress by acting, making mistakes, and correcting course. A guided torpedo arrives at its target literally by making a series of mistakes and continually correcting its course. You cannot correct your course if you are standing still. You cannot change or correct "nothing." You must consider the known facts in a situation, imagine possible conse-quences of various courses of action, choose one that seems to offer the best solution, and bet on it. You can correct your course as you go.

Consider some of today's most successful actors. Kevin Costner. Do you recall the film *Waterworld*? Tom Hanks. A film called *Joe and the Volcano*. We could go down the list. Every Oscar-winner, every Hollywood powerhouse has at least one such epic mistake on their resume.

More significantly, consider all the endeavors in which even the most successful participants are "wrong" more than they are "right."

Coaching a football game and calling plays or playing quarter-back and executing them: In most games, the victor has stacked up many more unsuccessful plays than successful ones.

Managing an investment portfolio: Typically, more stocks in "the basket" may go down than go up, but those that do go up pro-duce sufficient gains for overall profit.

Drilling for oil.

Developing advertisements.

In most environments, the victors are certainly not right 100% of the time! Often not even 50% of the time.

One of the most successful entrepreneurs I ever met, who brought 18 very successful new products to market in the space of a few years, and took his company from near-zero to over $200-million dollars in worth by age 38, remarked that few take note of the 100 other products he brought to market in that same time frame, all of which failed miserably. He describes his secret to success this way: *I fail forward faster.*

In the world of mail order, two of the legends are Ted Nicholas and Joseph Sugarman. Ted Nicholas is perhaps best known for a full-page advertisement that made his self-published book, *How To Form Your Own Corporation Without A Lawyer,* a million-copy bestseller. For a number of years, you could not open a business or financial publication, even an airline magazine without seeing that ad as well as many other ads, for Ted's other books and products. However Ted freely admits that for every profitable ad he created, he created eight or more that, when tested, flopped.

Joseph Sugarman was the first mail-order entrepreneur to accept credit card orders by telephone, using toll-free 800 numbers. He made his first fortune selling electronic gadgets with full-page advertisements, and was the first to sell a pocket calculator by mail order. More recently, he made a giant success out of Blu-Blockers sunglasses. When Mr. Sugarman lectures, he delights in telling one story after another of his biggest mistakes, the products he invested in that proved unsalable, the advertisements he developed and placed with the highest of hopes that did not produce. In their businesses, these men live uncertainty—and dare not require being right the majority of the time.

Only "Little Men" Are "Never Wrong." Another help in overcoming uncertainty is to realize the role that self-esteem and the protection of self-esteem play in indecisiveness. Many people are indecisive because they fear loss of self-esteem if they are proved wrong. Use self-esteem for yourself, instead of against yourself, by convincing yourself of this truth: Big men and big personalities make mistakes and admit them. It is the little man who is afraid to admit he has been wrong. (This, of course, applies equally to women.)

Success through the Process of Elimination. I've enjoyed reading Arthur Conan Doyle's tales of the great detective Sherlock Holmes' exploits. Holmes' trusty helpmate Dr. Watson, a man of many fine qualities but woefully little imagination, is frequently befuddled and amazed as Holmes "disappears into his own imagination" and emerges with the solution to the most mystifying of crimes. In his imagination, Holmes engages in the pedantic, dogged process of elimination, ultimately arriving at the one, best conclusion he cannot eliminate. Then that becomes his target, engaging all of the powers of his Automatic Success Mechanism in uncovering the clues, facts, and evidence that prove it true; i.e., he arrives at the target. A lesser detective would, instead, remain mired in the massive difficulty of the task and the confusing, even conflicting testimonies, thus engaging his Automatic Failure Mechanism instead of his Automatic Success Mechanism.

It's also worth noting that Holmes is willing to be wrong and, when his first attempts at and proclamations of deduction prove far off course, he does not collapse in embarrassment or humiliation, or give control over to frustration and aggression, nor does he retreat into isolation. He virtually shrugs off his mistakes and quickly refocuses, zigging and zagging his way toward his ultimate objective.

Thomas Edison's wife once observed that, "Mr. Edison worked endlessly on a problem, using the method of elimination. If a person asked him whether he were discouraged because so many attempts proved unavailing, he would say, 'No, I am not discouraged, because every wrong attempt discarded is another step forward.'"

If outcomes were preordained and certain, no one would play a game, nor would thousands of spectators tune in to television to watch it contested.

We must learn to embrace the short-term uncertainties of the game, while staying connected to the targets we choose, and trusting that we will achieve our overriding objectives, albeit by zigging and zagging rather than a straight line.

Reassure yourself that you are *not* your mistakes, so that you can freely acknowledge them, extract whatever useful feedback can be found in them, correct course, and continue moving forward.

Resentment

When the Automatic Failure Mechanism looks for a scapegoat or excuse for failure, it often serves up society, "the system," life, the "breaks," luck, the boss, the spouse, even the customer! People in the firm grip of their Automatic Failure Mechanisms resent the success and happiness of others because they are proof that life is short changing them and they are being treated unfairly. Resentment is an attempt to make our own failure palatable by explaining it in terms of unfair treatment, injustice. But, as a salve for failure, resentment is a cure that is worse than the disease. It is a deadly poison to the spirit, makes happiness impossible, and uses up tremendous energy that could go into accomplishment.

Quite often, when people came to me in my practice, requesting surgical correction of insignificant imperfections on their faces magnified by their imaginations, conversations with them lead to a realization: They disliked what they saw when they looked in the mirror not due to the reality of the reflection, but the resentment harbored for just about everyone in their life and their life circumstances.

Resentment Is a Way That Fails. Resentment is also a way of making us feel important. Many people get a perverse satisfaction from feeling wronged. The victim of injustice, the one who has been unfairly treated, is morally superior to those who caused the injustice.

Resentment is also a way, or an attempt, to wipe out or eradicate a real or fancied wrong or injustice that has already happened. The resentful person is trying to "prove a case" before the court of life, so to speak. If he can feel resentful enough and thereby "prove" the injustice, some magic process will reward him by making the event or circumstance that caused the resentment "not so." In this sense, resentment is a mental resistance to, a nonacceptance of, something that has already happened. The word itself comes from two Latin words: *re*, meaning back, and *sentire*, meaning to feel. Resentment is an emotional rehashing or refighting of some event in the past. You cannot win, because you are attempting to do the impossible—change the past.

Resentment Creates an Inferior Self-Image. Resentment, even when based on real injustices and wrongs, is not the way to win. It soon becomes an emotional habit. Habitually feeling that you are a victim of injustice, you begin to picture yourself in the role of a victimized person. You carry around an inner feeling that is looking for an external peg to hang itself on. It is then easy to see "evidence" of injustice, or fancy you have been wronged, in the most innocent remark or neutral circumstance.

Habitual resentment invariably leads to self-pity, which is the worst possible emotional habit anyone can develop. When these habits have become firmly ensconced, a person does not feel "right" or "natural" when they are absent. They then literally begin to search for and look for "injustices." Someone has said that such people feel good only when they are miserable.

Emotional habits of resentment and self-pity also go with an ineffective, inferior self-image. You begin to picture yourself as a pitiful person, a victim, who was meant to be unhappy.

The Real Cause of Resentment. Remember that your resentment is not caused by other persons, events, or circumstances. It is caused by your own emotional response, your own reaction. You alone have power over this, and you can control it if you firmly convince yourself that resentment and self-pity are not ways to happiness and success, but ways to defeat and unhappiness.

As long as you harbor resentment, it is literally impossible for you to picture yourself as a self-reliant, independent, self-determining person who is "the Captain of his soul, the master of his Fate." The resentful person turns over his reins to other people. They are allowed to dictate how he shall feel, how he shall act. He is wholly dependent on other people, just as a beggar is. He makes unreasonable demands and claims on other people. If everyone else should be dedicated to making you happy, you will be resentful when it doesn't work out that way. If you feel that other people "owe" you eternal gratitude, undying appreciation, or continual recognition of your superlative worth, you will feel resentment when these debts are not paid. If life owes you a living, you become resentful when it isn't forthcoming.

Resentment is therefore inconsistent with creative goal-striving. In creative goal-striving *you* are the creator, not the passive recipient. *You* set your goals. No one owes you anything. You go out after your own goals. You become responsible for your own success and happiness. Resentment doesn't fit into this picture, and because it doesn't it is a failure mechanism.

In a sense, there is no justice, but we may manufacture just results for ourselves. It is fact that by the very act of birth, one person is unjustly set out to begin a hard life in a ghetto filled with street crime, while another, born in a cross-town hospital that same moment, will begin life in a safe suburb. One will go to a school in disrepair, the other to a school with every modern advantage. Similarly, it is a fact that, in many sales offices, leads are disproportionately or unjustly distributed by the sales manager to her "pets" and those in her "doghouse." It is a fact that promotion in corporate settings frequently occurs due to factors other than pure merit. We could go on and on. There's no denying injustice. If you intend to insist on justice in order to live a successful and happy life, you will not do so in this lifetime, on this planet.

The other day, just after emerging from my New York town-house, wearing a brand new, beautifully tailored suit out of the wrapper for the very first time, en route to an important luncheon engagement, a passing taxi cab roared through a muddy puddle and splashed dirty water all over my pants. It occurred to me a more just arrangement would be if taxi cabs only splashed puddle water onto people wearing old work clothes already soiled, only if on their way home so that changing out of them would pose no inconvenience. Maybe I should lobby the mayor to pass such a law!

Of course, I was helpless to undo this unjust incident or to do anything to eradicate this injustice in general from being part and parcel of living in the city. I could certainly be more careful in the future, but that was neither here nor there. The immediate choice before me was to spend the rest of my day frustrated, angry, bitter and resentful, or to recalibrate and take whatever constructive actions possible to get back on track toward an enjoyable and productive meeting.

I admit, it's easier to react this way to such a minor injustice as taxi cabs, puddles, and soiled trousers than to racial injustice in society or bureaucratic injustice in your career. But the outcome will be the same. The fundamental choices are the same. And you can enjoy the powers of your Automatic Success Mechanism only if you choose to rise above injustice, small or large.

Over years, Psycho-Cybernetics has found its way into quite a number of prison inmate counseling programs, classes, halfway house classes, and the like. I suppose thousands of copies of my books have been donated to prisons and to individual prisoners. Even today, The Psycho-Cybernetics Foundation does not deny sincere requests from inmates for the book. As a result, I've had many conversations with wardens, counselors, pastors, and others working in this environment and naturally the subject of recidivism comes up often. A great cost to individuals, families, and society is the majority of prisoners who, once released after serving time, fail to stay straight and wind up back in prison again. And again. I have become convinced that recidivism is nothing more than resentment realized. If a person emerges from prison into society with his resentments intact—resentment against his upbringing and background, his prosecutors and jailers, his current lack of resources, the difficulty he faces in gaining others' acceptance and trust, etc.—he is nearly certain to commit new crimes and return himself to prison. Only the rare individual who manages to cleanse herself of these resentments and recalibrate is able to stay straight. Similarly, any individual who permits resentment to control her thoughts locks herself and her potential into a prison of her own making. She is her own hanging judge, discompassionate jury, and jailer.

Emptiness

Perhaps as you read this chapter you thought of someone who had been "successful" in spite of frustration, misdirected aggressiveness, resentment, etc. But do not be too sure. Many people acquire the outward symbols of success but when they go to open the long sought-for treasure chest, they find it empty. It is as if the money they have strained so hard to attain turns to counterfeit in their hands. Along the way, they *lost the capacity to enjoy*. And when you have lost the capacity to enjoy, no amount of wealth or anything else can bring success or happiness. These people win the nut of success but when they crack it open it is empty.

Those who have the capacity to enjoy still alive within them find enjoyment in many ordinary and simple things in life. They also enjoy whatever success in a material way they have achieved. Those in whom the capacity to enjoy is dead can find enjoyment in nothing, be it a one-dollar ice cream cone or a million-dollar mansion. No goal is worth working for. Life is a terrible bore. Nothing is worthwhile. You can see these people by the hundreds night after night knocking themselves out in night clubs trying to convince themselves they are enjoying it. They travel from place to place, become entangled in a whirl of parties, hoping to find enjoyment, always finding an empty shell. The truth is that joy is an accompaniment of creative function, of creative goal striving. It is possible to win a fake "success," but when you do you are penalized with an empty joy.

Life Becomes Worthwhile When You Have Worthwhile Goals. This is the Psycho-Cybernetic secret to keeping your Automatic

Failure Mechanism safely asleep, not troubled by any assignment from you and not troubling you with the results of its labors.

**Life is worthwhile only when you have
firmly fixed in your sights worthwhile goals.**

Emptiness is a symptom that you are not living creatively. You either have no goal that is important enough to you, or you are not using your talents and efforts in striving toward an important goal. The person who has no purpose of her own pessimistically concludes, "Life has no purpose." The person who has no goal worth working for concludes, "Life is not worthwhile." The person with no important job to do complains, "There is nothing to do." The individual who is actively engaged in striving toward an important goal or goals does not come up with pessimistic philosophies concerning the meaninglessness or the futility of life in general or his life in specific.

Even the most elderly can—and do—operate as goal-striving, optimistic people. A wonderful trend has been the migration of retirees to small college towns, where they pursue goals of learning, education, mastery of interesting subjects, acquiring some skill they never found time to previously pursue, even mentoring others. Earlier in this book I described the four steps of the learning process; aliveness is based on constantly setting new goals and then moving up that four-step ladder of learning in order to effectively pursue them.

Emptiness Is Not a Way That Wins. Emptiness, once experienced, can become a way of avoiding effort, work, and responsibility. It becomes an excuse or a justification for noncreative living. If all is vanity, if there is no new thing under the sun, if there is no joy to be found anyway, why bother? Why try? If life is just a treadmill, if we work eight hours a day so that we can afford a house to sleep in, so that we can sleep eight hours to become rested for another day's work, why get excited about it? All these intellectual "reasons" vanish, however, and we experience joy and satisfaction, when once we get off the treadmill, stop going around and around in circles, and select a goal worth striving for—and go after it.

Emptiness and an Inadequate Self-Image Go Together. Emptiness may also be the symptom of an inadequate self-image. It is impossible to psychologically accept something that you feel does not belong to you or that is not consistent with your self. Those who hold an unworthy and undeserving self-image may hold their negative tendencies in check long enough to achieve a genuine success, then be unable to accept it psychologically and enjoy it. They may even feel guilty about it, as if they had stolen it. Their negative self-image may even spur them on to achievement by the well-known principle of overcompensation. But I do not subscribe to the theory that one should be proud of an inferiority complex or thankful for it just because it sometimes leads to the external symbols of success. When "success" finally comes, such persons feel little sense of satisfaction or accomplishment. They are unable to take credit in their own minds for their accomplishments. To the world they are a success. They themselves still feel inferior, undeserving, almost as if they were thieves and had stolen the status symbols that they thought were so important. "If my friends and associates really knew what a phony I am," they think.

This reaction is so common that psychiatrists refer to it as the "success rejection syndrome," the man who feels guilty, insecure and anxious, when he realizes he has succeeded.

Only striving for goals that are important to you—not as status symbols, but because they are consistent with your own deep inner wants—is healthful. Striving for real success—for your success through creative accomplishment—brings a deep inner satisfaction. Striving for a phony success to please others brings a phony satisfaction.

MENTAL TRAINING EXERCISES

Awareness, acknowledgment, and prompt reaction to a slumbering Automatic Failure Mechanism awakening and attempting to distract you with F-A-I-L-U-R-E is important.

Glance at Negatives, But Focus on Positives

Automobiles come equipped with "negative indicators" placed directly in front of the driver, to tell you when the battery is not charging, when the engine is becoming too hot, when the oil pressure is becoming too low, etc. To ignore these negatives might ruin your car. However, there is no need to become unduly upset if a negative signal flashes. You merely stop at a service station or a garage, and take positive action to correct the problem. A negative signal does not mean the car is no good. All cars overheat at times.

However, the driver of the automobile does not look at the control panel exclusively and continuously. To do so might be disastrous. She must focus her gaze through the windshield, look where she is going, and keep her primary attention on her goal—*where she wants to go*. She merely glances at the negative indicators from time to time. When she does, she does not fix on them or dwell on them. She quickly focuses her sight ahead again and concentrates on the positive goal of where she wants to go.

How to Use Negative Thinking

We should adopt a similar attitude about our own negative symptoms. I am a firm believer in "negative thinking" when used correctly. We need to be aware of negatives so that we can steer clear of them. A golfer needs to know where the bunkers and sand traps are, but he doesn't think continuously about the bunker—where he doesn't want to go. His mind glances at the bunker, but dwells on the green. Used correctly, this type of negative thinking can work for us to lead us to success, if:

1. We are sensitive to the negative to the extent that it can alert us to danger.

2. We recognize the negative for what it is—something undesirable, something we don't want, something that does not bring genuine happiness.

3. We take immediate corrective action and substitute an opposite positive factor from the Success Mechanism. Such practice will in time create a sort of automatic reflex that becomes a part of our inner guidance system. Negative feedback will act as a sort of automatic control, to help us steer clear of failure and guide us to success.

Take a few minutes toward the conclusion of each day, or midday and at day's end if you can. Find a quiet place, close your eyes, enter your imagination so as to revisit the day's events and your behavior. Congratulate yourself on all your Automatic Success Mechanism reflective actions but take note of Automatic Failure Mechanism warning lights quietly flashing on the dashboard! Tell yourself that Automatic Failure Mechanism behavior is "not you" and is not to be tolerated. If corrections can be made for any that occurred, by all means make them. Be the bigger person by calling or going to see anyone who may deserve your apology, your gratitude, or your congratulations.

Analyze your thoughts and actions of the day in terms of contributing toward achieving your goals, even measure your ratio of Automatic Success Mechanism-versus Automatic Failure Mechanism-driven activity; then resolve to improve that ratio.

Do not fear self-analysis. Stick with self-coaching, avoid self-loathing. Conclude your private critique of the day by identifying positives you can build on and the recommitment to your goals and ideals.

CHAPTER TEN

How to Remove Emotional Scars and Give Yourself an Emotional Facelift

Anger is really disappointed hope.

—Erica Jong

The facelift business is booming. Cosmetic surgery profession revenues have increased by double-digit percentages each year for the past handful of years. You now see mass television advertising offering any combination of procedures desired—nose, ears, throat, whole facelift, breast enlargement, buttocks improvement, tummy tuck—for a set monthly payment, akin to buying a car on payments! Still, many people seeking emotional salvation and satisfaction from the surgical scalpel will wake up with a new face or better sculpted body but with old disappointment and frustration.

I and others have learned a great deal about Psycho-Cybernetics in the more than fifty years that have passed since I first began drawing the connection between patients coming to my office seeking to correct scars in their outer image and the existence of "scars" hidden away on their inner image or self-image. However, the fundamental analogy is every bit as valid as when first uncovered and recognized.

As a medical doctor and surgeon, I have performed countless operations of reconstructive as well as cosmetic facial surgery, and been privileged to lecture on such clinical techniques all over the world. Yet I have never become jaded about the miraculous systems built into the human body. For example, when you receive a physical

180

injury, such as a cut on the face, your body automatically forms scar tissue, which is both tougher and thicker than the original flesh. The purpose of the scar tissue is to form a protective cover or shell, nature's way of insuring against another injury in the same place. If an ill-fitting shoe rubs against a sensitive part of your foot, the first result is pain and sensitiveness. But, again, nature protects against further pain and injury by forming a callus, a protective shell.

We are inclined to do very much the same thing whenever we receive an emotional injury, when someone hurts us or rubs us the wrong way. We form emotional or spiritual scars for self-protection. We are very apt to become hardened of heart, callous toward the world, and to withdraw within a protective emotional shell of one kind or another.

What We Can Learn, When Nature Needs an Assist

In forming scar tissue, it is nature's intention to be helpful. In our modern society, however, scar tissue, especially on the face, can work against us instead of for us. Take George T., for example, a promising young attorney. He was affable, personable, and well on his way to a successful career, when he had an automobile accident, which left him with a horrible scar from midway on his left cheek to the left corner of his mouth. Another cut, just over his right eye, pulled his upper eyelid up tightly when it healed, which gave him a grotesque "glaring" appearance. Every time he looked in the bathroom mirror he saw a repulsive image. The scar on his cheek gave him a perpetual leer, or what he called an "evil look." After leaving the hospital, he lost his first case in court, and was sure that his evil and grotesque appearance had influenced the jury. He felt that old friends were repelled and repulsed by his appearance. Was it only his imagination that even his own wife flinched slightly when he kissed her?

George T. began to turn down cases. He started drinking during the day. He became irritable, hostile, and something of a recluse.

The scar tissue on his face formed a tough protection against future automobile accidents. But in the society in which George lived, physical injuries to his face were not the primary hazard. He was more vulnerable than ever to social cuts, injuries, and hurts. His scars were a liability instead of an asset.

Had George been a primitive man and suffered facial scars from an encounter with a bear or a saber-toothed tiger, his scars would have probably made him more acceptable to his fellows. Even in fairly recent times old soldiers have proudly displayed their scars of battle. I suspect the same is true of young toughs in inner city gangs.

In George's case, nature had good intentions, but nature needed an assist. I gave George back his old face by plastic surgery, which removed the scar tissue and restored his features.

Following surgery, the personality change in him was remarkable. He became his good-natured, self-confident self again. He stopped drinking. He gave up his lone wolf attitude, moved back into society, and became a member of the human race again. He literally found a new life.

This new life, however, was brought about only indirectly by plastic surgery on physical tissue. The real curative agent was the removal of emotional scars, the security against social cuts, the healing of emotional hurts and injuries, and the restoration of his self-image as an acceptable member of society, which in his case surgery made possible.

Most people build up a considerable amount of scar tissue on their self-images with no correlation whatsoever to actual physical disfigurement that can be solved by a skilled surgeon with a scalpel.

How Emotional Scars Alienate You from Life

Many people have inner emotional scars who have never suffered physical injuries. And the result on personality is the same. These people have been hurt or injured by someone in the past. To guard against future injury from that source they form a spiritual callus, an emotional scar to protect their ego. This scar tissue, however, "protects" them not only against the individual who originally hurt them, but also all other human beings. An emotional wall is built through which neither friend nor foe can pass.

Zig Ziglar tells an amusing story about a cat who innocently traipses across a stove top and lands on a burner still hot from recent use. With a loud yelp, the cat leaps off the stove and sulks away to nurse its tender paws. Zig says, not only won't that cat ever climb up on that stove again, he'll never even go into the kitchen!

Emotional scar tissue built up on the self-image affects people like scorched paws affect that cat. Given several repeats of an unpleasant, embarrassing or frustrating "scarring" experience, the affected individual not only avoids the precise situation, he avoids the general area in which it might occur. For example, I once counseled a very capable executive, rising up the ranks in a big corporation, who had been repeatedly chastened by his mentor and boss for sitting as quiet as a church mouse through meeting after meeting, only a spectator, not a participant. This fellow had very good ideas and input to offer, often did so privately, and often missed any credit for his contributions. In fact, most of his colleagues viewed him as "dead wood" and wondered about the boss' motives for having this fellow on the payroll.

You can probably do your own diagnosis at this point and guess right. This fellow had, throughout his junior and senior high school years, stuttered nervously if called on in class, suffered ridicule from other students, and, as a result, withdrawn from active participation in his classes, doing his level best to be "invisible" at all times. Call that the first layer of self-image scar tissue. Fast forward to his first marriage. Both his ex-wife and ex-mother-in-law were domineering personalities, quite possibly abusive, both constantly criticizing this fellow's ideas, whether choice of clothes, political opinion, even an opinion about a book or TV program. Early in this marriage he adopted a keep-it-to-himself attitude. This became a second layer of scar tissue.

Fast forward to a very recent year, when, active in his community association, he found himself at odds over an issue with a very influential, egotistical, uncompromising, bullying, and far more persuasive neighbor. His adversary attacked any idea this fellow proposed thoroughly and aggressively, and turned enough others against this fellow that he was summarily voted off the council at the end of his first year's term. Layer number three.

It didn't matter now that he was not dealing with school children, an abusive mother-in-law, or neighbors, that he was in a very different environment, that he had the full support of a powerful mentor and boss, that his suggestions would be listened to with respect, and that it was far more important for him to assert himself than at any of these other times. It didn't matter that this situation was very different from the others. Like the entire kitchen is to one stove top burner, this situation was still in the general area of the others. Close enough to be threatening to his self-image. Consequently, instead of representing the self-image of the smart, competent, promising executive he was, in these circumstances, he represented the self-image of a "scaredy cat."

Putty, Not Plaster

Could this man scrape away all this scar tissue and liberate his self-image? Absolutely, using all the tools of Psycho-Cybernetics we have discussed—awareness, rational thought, deliberate decision (i.e., establishing the target), purposeful use of the imagination, including the Theater of the Mind mental rehearsal techniques.

In his fine book *Profiles of Success and Power,* Dr. Gene Llundrum writes: "Self-Image is not set in plaster, it is set in putty."

I'm known as a plastic surgeon, but as an amateur sculptor for many years, I enjoy taking scalpel to clay and have often sculpted, unsculpted, and resculpted a face in clay until it was exactly as I imagined. The clay or putty-like material stays soft and malleable enough to do so many, many times. In his infinite wisdom, God manufactured the self-image of similar material, so it remains malleable throughout our entire lives. No one is ever too old, too jaded, too frightened, or too traumatized to "wet the clay" and begin remaking it as they imagine and desire.

Do Not Overprotect Yourself

As in the case of a facial scar, excessive protection against the original source of injury can make us more vulnerable and do us even more damage in other areas. The emotional wall that we build as protection against one person or one situation cuts us off from all other human beings, from many opportunities, even from our real selves. As we have pointed out previously, the person who feels "lonely" or out of touch with other human beings also feels out of touch with his real self and with life.

These listed techniques of Psycho-Cybernetics, all combined, place in your hands a most powerful, magical emotional scalpel, and they infuse your hands with the dynamic talent and ability of a world-class emotional surgeon, so that you may remove whatever emotional scars now inhibit your self-image. But to do so, you must take a risk. You must risk "bumps in the road," disappointment, rejection, and mistakes with the certainty that they will occur but will not deter you from your overriding goals.

Don't Underestimate the Power of Emotional Scars

Built-up emotional scars, one atop the other, make the self-image a threatened and vulnerable entity that triggers "survival mode behavior" from the servo-mechanism—flee or fight, fear or pugnacious aggressiveness—whenever confronted with a situation it senses might harm it in the same way as the past incidents that left scars.

In a book titled *Anxiety Disorders and Phobias*, the authors,[1] including a cognitive therapist, state that, "...the same apparatus that prevents a person from venturing into physical danger also deters him from exposing himself to psychological danger." In other words, the servo-mechanism may not be able to accurately assess the relativity of dangers. For example, you are not in any physical danger due to social embarrassment at a dinner party by not being able to hold up your end of a conversation, perhaps because you make less money than the other guests and feel inferior because of it, and are therefore fearful of being asked about your job or investments. Yet the situation may trigger the same kind of anxiety and inhibition as being confronted by a mugger in a dark alley. In the case of the mugger, meekly taking out your wallet and throwing it toward or past the mugger and running as fast as you can in the opposing direction may be appropriate. In the social situation, throwing away all opportunity for a pleasant evening and fleeing into silence or monosyllabic responses is wholly inappropriate and may lead to the exact result you are worried about—being perceived badly by hosts and other guests alike. The social situation is most likely to trigger this survival reaction if it closely resembles some situations that have left scar tissue on the self-image.

I would like to make one point addressed earlier in the book: You do not necessarily have to painstakingly revisit every incident or influence all

---

[1] Aaron T. Beck, M.D. and Gary Emery, Ph.D., with Ruth L. Greenberg, Ph. D. (New York: Basic Books, 1990 reprint edition

the way to early childhood in order to perform the emotional surgery needed to liberate a scarred self-image from this compulsive triggering of survivalist behavior in situations where it is inappropriate and counterproductive. You can begin with fresh programming, using recall of successes, mental movies, mental rehearsal, and other Psycho-Cybernetics techniques. Acceptance of the new by the self-image will automatically remove the old scars. Remember the term "solution-oriented therapy" or better yet "do it yourself solution-oriented therapy" and think in those terms rather than the cliché of 30 years of weekly visits to the couch.

Emotional Scars Help Make Juvenile Delinquents

Psychiatrist Bernard Holland has pointed out that, although juvenile delinquents appear to be very independent and have the reputation of being braggarts, particularly about how they hate everyone in authority, they protest too much. Underneath this hard exterior shell, says Dr. Holland, "is a soft vulnerable inner person who wants to be dependent upon others." However, they cannot get close to anyone because they will not trust anyone. Sometime in the past they were hurt by a person important to them, and they dare not leave themselves open to be hurt again. They always have their defenses up. To prevent further rejection and pain, they attack first. Thus, they drive away the very people who would love them, if given half a chance, and could help them.

A popular staple of daytime television talk shows these days is the theme show featuring "teens out of control," teens swearing, abusing their parents, skipping school, drinking, using drugs, engaging in promiscuous sex, even shoplifting and stealing cars. The show host and the parents turn these out-of-control teens over to military-type "juvenile boot camp" leaders who drag them off stage and take them away to "boot camp." Weeks later, they return, many dramatically changed. This is all controversial, yet there is considerable evidence of it getting positive and lasting results more often than not. When it works, why does it work? Even at a young age, these youngsters have piled on layer on layer on layer on layer of scar tissue, so that their self-image has totally handed over the reins to negative, Automatic Failure Mechanism emotions, notably including aggression to the nth degree. You've no doubt heard the saying "desperate circumstances require desperate measures." These boot camp interventions are desperate, last-resort measures—in a sense, incredibly sharp emotional scalpels. To slice away all the protective, hardened scar tissue on these self-images requires these heavy-handed, confrontive techniques.

Bottom-line: Most delinquency is symptomatic of severe emotional scarring, a profoundly unhealthy self-image, an Automatic Failure Mechanism unleashed and unchecked.

Carefully consider *all* your own habitual or repetitive behaviors and life experiences. Do you suffer through one disappointing intimate relationship after another? Do you find one group of co-workers after another disagreeable? Are all your clients cheapskates or "difficult"? And so on. Whether avoidance or aggression, self-image scarring is involved.

Can We Prevent Future Emotional Scarring?

There is a cowboy saying that is a favorite of this book's editor: "The first step to getting out of a hole is to stop digging." We might say that the first step to liberating a scarred self-image is to stop piling on more scar tissue. Can we do so? Certainly. New knowledge about why you respond to certain stimuli as you do, heightened emphasis on rational thinking, and maturity can be your allies. Just as there are smart things you can do, that are within your sphere of control, to strengthen your physical immune system, such as eating certain foods and avoiding others, taking antioxidant vitamin supplements, regularly exercising, there are things you can do to strengthen your emotional immune system as well.

Three Prescriptions for Immunizing Yourself Against Emotional Hurts

Be Too Big to Feel Threatened

Many people become "hurt" terribly by tiny pinpricks or what we call social slights. Everyone knows someone in the family, office, or circle of friends who is so thin-skinned and sensitive that others must be continually on guard, lest offense be taken at some innocent word or act.

It is a well-known psychological fact that the people who become offended the easiest have the lowest self-esteem. We are hurt by things we conceive of as threats to our ego or self-esteem. Fancied emotional thrusts that go unnoticed by the person with wholesome self-esteem slice these people up terribly. Even real digs and cuts, which inflict a terrible injury to the ego of the person with low self-esteem, do not make a dent in the ego of those who think well of themselves. The person who feels undeserving, who doubts his own capabilities, and who has a poor opinion of himself becomes jealous at the drop of a hat. The person who secretly doubts her own worth and who feels insecure within herself, who sees threats to her ego where there are none exaggerates and overestimates the potential damage from real threats.

We all need a certain amount of emotional toughness and ego security to protect us from real and fancied ego threats. It wouldn't be wise for our physical body to be covered over completely with a hard callus or a shell like a turtle's. We would be denied the pleasure of all sensual feeling. But our body does have a layer of outer skin, the epidermis, for the purpose of protecting us from invasion of bacteria, small bumps and bruises, and small pinpricks. The epidermis is thick enough and tough enough to offer protection against small wounds, but not so thick or hard that it interferes with all feeling. Many people have no epidermis on their ego. They have only the thin, sensitive inner skin. They need to become thicker-skinned, emotionally tougher, so that they will simply ignore petty cuts and minor ego threats.

Also, they need to build up their self-esteem, get a better and more adequate self-image of themselves so that they will not feel threatened by every chance remark or innocent act. A big strong person does not feel threatened by a small danger; a weak, little person does. In the same way a healthy strong self-image does not feel itself threatened by every innocent or offhand remark.

It seems that some people literally go through life waiting to be offended. They are rarely disappointed!

Healthy Self-Images Do Not Bruise Easily

The person who feels his self-worth is threatened by a slighting remark has a small weak ego and a small amount of self-esteem. He is self-centered, self-concerned, hard-to-get-along with, and what we call egotistic. But we do not cure a sick or weak ego by beating it down, undermining it, or making it even weaker through self-abnegation or trying to become selfless. Self-esteem is as necessary to the spirit as food is to the body. The cure for self-centeredness, self-concern, "egotism" and all the ills that go with it is the development of a healthy, strong ego by building up self-esteem. When a person has adequate self-esteem, little slights offer no threat at all; they are simply passed over and ignored. Even deeper emotional wounds are likely to heal faster and cleaner, with no festering sores to poison life and spoil happiness.

Don't Take Things So Personally

I remember when Polish jokes were the rage, and having a real estate agent tell me that her office colleagues all disliked her for some reason and made fun of her at every opportunity. When I asked for the evidence she cited their telling of Polish jokes. This woman was married, however, and did not use her maiden name, which clearly revealed her Polish heritage. I had not known she was Polish until she told me.

One of the businessmen I occasionally went to the driving range with delighted in telling me doctor jokes. I found them amusing, and never did it occur to me that he was secretly trying to wound me personally. The two situations weren't that different but the two self-images involved certainly were.

When you habitually personalize every slight, every overheard conversation, even things you read or hear in media, you reveal a very thin-skinned self-image with the weakest of immunities.

Be bigger than such things. Have bigger fish to fry, as the saying goes. The person in hot pursuit of meaningful, rewarding goals and a calendar of important things to do has little time to obsess over trivial slights and offenses. Most dumb, insensitive remarks are dumb, insensitive remarks; they have no hidden meaning, and searching for it— certainly being offended by it—is an utter waste of time.

The popular writer of pulp westerns, Louis L'Amour, was once asked in an interview to reveal the hidden meaning behind the fact that none of the villains in any of his hundreds of books ever died from the first bullet. The interviewer thought he was onto something. The novelist answered, "Because in those days, we got paid by the word." I am not getting paid by the word, so I'll move on!

MENTAL TRAINING EXERCISE

Visit the supermarket. Find and buy two potatoes, the smallest, most stunted one, and the biggest one. Set them side by side on your desk or somewhere frequently visible to you during the day. You might even take a Polaroid photograph of the two of them side by side and post it on your automobile visor or dashboard, inside your briefcase, someplace you will see it. Let it trigger the thought that your self-image is bigger than a tiny, stunted potato, and ask yourself if you are acting as a big potato or a shrunken spud today!

A Self-Reliant, Responsible Attitude Makes You Less Vulnerable

As Dr. Holland has pointed out, the juvenile delinquent with the hard outer shell has a soft, vulnerable inner person who wants to be dependent on others and wants to be loved by others.

Sales professionals tell me that those who put up the most sales resistance at the outset are frequently "easy" sells once you get past their defenses; that people who feel called on to put up "No salesmen allowed" signs do so because they know they are soft touches and need protection.

The person with the hard, gruff, exterior, usually develops it because instinctively he realizes that he is so soft inside that he needs protection.

The person who has little or no self-reliance, who feels emotionally dependent on others, makes herself most vulnerable to emotional hurts. Every human being wants and needs love and affection. But the creative, self-reliant person also feels a need to give love. Her emphasis is as much or more on the giving, as on the getting. She doesn't expect love to be handed to her on a silver platter. Nor does she have a compulsive need that "everybody" must love her and approve of her.

The passive-dependent person turns her entire destiny over to other people, circumstances, luck. Life owes her a living and other people owe her consideration, appreciation, love, happiness. She makes unreasonable demands and claims on other people and feels cheated, wronged, hurt when they aren't fulfilled. Because life just isn't built that way, she is seeking the impossible and leaving herself "wide open" to emotional hurts and injuries.

Once, while speaking to a large convention of salespeople, I met another professional speaker I had heard quite a bit about. He was very successful and in considerable demand in the sales world, but he told me that he rarely got fan mail and almost never got rounds of hearty applause when he concluded his presentations. And he seemed oddly proud of the fact. When I asked about this, he explained "It's because I make 'em mad." He went on to quote the Harry Truman "give 'em hell" quote; Truman reportedly said, "I don't give 'em hell. I tell them the truth and they think it's hell." Or something like that. Anyway, this fellow was one of the busiest, highest paid, *least* beloved speakers in the business—and proud of it! His corporate clients who paid his fees loved having him lay into the troops. Often, his pot-stirring of indignation converted into heightened sales performance immediately, as many of the salespeople determined to "show that s.o.b. something." This is somewhat the equivalent of the football coach posting a newspaper clipping in the locker-room quoting players from the next opposing team "dissing" them. I'll freely admit, it's not a role as a speaker I would seek out or enjoy. But it is interesting how self-reliant and immune his self-image is to the lack of love in the room!

It is up to you to develop a more self-reliant attitude. Assume responsibility for your own life and emotional needs. We have a saying, "Give yourself your own gold stars." As emotionally immature children, we look to parents and teachers for gold stars. Draw or color a picture, immediately race to take it to Mom, who ooh's and aah's over it and proudly displays it on the refrigerator door with magnets. As an adult, you must graduate from such urgent neediness. You must be able to admire your own good work and recognize your own achievements.

This loops back to the discussion about your AQ in Chapter 8. The refusal to blame ourselves or others or to accept a problem as beyond our influence gives us resiliency in the face of adversity.

Relax Away Emotional Hurts

I once had a patient ask me, "If the forming of scar tissue is a natural and automatic thing, why doesn't scar tissue form when a plastic surgeon makes an incision?"

The answer is that if you cut your face and it heals naturally, scar tissue will form, because a certain amount of tension in the wound and just underneath the wound pulls the surface of the skin back, creates a gap, which is filled in by scar tissue. A plastic surgeon who operates and not only pulls the skin together closely by suturing, but also cuts out a small amount of flesh underneath the skin so that there is no tension present. The incision heals smoothly, evenly, and with no distorting surface scar. It is interesting to note that the same thing happens in the case of an emotional wound. If there is no tension present, there is no disfiguring emotional scar left.

Have you ever noticed how easy it is to get your feelings hurt, or take offense, when you are suffering tensions brought about by frustration, fear, anger, or depression?

We go to work feeling out of sorts or down in the dumps, or with self-confidence shaken because of some adverse experience. A friend comes by and makes a joking remark. Nine times out of ten we would laugh, think it funny, "think nothing about it," and make a good-natured crack in return. But not today.

Today, we are suffering tensions of self-doubt, insecurity, anxiety. We take the remark in the wrong way, become offended and hurt, and an emotional scar begins to form.

This simple, everyday experience illustrates very well the principle that we are injured and hurt emotionally not so much by other people or what they say or don't say, but by our own attitude and our own response.

Relaxation Cushions Emotional Blows

When we feel hurt or offended, the feeling is entirely a matter of our own response. In fact, the feeling *is* our response.

It is our own responses that we have to be concerned about, not other people's. We can tighten up, become angry, anxious, or resentful and feel hurt. Or we can make no response, remain relaxed and feel no hurt. Scientific experiments have shown that it is absolutely impossible to feel fear, anger, anxiety, or negative emotions of any kind while the muscles of the body are kept perfectly relaxed. We have to do something to feel fear, anger, anxiety. "No man is hurt but by himself," said Diogenes.

"Nothing can work me damage except myself," said St. Bernard. "The harm that I sustain I carry about with me, and am never a real sufferer but by my own fault."

You alone are responsible for your responses and reactions. You do not have to respond at all. You can remain relaxed and free from injury.

PRESCRIPTION

Take time each and every day to apply these three principles. Take time to relax and destress. Make notes, even written notes, of your accomplishments and progress toward your goals. A written "success diary" is a very simple tool for building a stronger self-image. Create a visualization, a mental picture or two to call up and assist you when confronted by unjust criticism, "catty" remarks, or other attacks on your self-image. One patient of mine told me he would call up a cartoon-like image of his head on Superman's body, standing in the classic Superman pose, chest stuck out, bullets bouncing off, cape flying in the wind.

How to Remove Old Emotional Scars

We can prevent, and immunize ourselves against, emotional scars by practicing the three foregoing rules. But what about the old emotional scars formed in the past—the old hurts, grudges, grievances against life, resentments?

Once an emotional scar has formed, there is but one thing to do and that is to remove it by surgery, the same as a physical scar.

Give Yourself a Spiritual Facelift

In removing old emotional scars, you alone can do the operation. You must become your own plastic surgeon, and give yourself a spiritual face lift. The results will be new life and new vitality, a newfound peace of mind and happiness.

To speak of an emotional facelift and the use of mental surgery is more than a simile.

Old emotional scars cannot be doctored or medicated. They must be "cut out," given up entirely, eradicated. Many people apply various kinds of salve or balm to old emotional wounds, but this simply does not work. They may self-righteously forego overt and physical revenge, yet "take it out" or "get even" in many subtle ways. A typical example is the wife who discovers her husband's infidelity. Upon the advice of her minister and/or psychiatrist, she agrees she should forgive him. Accordingly she does not shoot him. She does not leave him. In all overt behavior she is a dutiful wife. She keeps the house neatly; she prepares meals well; and so on. But she makes his life hell on earth in many subtle ways by the coldness of her heart and by flaunting her moral superiority. When he complains, her answer is, "Well, dear, I did forgive you—but I cannot forget." Her very "forgiveness" becomes a thorn in his side, because she is conscious of the fact that it is proof of her moral superiority. She would have been more kind to him, and been happier herself, had she refused this type of forgiveness and left him.

Forgiveness Is a Scalpel That Removes Emotional Scars

"'I can forgive, but I cannot forget,' is only another way of saying 'I will not forgive,'" said Henry Ward Beecher. "Forgiveness ought to be like a canceled note—torn in two, and burned up, so that it never can be shown against one."

Forgiveness, when it is real and genuine and complete, and forgotten—is the scalpel which can remove the pus from old emotional wounds, heal them, and eliminate scar tissue.

Forgiveness which is partial, or half-hearted, works no better than a partially completed surgical operation on the face. Pretended forgiveness, which is entered into as a duty, is no more effective than a simulated facial surgery.

Your forgiveness should be forgotten, as well as the wrong which was forgiven. Forgiveness which is remembered, and dwelt upon, re-infects the wound you are attempting to cauterize. If you are too proud of your forgiveness, or remember it too much, you are very apt to feel that the other person owes you something for forgiving him. You forgive him one debt, but in doing so, he incurs another, much like the operators of small loan companies who cancel one note and make out a new one every two weeks.

Forgiveness Is Not a Weapon

There are many common fallacies regarding forgiveness, and one of the reasons that its therapeutic value has not been more recognized is the fact that real forgiveness has been so seldom tried. For example, many writers have told us that we should forgive to make us "good." We have seldom been advised to forgive that we might be happy. Another fallacy is that forgiveness places us in a superior position or is a method of winning out over our enemy. This thought has appeared in many glib phrases, such as "Don't merely try to 'get even'—forgive your enemy and you 'get ahead' of him." Tillotson, the former Archbishop of Canterbury, tells us, "A more glorious victory cannot be gained over another man, than this, that when the injury began on his part, the kindness should begin on ours." This is just another way of saying that forgiveness itself can be used as an effective weapon of revenge, which it can. Revengeful forgiveness, however, is not therapeutic forgiveness.

Therapeutic forgiveness cuts out, eradicates, cancels, makes the wrong as if it had never been. Therapeutic forgiveness is like surgery.

Give Up Grudges as You Would a Gangrenous Arm

First, the wrong—and particularly our own feeling of condemnation of it—must be seen as an undesirable thing rather than a desirable thing. Before anyone can agree to have an arm amputated, he must cease to see the arm as a desirable thing to be retained, but as an undesirable, damaging, and threatening thing to be given up.

In facial surgery there can be no partial, tentative, or halfway measures. The scar tissue is cut out, completely and entirely. The wound is allowed to heal cleanly. And care is taken to see that the face will be restored in every particular, just as it was before injury and just as if the injury had never been.

You Can Forgive—If You're Willing

Therapeutic forgiveness is not difficult. The only difficulty is to secure your own willingness to give up and do without your sense of condemnation—your willingness to cancel out the debt—with no mental reservations.

We find it difficult to forgive only because we like our sense of condemnation. We get a perverse and morbid enjoyment out of nursing our wounds. As long as we can condemn others, we can feel superior to them. No one can deny that there is also a perverse sense of satisfaction in feeling sorry for yourself.

Your Reasons for Forgiveness Are Important

In therapeutic forgiveness we cancel out the debt of the other person, not because we have decided to be generous, do a favor, or we are a morally superior person. We cancel the debt, mark it "null and void," not because we have made the other person "pay" sufficiently for the wrong, but because we have come to recognize that the debt itself is not valid. True forgiveness comes only when we are able to see, and emotionally accept, that there is and was nothing for us to forgive. We should not have condemned or hated the other person in the first place.

Not long ago I went to a luncheon also attended by a number of clergy. The subject of forgiveness came up in general, and then the case of the adulterous woman whom Jesus forgave in particular. I listened to a very learned discussion of why Jesus was able to "forgive" the woman, how he forgave her, how his forgiveness was a rebuke to the church men of his time who were ready to stone her, etc. etc.

Jesus Didn't "Forgive" the Adulterous Woman

I resisted the temptation to shock these gentlemen by pointing out that actually Jesus never forgave the woman at all. Nowhere in the narrative, as it appears in the New Testament, is the word "forgive" or "forgiveness" used, or even hinted at. Nor can it be reasonably implied from the facts as given in the story. We are told merely that after her accusers had left, Jesus asked the woman, "Hath no man condemned thee?" When she answered in the negative, he said, "Neither do I condemn thee. Go and sin no more."

You cannot forgive others unless you have first condemned them. Jesus never condemned the woman in the first place; so there was nothing for him to forgive. He recognized her sin or her mistake, but did not feel called on to hate her for it. He was able to see, before the fact, what you and I must see after the fact in practicing therapeutic forgiveness: that we ourselves err when we hate others because of their mistakes, when we condemn them, or when we classify them as certain types, confusing the person with the behavior, or when we mentally incur a debt that others must "pay" before being restored to our good graces and our emotional acceptance.

Whether you ought to do this, whether you should do it, or whether you can reasonably be expected to do it is a matter outside the scope of this book and my own field. I can only tell you as a doctor that if you will do it, you will be far happier and healthier, and you will attain more peace of mind. However, I would like to point out that this is what therapeutic forgiveness is, and that it is the only type of forgiveness that really works. And if forgiveness is anything less than this, we might as well stop talking about it.

Forgive Yourself as Well as Others

Not only do we incur emotional wounds from others; most of us inflict them on ourselves.

We beat ourselves over the head with self-condemnation, remorse, and regret. We beat ourselves down with self-doubt. We cut ourselves up with excessive guilt.

Remorse and regret are attempts to emotionally live in the past. Excessive guilt is an attempt to make right in the past something we did wrong or thought of as wrong in the past.

Emotions are used correctly and appropriately when they help us to respond or react appropriately to a reality in the present environment. Since we cannot live in the past, we cannot appropriately react emotionally to the past. The past can be simply written off, closed, forgotten, insofar as our emotional reactions are concerned. We do not need to take an "emotional position" one way or the other regarding detours that might have taken us off course in the past. The important thing is our present direction and our present goal.

We need to recognize our own efforts as mistakes. Otherwise we could not correct course. "Steering" or "guidance" would be impossible. But it is futile and fatal to hate or condemn ourselves for our mistakes. A study on guilt conducted at Case Western Reserve University, reported in *Reader's Digest* (September 1997) found that the average person spends *two hours a day feeling guilty*! Much of this is even present moment guilt: the working mother who feels guilty while at work about not being at home with her children, then guilty if at home in the afternoon with her children for not pulling her weight at work; the exhausted son or daughter of an aging, infirm parent, guilty for feeling a bit irritable; the traveling executive who feels guilty about missing his daughter's recital at school.

You cannot see your future with optimistic eyes if you cannot view your present and past with kind eyes. This is not to suggest simply letting yourself off the hook at every turn. Responsibility is important. But what I call The Critic Within is so much more powerful than other critics, we must take care not to let it run roughshod over our self-image.

Once, after lecturing to a large group of inmates at an Oklahoma prison, I came away with a realization: Here I had been in the company of robbers, murderers, people who had made horrendous mistakes, in some cases repeatedly, yet most did not blame or punish themselves as much as many people on the outside do, for much less serious missteps in a life 99% made up of honest, ethical behavior. It is common for inmates to be jail house lawyers, fighting for their rights inside prison, while many good citizens deprive themselves of their basic, inalienable rights to pursue happiness solely through their own excessive self-criticism and self-punishment. As we drove away from the prison with its huge concrete walls, rolls of barbed wire on the top of the walls, and armed guards in towers, I thought to myself that many people build prisons far more intimidating than these, then lock themselves up in them, all because of some past "sin." I am not a great believer in sin, but if there is sin, it is for people who waste their lives chastising themselves for mistakes they've made, mistakes that are only human.

You Make Mistakes—Mistakes Do Not Make "You"

In thinking of our own mistakes (or those of others) it is helpful, and realistic, to think of them in terms of what we did or did not do, rather than in terms of what the mistakes made us.

One of the biggest mistakes we can make is to confuse our behavior with our self, to conclude that because we did a certain act it characterizes us as a certain sort of person. It clarifies thinking if we can see that mistakes involve something we do: They refer to actions, and to be realistic we should use verbs denoting action, rather than nouns denoting a state of being in describing them.

For example, to say "I failed" (verb form) is but to recognize an error, and can help lead to future success.

But to say, "I am a failure" (noun form) does not describe what you did, but what you think the mistake did to you. This does not contribute to learning, but tends to fixate the mistake and make it permanent. This has been proved over and over in clinical psychological experiments.

We seem to recognize that all children, in learning to walk, will occasionally fall. We say he "fell" or she "stumbled." We do not say "he is a faller" or "she is a stumbler."

However, many parents fail to recognize that all children, in learning to talk, also make mistakes or "nonfluences"—hesitation, blocking, repetition of syllables and words. It is a common experience for an anxious, concerned parent to conclude, "He is a stutterer." Such an attitude, or a judgment—not of the child's actions but of the child—gets across to the child, who begins to think of himself as a stutterer. His learning is fixated, and the stutter tends to become permanent.

According to Dr. Wendell Johnson, the nation's foremost authority on stuttering at the time I wrote the original edition of this book, this sort of thing is the cause of stuttering. He found that the parents of nonstutterers are more likely to use descriptive terms ("He did not speak"), whereas the parents of stutterers were inclined to use judgmental terms ("He could not speak"). Writing in the *Saturday Evening Post* (January 5, 1957), Dr. Johnson said, "Slowly we began to comprehend the vital point that had been missed for so many centuries. Case after case had developed after it had been diagnosed as stuttering by over-anxious persons unfamiliar with the facts of normal speech development. The parents rather than the child, the listeners rather than the speakers, seemed to be the ones most requiring understanding and instruction."

Dr. Knight Dunlap, who made a twenty-year study of habits, their making, unmaking, and relation to learning, discovered that the same principle applied to virtually all "bad habits," including bad emotional habits. It was essential, he said that patients learn to stop blaming themselves, condemning themselves, and feeling remorseful over their habits—if they were to cure them. He found particularly damaging the conclusion, "I am ruined," or "I am worthless," because the patient had done, or was doing, certain acts.

So remember you make mistakes. Mistakes don't make you—anything!

What you do need not define who you are or what you will do!

You Are *Not* Your Mistakes.

Who Wants to Be an Oyster?

One final word about preventing and removing emotional hurts. To live creatively, we must be willing to be a little vulnerable. We must be willing to be hurt a little, if necessary, in creative living. A lot of people need a thicker and tougher emotional skin than they have. But they need only a tough emotional hide or epidermis, not a shell. To trust, to love, to open ourselves to emotional communication with other people is to run the risk of being hurt. If we are hurt once, we can do one of two things. We can build a thick protective shell, or scar tissue, to prevent being hurt again, live like an oyster, and not be hurt.

Or we can "turn the other cheek," remain vulnerable and go on living creatively.

An oyster is never hurt. It has a thick shell that protects it from everything. It is isolated. An oyster is secure, but not creative. It cannot go after what it wants, it must wait for it to come to it. An oyster knows none of the hurts of emotional communication with the environment, but neither can an oyster know the joys.

An Emotional Facelift Makes You Look and Feel Younger

As this edition is being written, the so-called "baby boomer" generation is hitting the 50-year-old mark and is more obsessed with stopping the clock, even turning back the clock, than any generation before. Fortunes are spent on cosmetic surgery, liposuction, fitness gyms and devices, personal trainers, lotions and potions, growth hormone injections, on and on.

I have a different prescription! Try giving yourself a spiritual facelift. It is more than a play on words. It opens you up to more life, more vitality, the stuff that youth is made of. You'll feel younger. You'll actually look younger. Many times I have seen a man or woman apparently grow five or ten years younger in appearance after removing old emotional scars. Look around you. Who are the youthful looking people you know over the age of forty? The grumpy? Resentful? The pessimistic? The ones who are soured on the world? Or are they the cheerful, optimistic, good-natured people?

Remember I am a medical doctor, a plastic surgeon. I am absolutely serious and sincere when I tell you that you can look years younger in face and posture, and feel years younger in health and vitality, thanks to emotional surgery and self-image strengthening with Psycho-Cybernetics!

Carrying a grudge against someone or against life can bring on the old age stoop, just as much as carrying a heavy weight around on your shoulders would. People with emotional scars, grudges, and the like are living in the past, which is characteristic of old people. The youthful attitude and youthful spirit that erases wrinkles from the soul and the face, and that puts a sparkle in the eye, looks to the future and has a great expectation to look forward to.

So why not give yourself a facelift? Your do-it-yourself kit consists of the relaxation of negative tensions to prevent scars, therapeutic forgiveness to remove old scars, providing yourself with a tough (but not a hard) epidermis instead of a shell, creative living, a willingness to be a little vulnerable, and a nostalgia for the future instead of the past.

MENTAL TRAINING EXERCISES

By far, the most challenging and rewarding exercises of all suggested in this book are these involving forgiveness. Choose one or two persons for whom you've long carried resentment over past slights and find a way in your heart to truly, completely forgive them, no strings attached, and ultimately do so via your actions toward them. Also, identify some past error or situation you have been carrying a grudge against yourself for, and forgive yourself, and finally, once and for all, banish this from your thoughts. This may very well require considerable work in your imagination factory. Invest 30 minutes a day for 21 consecutive days on quiet reflection, working on this with yourself, in solitude.

Key Ideas for Do–It–Yourself Emotional Surgery to Remove Self-Image Scars with Psycho-Cybernetics

Your Talents

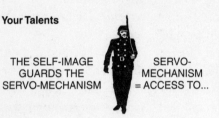

THE SELF-IMAGE
GUARDS THE
SERVO-MECHANISM

SERVO-
MECHANISM
= ACCESS TO...

TALENTS	ACTION
ABILITIES	FOLLOW THROUGH
SKILL	ENTHUSIAM
CONFIDENCE	ENDURANCE

CHAPTER ELEVEN

How to Unlock Your Real Personality

To avoid criticism, do nothing, say nothing, be nothing.
—Elbert Hubbard

*P*ersonality, that magnetic and mysterious something that is easy to recognize but difficult to
define, is not so much acquired from without as *released* from within.

What we call "personality" is the outward evidence of that
unique and individual creative self, made in the image of God, that
spark of divinity within us or what might be called the free and full
expression of your real self.

This real self within every person is attractive. It *is* magnetic. It
does have a powerful impact and influence on other people. We have
the feeling that we are in touch with something real and basic, and it
does something to us. On the other hand, a phony is universally disliked and detested.

Why does everyone love babies? Certainly not for what babies
can do, or what they know or have, but simply because of what they
are. Infants have "personality plus." There is no superficiality, no
phoniness, no hypocrisy. In their own language, which consists mostly
of either crying or cooing, they express their real feelings. They "say
what they mean." There is no guile. Babies are emotionally honest.
They exemplify to the *n*th degree the psychological dictum, "Be yourself." They have no qualms about expressing themselves. They are not
in the least inhibited.

Babies are proof that all inhibition is learned, taught to the self-image, not born within the self-image.

Everyone Has a Dynamic Personality Locked Up Within Him

Every human being has the mysterious something we call personality.

When we say that people have a "good personality," what we really mean is that they have freed and released the creative potential within them and are able to express their real self.

"Poor personality" and "inhibited personality" are one and the same. Individuals with a "poor personality" do not express the creative self within. They have restrained it, handcuffed it, locked it up, and thrown away the key. The word "inhibit" literally means to stop, prevent, prohibit, restrain. The inhibited personality has imposed a restraint on the expression of the real self. For one reason or another the person is afraid to express himself, afraid to be himself, and has locked up his real self within an inner prison. The symptoms of inhibition are many and varied: shyness, timidity, self-consciousness, hostility, feelings of excessive guilt, insomnia, nervousness, irritability, inability to get along with others.

Frustration is characteristic of practically every area and activity of the inhibited personality. The real and basic frustration is the failure to "be himself" and the failure to adequately express himself. But this basic frustration is likely to color and overflow into all that he does.

Excessive Negative Feedback Equals Inhibition

The science of cybernetics gives us a new insight into the inhibited personality, and shows us the way toward disinhibition, freedom, and how to release our spirits from self-imposed prisons.

Negative feedback in a servo-mechanism is equivalent to *criticism*. Negative feedback says in effect, "You are wrong, you are off course, you need to take corrective action to get back on the beam."

The purpose of negative feedback, however, is to *modify* response, and change the course of forward action, not to stop it altogether.

If negative feedback is working properly, a missile or a torpedo reacts to "criticism" just enough to correct course and keeps going forward toward the target. This course will be, as we have previously explained, a series of zig-zags.

However, if the mechanism is too sensitive to negative feedback, the servo-mechanism overcorrects. Instead of progressing toward the target, it will perform exaggerated lateral zig-zags or stop all forward progress altogether.

Our own built-in servo-mechanism works in the same way. We must have negative feedback in order to operate purposely, in order to steer our way or be guided to a goal.

Negative feedback always says in effect, "Stop what you're doing or the way you're doing it, and do something else." Its purpose is to modify response or change the degree of forward action, not to stop all action. Negative feedback does not say, "Stop—period!" It says, "What you are doing is wrong," but it does not say, "it is wrong to do anything."

Yet where negative feedback is excessive or where our own mechanism is too sensitive to negative feedback, the result is not modification of response—but total inhibition of response.

Inhibition and excessive negative feedback are one and the same. When we overreact to negative feedback or criticism, we are likely to conclude that not only is our present course slightly off beam, or wrong, but that it is wrong for us even to want to go forward.

A hiker or a hunter often gets back to the automobile by picking out some prominent landmark near the car, such as an extra tall tree that can be seen for miles. When returning to the car, the hiker looks for the tree (or target) and starts walking toward it. From time to time the tree may be lost from his view, but the course can be checked by comparing the hiker's direction with the location of the tree. If the course is 15 degrees to the left of the tree, what the hiker is doing is "wrong." He immediately corrects the course and again walks directly toward the tree. *He does not, however, conclude that it is wrong for him to walk.*

Yet many of us are guilty of just so foolish a conclusion. When it comes to our attention that our manner of expression is off course, missing the mark, or "wrong," we conclude that self-expression itself is wrong or that success for us (reaching our target tree) is wrong.

Keep in mind that excessive negative feedback has the effect of interfering with, or stopping completely, the appropriate response.

Stuttering as a Demonstration of Inhibition

Stuttering offers a good illustration of how excessive negative feedback brings on inhibition and interferes with appropriate response.

While most of us are not consciously aware of the fact, when we talk we receive negative feedback data through our ears by listening to or "monitoring" our own voice. This is the reason that totally deaf individuals seldom speak well. They have no way of knowing whether their voice is coming out as a shriek, a scream, or an unintelligible mumble. This is also the reason that persons born deaf do not learn to talk at all, except with special tutoring. If you sing, perhaps you have been surprised to find that you could not sing on key, or in harmony with others, while suffering temporary deafness or partial deafness because of a cold.

Thus, negative feedback itself is no bar or handicap to speech. On the contrary, it *enables* us to speak and speak correctly. Voice teachers advise that we record our own voices on a tape recorder and listen to them as a method of improving tone, enunciation, etc. By doing this we become aware of errors in speech that we had not noticed before. We are able to see clearly what we are doing "wrong," and we can make correction.

However, if negative feedback is to be effective in helping us talk better, it should (1) be more or less automatic or subconscious, (2) it should occur spontaneously, or *while we're talking*, and (3) response to feedback should not be so sensitive as to result in inhibition.

If we are consciously overcritical of our speech, or if we are too careful in trying to avoid errors in advance, rather than reacting spontaneously, stuttering is likely to result.

If the stutterer's excessive feedback can be toned down, or if it can be made spontaneous rather than anticipatory, improvement in speech will be immediate.

Video tape has provided an extraordinarily valuable feedback tool for people seeking to improve their communication effectiveness. Chiropractors and dentists role-play their case presentations to patients on video, with consultants acting as the skeptical patients, then study the video replay. Sales professionals do the same. Speakers, seminar leaders, politicians, and their speech coaches make similar use of it. Golfers' swings can be better analyzed and the golfers' better coached by video taping the swing. Football players "study film." This is extremely valuable only to the person with a sufficiently healthy self-image not to obsess over every mistake and flaw observed, and able to focus on "course correction" through observation.

What many people and coaches do not fully understand about such feedback, about capturing performance on tape for careful observation and analysis, is that it is equally important and often more useful to identify, focus on, and imprint the "positives" rather than the "negatives."

Care must be taken not to overly emphasize a flaw in performance to such a degree that it becomes mistakenly received by the servo-mechanism as the "target." You might think of this in the context of the old mind trick: Tell people to close their eyes for 60 seconds and think of anything but a dancing pink elephant in red boxer shorts on roller skates. Invariably, what mental picture dominates? Be careful you do not manufacture "pink elephants" for yourself or permit coaches to do it for you.

Conscious Self-Criticism Makes You Do Worse

This has been proved by Dr. E. Colin Cherry of London, England. Writing in the British scientific journal, *Nature*, Dr. Cherry stated his belief that stuttering was caused by "excessive monitoring." To test his theory he equipped 25 severe stutterers with earphones through which a loud tone drowned out the sound of their own voices. When asked to read aloud from a prepared text under these conditions, which eliminated self-criticism, the improvement was "remarkable." Another group of severe stutterers was trained in "shadow-talk"—to follow as closely as possible and attempt to "talk with" a person reading from a text or a voice on radio or TV. After brief practice the stutterers learned to shadow-talk easily, and most of them were able to speak normally and correctly under these conditions, which obviated advance criticism and literally forced them to speak spontaneously or to synchronize speaking and "correcting." Additional practice in shadow-talk enabled the stutterers to "learn" how to speak correctly at all times, proving to the self-image that the previously believed "truth" ("I'm a stutterer") was incorrect.

When excessive negative feedback or self-criticism was eliminated, inhibition disappeared and performance improved. When there was no time for worry, or too much carefulness in advance, expression immediately improved. This gives us a valuable clue as to how we may disinhibit or release a locked-up personality and improve performance in other areas.

How the Dale Carnegie Program, Toastmasters International and Network Marketing or MLM Companies Provide Just the Right Balance of "Course Correction" Feedback

Countless business leaders have graduated from the Dale Carnegie Program, notably Lee Iacocca, who in turn has encouraged thousands to enroll. Many top professional speakers, as well as countless sales professionals, executives, pastors, and community leaders, have gone from awkward, nervous, inhibited, stumbling speakers to confident and persuasive speakers through participation in Toastmasters. It is almost the norm in the world of network marketing for the inhibited person who believes and insists that she "can't" sell and "can't" speak in front of a group to flower and bloom and metamorphose into a dynamic, convincing salesperson, and to become such a "ham" on stage it's hard to pry the microphone from her fingers!

Why and how does this happen with such consistency and frequency in these environments?

The individuals' experiences in these environments provide what you might call *gentle* course-correction feedback, so that the individuals have a safe, encouraging opportunity to test and challenge their limiting beliefs, to let their suppressed personality come out into the light little by little, to discover their true self, ultimately showing proof of greater abilities to their self-image, thus moving that little dotted line of self-imposed limits and giving themselves more room for creative self-expression.

In these environments, individuals are more cajoled than forced into self-expression, then they are applauded and congratulated often for each small step forward, each small victory. Course-correction feedback is well balanced with recognition of positive aspects of performance. There's never a band of jackals leaping at persons when they err, screaming "I told you so—you can't do this!" To the contrary, even those who go on stage and stumble, forget their place, flush beet red will get applause and encouragement. In this safe environment, they can risk improvement rather than choose isolation. More often than not, they quickly discover that their "I can't" beliefs are merely self-imposed limits, not actual limits.

Such a discovery can have extraordinary results.

A Sales Manager "Cons" His Own Salesperson

A manager of a direct sales force told me of his "conning" one of his own salespeople into improved performance, and while I cannot condone the strategy, its result is fascinating and provocative. This particular salesperson was in a severe slump, going on appointment after appointment after appointment, and returning night after night empty-handed. Her self-image was rapidly shrinking to the size of a tiny spud, and the manager realized he needed to employ some powerful, fast-acting medicine—or fire her.

The next night he engineered two appointments back to back that were "rigged." He sent her to friends' homes. That afternoon, he rehearsed his friends and gave them the money to make their purchases, so the actual sales took place on which commissions would be paid. When she arrived at the first home, and began rather timidly going through her presentation, she discovered unusually receptive and responsive prospects. Their positive feedback helped her warm to the task, and by the end of her presentation she was humming along. She closed the sale and left with signed order and a $300 check in her attaché case. At the second appointment, everything went as if scripted, and her prospects were performing perfectly. Another $300 check.

Over the next four nights, from eight appointments, she chalked up six sales. By month's end, she had batted over 70% for the entire month, earned her biggest month's income ever (although a small bit of it came secretly from her sales manager's wallet!), and even won a "getaway weekend" in the company's sales contest. As he said, "a star was reborn."

We must find opportunities and environments where we can operate without fear or inhibition, to prove our competence to our self-images. Then we can trust our servo-mechanism to deliver peak performance even as we move into rougher seas.

Excessive "Carefulness" Leads to Inhibition and Anxiety

Have you ever tried to thread a needle? If so, and if you are inexperienced at it, you may have noticed that you could hold the thread steady as a rock *until* you approached the eye of the needle and attempted to insert it into the very small opening. Each time you tried to place the thread through the small opening, your hand unaccountably shook and the thread missed the mark.

Attempting to pour a liquid into the mouth of a very small necked bottle often results in the same kind of behavior. You can hold your hand perfectly steady, until you try to accomplish your purpose; then for some strange reason you quiver and shake.

In medical circles, we call this "purpose tremor."

It occurs in normal people when they try too hard or are "too careful" not to make an error in accomplishing a purpose. In certain pathological conditions, such as injury to certain areas of the brain, purpose tremor can become very pronounced. A patient, for example, may be able to hold his hand steady as long as he is not trying to accomplish anything. But let him try to insert a key into the door lock and his hand may zig-zag back and forth as much as six to ten inches. He may be able to hold a pen steady enough until he attempts to sign his name. Then his hand tremors uncontrollably. If he is ashamed of this, and becomes even more "careful" not to make an error in the presence of strangers, he may not be able to sign his name at all.

These people can be helped, and often remarkably, by training in relaxation techniques where they learn to relax from excessive effort and "purposing" and not to be overly careful in trying to avoid errors or failures.

Excessive carefulness, or being too anxious not to make an error, is a form of excessive negative feedback. As in the case of the stutterer, who attempts to anticipate possible errors and be overly careful not to make them, the result is inhibition and deterioration of performance. Excessive carefulness and anxiety are close kin. Both have to do with too much concern for possible failure, doing the wrong thing, and making too much of a conscious effort to do right.

"I don't like these cold, precise, perfect people, who, in order not to speak wrong, never speak at all, and in order not to do wrong, never do anything," said Henry Ward Beecher.

Apparently, the public prefers "authentic" to "forcibly inhibited" as well. One of the most popular presidents ever, dubbed The Great Communicator, Ronald Reagan, if unknown to a team of speech and presentation experts reviewing him on film, would be the subject of much criticism for his many performance flaws. His habit, for example, of starting sentence after sentence with "Well," is a professional speaking no-no. The longest running television show, "The Tonight Show," has been hosted by a sequence of people—Jack Parr, Johnny Carson, Jay Leno—who all violate many so-called rules of performance and perhaps of even greater importance, are all undeterred by their flubs, the jokes that are dead on arrival. This show has no laugh track to support pretending something is working when it is not. I have noticed time and again, in public speaking, in entertainment and in politics, the person who is excessively careful, trying to match some "perfect" standard or ideal, rarely succeeds.

Self-Consciousness Is Really Others' Consciousness

The cause-and-effect relationship between excessive negative feedback and what we call self-consciousness can be readily seen.

In any sort of social relationship we constantly receive negative feedback data from other people. A smile, a frown, a hundred different subtle clues of approval or disapproval, interest or lack of interest, continually advise us of "how we're doing," whether we're getting across, whether we're hitting or missing the mark, so to speak. In any sort of social situation there is a constant interaction going on between speaker and listener, actor and observer. And without this constant communication, back and forth, human relations and social activities would be virtually impossible. And if not impossible, it would certainly be dull, boring, noninspiring, and dead—without "sparks."

Good actors, actresses, and public speakers can sense this communication from the audience, and it helps them perform better. Persons with "good personalities," who are popular and magnetic in social situations, can sense this communication from other people and they automatically and spontaneously react and respond to it in a creative way. The communication from other people is used as negative feedback, and enables the person to perform better socially. Unless a person can respond to this communication from other people, she is a "cold fish" type, the "reserved" personality who does not warm up to other people. Without this communication you become a social dud, the hard-to-get-to-know type who interests no one.

However, this type of negative feedback, to be effective, should be creative. That is, it should be more or less subconscious, automatic, and spontaneous, rather than consciously contrived or thought about.

What Others Think Creates Inhibition

When you become too consciously concerned about what others think, when you become too careful to consciously try to please other people, when you become too sensitive to the real or fancied disapproval of other people, then you have excessive negative feedback, inhibition, and poor performance.

Whenever you constantly and consciously monitor your every act, word, or manner, again you become inhibited and self-conscious.

You become too careful to make a good impression, and in so doing choke off, restrain, inhibit your creative self and end up making a rather poor impression.

The best way to make a good impression on other people is: Never consciously try to make a good impression on them. Never act, or fail to act, purely for consciously contrived effect. Never wonder consciously what the others are thinking of you, how they are judging you.

How a Salesman Cured Self-Consciousness

James Mangan, the famous salesman, author, and lecturer, said that when he first left home he was painfully self-conscious, especially when eating in the dining room of a "ritzy" or high-class hotel. As he walked through the dining room he felt that every eye was on him, judging him, critical of him. He was painfully conscious of his every movement, motion and act, the way he walked, the way he sat down, his table manners, and the way he ate his food. And all these actions seemed stiff and awkward. He wondered why was he so ill at ease? He knew he had good table manners and knew enough social etiquette to get by. Why had he never felt self-conscious and ill at ease when eating in the kitchen with Ma and Pa?

He decided it was because when he was eating with Ma and Pa, he did not think or bother to wonder how he was acting. He was neither careful nor self-critical. He was not concerned about producing an effect. He had felt composed, relaxed, and had done all right.

James Mangan cured his self-consciousness by remembering how he had felt, and how he had acted, when he "was going to the kitchen to eat with Ma and Pa." Then, when he walked into a ritzy dining room, he would imagine or pretend that he "was going to eat with Ma and Pa"—and act that way.

Poise Comes When You Ignore Excessive Negative Feedback

Mangan also found that he could overcome his stage fright and self-consciousness when calling on big shots or in any other social situation by saying to himself, "I'm going to eat with Ma and Pa," conjuring up in his imagination how he had felt and how he had acted, and then "acting that way." In his book *The Knack of Selling Yourself*, Mangan advises salespeople to use the "I'm going home to eat supper with my Ma and Pa! I've been through this a thousand times—nothing new can happen here" technique.

This attitude of being immune to strangers or strange situations, this total disregard for all the unknown or unexpected, has a name. It is called *poise*. Poise is the deliberate shunting aside of all fears arising from new and uncontrollable circumstances.

You Need to Be More Self-Conscious

The late Dr. Albert Edward Wiggam, famous educator, psychologist, and lecturer, said that in his early years he was so painfully self-conscious he found it all but impossible to recite in school. He avoided other people and could not talk to them without hanging his head. He constantly fought his self-consciousness and tried hard to overcome it, all to no avail. Then one day he got a new idea. His trouble was not self-consciousness at all. It was really excessive others' consciousness. He was too painfully sensitive to what others might think of everything he said or did, every move he made. This tied him up in knots; he could not think clearly, and he could think of nothing to say. He did not feel this way when alone with himself. When alone, he was perfectly calm and relaxed, at ease, poised, and he could think of lots of interesting ideas and things to say. And he was also perfectly aware of and at home with his self.

Then he stopped fighting and trying to conquer his self-consciousness and instead concentrated on developing *more* self-consciousness: feeling, acting, behavior, thinking as he did when he was alone, without any regard to how some other person might feel about or judge him. This total disregard for the opinion and judgment of other people did not result in his becoming callous, arrogant, or entirely insensitive to others. There is no danger of entirely eradicating negative feedback, no matter how hard you may try. But this effort in the opposite direction did tone down his overly sensitive feedback mechanism. He got along better with other people, and went on to make his living counseling people and making public speeches to large groups, "without the slightest degree of anxiety."

The most liberating of all thoughts is disregard or "disconcern" for what other people think. Famous mail-order impresario and entrepreneur J. Peterman wrote (in his autobiography *Peterman Rides Again*); "Once you realize that most people are keeping up appearances and putting on a show, their approval becomes less important." Excessive concern over what other people think inhibits personality more than any other factor.

Truth be told, we tend to believe other people think about us far more than they ever actually do. In the popular TV sitcom "Frasier," about a psychologist, the main character (Dr. Frasier) is receiving a Lifetime Achievement Award, and receives a floral arrangement and a congratulatory note from his old college professor. The note reads "Congratulations. You must be very proud." At first, Frasier is pleased to have received the congratulations from his old mentor. But then he begins to analyze it for its hidden meaning. Why didn't it read, "I am very proud of you" instead of "You must be very proud"? Etc. Soon he is off to the professor's office and confronts him, with a longwinded series of questions and interpretations of what the professor meant by his terse note. When Frasier finally runs out of steam and the professor can get a word in edgewise, he sheepishly tells Frasier, "Actually, I just told my secretary to send flowers and a card. She wrote the note."

You do the same. So do I. One evening, on a drive home after a party at a friend's home, I was mulling over an offhand remark someone there had made to me, trying to discern its hidden meaning and asking my wife Anne, "Do you think he meant this? Or did he mean that? Why would he think that about me?"

Anne finally said, "Maxie, he wasn't thinking anything at all. He was drunk."

How many times have you obsessed over what somebody's remark—or even their glance—meant, devoting hours to it? While you stew, the other person forgot the matter within seconds, and moved onto a myriad of other people, places, and things.

An Athlete's Comeback Based on a Liberated Self-Image

Her name is Jennifer Capriati, once a 14-year-old tennis phenom growing up in the spotlight of massive media attention, under the pressure of adult competition. In the first phase of her career, between 1990 and 1993, she reached three Grand Slam semifinals and captured the 1992 Olympic gold medal at Barcelona. But then her career and confidence took such a dramatic downturn, she left the tour for two years, and seriously considered giving up tennis altogether. In 1994, she made news with a drug arrest and a shoplifting incident.

Despite winning the Olympic gold medal in 1992, she traces her frustration and disillusionment to a year earlier, when she lost the Grand Slam semifinal to Monica Seles, in a close match she initially controlled. "I never played well after that, except for the Olympics."

After a two-year hiatus, Capriati returned, competing at top levels, this time proclaiming peace of mind instead of unbearable pressure. A journalist reporting on her return wrote (in *USA Today*), "There seem to be two key reasons for Capriati's renaissance—concluding it didn't matter what people believed about her and learning to stop believing bad things about herself."

In 2001, she beat Martini Hingis in the final of the Australian Open, winning her first ever Grand Slam tournament.

You, too, can experience the same lifting of emotional weight from your shoulders that this young tennis star has, by rationally concluding that others' opinions about you—real or magnified by imagination—are far less important than your own opinions about yourself!

What Makes You Think You Can Do That?

On November 4, 1998, long-time professional politician "Skip" Humphrey (son of Hubert Humphrey), the Attorney General of Minnesota, and Norman Coleman, mayor of St. Paul, were shocked as their opponent Jesse "The Body" Ventura had whipped them in the election and now took claim to the governor's mansion. The long-shot, third-party candidate, better known for his outrageous outfits and antics as a pro wrestler than for more cerebral pursuits, campaigning with far fewer resources, took 37% of the vote—more than enough to win in a tightly contested three-candidate election. What on earth made Jesse Ventura imagine he could actually beat the two parties' credible and experienced candidates?

If you have ever been asked "What makes you think you can do that?" you might have taken some satisfaction in Jesse Ventura's underdog, upset victory. All too often this question is asked of us by people who should be in our corner, building us up. Often they ask it with sincere concern for our well-being, sometimes with more concern for themselves, but it doesn't matter: The adverse effect is the same.

I can remember everyone I knew but my mother repeatedly asking me what made me think I could jump right into private practice and succeed? Wouldn't I be better advised to seek a position on the bottom rung, in someone else's practice or in a hospital? My mother, bless her soul, never raised such doubt and unwaveringly voiced her confidence that I could do anything I set my mind to do. Whether she had private, silent doubts or concerns I do not know, and am glad I did not know.

You will be asked this question (What makes *you* think…) just about any and every time you attempt anything of significance. Fortunately, you can succeed no matter what others' doubts may be, as long as you are not controlled by them. Your strong self-image that counsels you that you can do anything you set your mind to is a most important ally. Many a person with a cheering section of one has confounded critics, baffled skeptics, amazed even close friends and family members in achieving remarkable things. It is only when your cheering section's bleachers are devoid of the one true believer who matters most—yourself—that you are in truly dire straits.

Your Opinion Matters Most of All

In 1994, in his book *Six Pillars of Self-Esteem*, expert Dr. Nathaniel Branden defined self-esteem as "the reputation we acquire with ourselves."

Einstein had a reputation as a daydreamer and dullard in school; today he'd likely be diagnosed with ADD and given a drug. He had a reputation with his adult colleagues as being "dumb" at mathematics! It didn't interfere with his success.

What of the ex-convict attempting to go straight, secure a decent job, and build a constructive life? His reputation precedes him everywhere he goes and will be a very real obstacle for some time, but it will still ultimately be his own opinion of himself that will matter most, that will determine whether or not he will persevere. Recidivism is unfortunately high, but fortunately not 100%. People *do* emerge from criminal pasts and incarceration to build worthy lives. Certainly you can liberate your self-image from any prison of your own making, built of bricks from the past, to live a more fulfilling life!

Your reputation with others cannot jettison past mistakes, often gives unfair weight to mistakes while ignoring many other accomplishments and attributes, and is even colored by the biases of the people making judgments. You cannot change that except through time and performance. But you certainly do not have to accept that same reputation. You know better. You have all the facts. And only you can know the current level of commitment to certain ideals. Determine for yourself what your reputation will be with yourself tomorrow and live up to it today, as the axiom goes "one day at a time."

"Conscience Doth Make Cowards of Us All"

So said Shakespeare. And so say modern-day psychiatrists and enlightened ministers.

Conscience itself is a learned negative feedback mechanism having to do with morals and ethics. If the learned and stored data is correct (concerning what is "right" and what is "wrong") and if the feedback mechanism is not overly sensitive but realistic, the result (just as with any other goal-striving situation) is that we are relieved from the burden of having to "decide" constantly as to what is right and wrong. Conscience steers us, or guides us, down the "straight and narrow" to the goal of correct, appropriate, and realistic behavior insofar as ethics and morals are concerned. Conscience works automatically and subconsciously, as does any other feedback system.

However, as Dr. Harry Emerson Fosdick says, "Your conscience can fool you." Your conscience itself can be wrong. It depends on your own basic beliefs concerning right and wrong. If your basic beliefs are true, realistic, and sensible, conscience becomes a valuable ally in dealing with the real world and in sailing on the ethical sea. It acts as a compass that keeps you out of trouble, as a mariner's compass keeps the ship off the reefs. But if your basic beliefs are themselves wrong, untrue, unrealistic, or irrational, these declinate your compass and pushes it off true north, just as magnetic bits of metal can disturb the compass of the mariner, and guide the ship into trouble rather than away from it.

Conscience can mean many things to many people. If you are brought up to believe, as some people are, that it is sinful to wear buttons on your clothes, your conscience will bother you when you do. If you are brought up to believe that cutting off another human's head, shrinking it, and hanging it on your wall is right, proper, and a sign of manhood, then you will feel guilty, unworthy, and undeserving if you haven't managed to shrink a head. (Head-shrinking savages would no doubt call this a sin of omission.)

Conscience's Job Is to Make You Happy, Not Miserable

The purpose of conscience is to help make us happy and productive, not the other way around. But if we are to let our conscience be our guide, our conscience must be based on truth. It must point to true north. Otherwise, blindly obeying conscience can only get us into trouble, rather than out of it, and make us unhappy and unproductive in the bargain.

Self-Expression Is Not a Moral Issue

Much mischief results from our taking a "moral" position on matters that are not basically moral matters at all.

For example, self-expression, or the lack of it, is not basically an ethical question, aside from the fact that it is our duty to use the talents our Creator gave us.

Yet self-expression may become morally wrong as far as your conscience is concerned, if you were squelched, shut up, shamed, humiliated, or perhaps punished as a child for speaking up, expressing your ideas, "showing off." Such a child learns that it is wrong to express herself, to hold herself out as having any worthwhile ideas, or perhaps to speak at all.

If a child is punished for showing anger, or shamed too much for showing fear, or perhaps made fun of for showing love, she learns that expressing her real feelings is wrong. Some children learn that it is sinful or wrong only to express the "bad emotions"—anger and fear. But, when you inhibit bad emotions, you also inhibit the expression of good emotions. And the yardstick for judging emotions is not "goodness" or "badness," as such, but appropriateness and inappropriateness. It is appropriate for the man who meets the bear on the trail to experience fear. It is appropriate to experience anger if there is a legitimate need to destroy an obstacle by sheer force and destructiveness. Properly directed and controlled, anger is an important element of courage.

If every time a child comes up with an opinion, she is squelched and put in her place, she learns that it is "right" for her to be a nobody and wrong to want to be a somebody.

Such a distorted and unrealistic conscience does indeed make cowards of us all. We can become overly sensitive and too carefully concerned with whether we have a right to succeed in even a worthwhile endeavor. We become too carefully concerned about whether or not "I deserve this." Many people, inhibited by the wrong kind of conscience, hold back or take a back seat in any kind of endeavor, even in church activities. They secretly feel it would not be right for them to hold themselves out as a leader or presume to be somebody, or they are overly concerned with whether other people might think they were showing off.

Stage fright is a common phenomenon. It becomes understandable when seen as excessive negative feedback coming from a "declinated conscience." Stage fright is the fear that we will be punished for speaking up, expressing our own opinion, presuming to be somebody, or showing off—things that most of us learned were "wrong" and punishable as children. Stage fright illustrates how universal is the suppression and inhibition of self-expression.

Disinhibition— A Long Step in the Opposite Direction

If you are among the millions who suffer unhappiness and failure because of inhibition, you need to deliberately practice *disinhibition*. You need to practice being less careful, less concerned, less conscientious. You need to practice speaking before you think instead of thinking before you speak, acting without thinking, instead of thinking or considering carefully before you act.

Commonly, when I advise a patient to practice disinhibition (and the most inhibited object the most), I am likely to hear something like this: "But surely you do not think that we need to exercise no care at all, no concern, no worry about results. It seems to me that the world needs a certain amount of inhibition, otherwise we would live like savages and civilized society would collapse. If we express ourselves without any restraint, freely expressing our feelings, we would go around punching people in the nose who disagreed with us."

"Yes," I say, "you are correct. The world does need a certain amount of inhibition. But not you. The key words are 'a certain amount.' You have such an excessive amount of inhibition, you are like a patient running a temperature of 108 degrees, who says, 'But surely body heat is necessary for health. Man is a warm-blooded animal and could not live without a certain amount of temperature. We all need temperature, yet you are telling me that I should concentrate completely and entirely on *reducing my temperature*, and ignore completely the danger of not having any temperature.'"

The stutterer, who is already so tied up with moral tensions, excessive negative feedback, self-critical analysis, and inhibition that he cannot talk at all, is prone to argue in the same way, when told to *totally ignore* negative feedback and self-criticism. He can cite you numerous proverbs, apothegms, and the like to prove that one should think before he speaks, that an idle and careless tongue gets you into trouble, and that one should be very careful of what he says and how he says it because "good speech is important" and "a word spoken cannot be recalled." All that he is saying in effect is that negative feedback is a useful and beneficial thing. But *not for him*. When he totally ignores negative feedback by either being deafened by a loud tone, or by shadow talk, he speaks correctly.

The Straight and Narrow Path Between Inhibition and Disinhibition

Someone has said that the inhibited, worry-warty, anxiously concerned personality "stutters all over."

Balance and harmony are what is needed. When the temperature has gone *too high*, the doctor attempts to lower it; when it has sunk too low, he attempts to raise it. When a person cannot sleep enough, a prescription is given to make the patient sleep more; when a person sleeps too much, a stimulant is prescribed to keep him awake, etc. It is not a question of which is best—a hot or cold temperature, or sleepfulness or wakefulness. The cure lies in taking a long step in the opposite direction. Here, the principle of cybernetics enters into the picture again. Our goal is an adequate, self-fulfilling, creative personality. The path to the goal is a course between too much inhibition and too little. When there is too much, we correct course by ignoring inhibition and practicing more disinhibition.

How to Tell Whether You Need Disinhibition

Here are the "feedback" signals which can tell you whether you are off course because of too much or too little inhibition:

If you continually get yourself into trouble because of overconfidence, if you habitually "rush in where angels fear to tread," if you habitually find yourself in hot water because of impulsive, ill-considered actions, if projects backfire on you because you always act first and ask questions later, if you can never admit you're wrong, if you are a loud talker and a blabbermouth, then you probably have *too little* inhibition. You need to think more of the consequences before acting. You need to stop acting like a bull in a china shop and plan your activities more carefully.

However, the great majority of people do not fall in this category. If you are shy around strangers; if you dread new and strange situations, if you feel inadequate, worry a lot, are anxious, overly concerned, if you are nervous and feel self-conscious, if you have any nervous symptoms such as facial tics, blinking your eyes unnecessarily, tremor, or difficulty in going to sleep, if you feel ill at ease in social situations, if you hold yourself back and continually take a back seat, then these are all symptoms showing that you have too much inhibition. You are too careful in everything, you plan too much. You need to practice St. Paul's advice to the Ephesians: "Be careful in nothing ..."

Mental Training Exercises

1. Don't wonder in advance what you are going to say. Just open your mouth and say it. Improvise as you go along. (Jesus advises us to give no thought as to what we would say if delivered up to councils, but that the spirit would advise us what to say at the time.)

2. Don't plan (take no thought for tomorrow). Don't think before you act. Act and correct your actions as you go along. This advice may seem radical, yet it is actually the way all servo-mechanisms must work. A torpedo does not "think out" all its errors in advance, and attempt to correct them in advance. It must act first—start moving toward the goal—then correct any errors that may occur.

3. Stop criticizing yourself. The inhibited person indulges in self-critical analysis continually. After each action, however simple, she says to herself, "I wonder if I should have done that." After she has gotten up courage enough to say something, she immediately says to herself, "Maybe I shouldn't have said that. Maybe the other person will take it the wrong way." Stop tearing yourself apart. Useful and beneficial feedback works subconsciously, spontaneously, and automatically. Conscious

self-criticism, self-analysis, and introspection is good and useful if undertaken perhaps once a year. But the continual, moment-by-moment, day-by-day, sort of second-guessing yourself—or playing Monday-morning quarterback to your past actions—is defeating. Watch for this self-criticism; pull yourself up short and stop it.

4. Make a habit of speaking louder than usual. Inhibited people are notoriously soft-spoken. Raise the volume of your voice. You don't have to shout at people and use an angry tone; just consciously practice speaking louder than usual. Loud talk in itself is a powerful disinhibitor. Experiments have shown that you can exert up to 15% more strength and lift more weight, if you shout, grunt, or groan loudly as you make the lift. The explanation of this is that loud shouting disinhibits and allows you to exert all your strength, including what has been blocked off and tied up by inhibition.

5. Let people know when you like them. The inhibited personality is as afraid of expressing "good" feelings as "bad" ones. If he expresses love, he is afraid it will be judged sentimentality; if he expresses friendship, he is afraid it will be considered fawning or apple polishing. If he compliments someone, he is afraid the other will think him superficial or suspect an ulterior motive.

Totally ignore all these negative feedback signals. Compliment at least three people every day. If you like what people are doing, or wearing, or saying, let them know it. Be direct. "I like that, Joe." "Mary, that is a very pretty hat." "Jim, that proves to me you are a smart person." And if you're married, just say to your spouse, "I love you" at least twice a day.

CHAPTER TWELVE

Do-It-Yourself Tranquilizers that Bring Peace of Mind

Worry affects the circulation, the heart, the glands, the whole nervous system, and profoundly affects health.
—Charles W. Mayo

Tranquilizer drugs, which have become so popular, bring peace of mind, and calmness; they reduce or eliminate nervous symptoms by an "umbrella action." Just as an umbrella protects us from the rain, the various tranquilizers erect a psychic screen between us and disturbing stimuli. Tranquilizers work because they greatly reduce, or eliminate, *our own response* to disturbing outside stimuli. But tranquilizers do not change the environment. The disturbing stimuli are still there. We are still able to *recognize* them intellectually, but we do not *respond* to them emotionally.

In chapter 7 on happiness, we said that our own feelings do not depend on externals, but on our own attitudes, reactions, and responses. Tranquilizers offer convincing evidence of this fact. In substance they reduce or tone down our overresponse to negative feedback.

I might add that today's medical community seems far too quick and liberal in resorting to drugs for every imaginable psychological malady, from children's attention deficit disorder to adult anxiety. The newest business of M.D. diagnosis and drug prescription via the Internet is most disturbing.

For the person who suffers from severe anxiety or compulsive behavior, Dr. Lucinda Bassett at the Midwest Anxiety Center has done some remarkable work perfectly in keeping with the principles of Psycho-Cybernetics. I recommend her self-help materials and services, including, as a starting point, her book *From Panic to Power.* The author suffered from acute anxiety disorders beginning in childhood and in 1981 was a full-blown agoraphobic. Using her own healing process as a framework, supplemented with thousands of case histories, she developed a program, expressed in her book, that helps even those with severe anxieties reclaim their true personalities.

For a great many people—probably you too—neither drugs nor advanced anxiety treatment measures are needed; the do-it-yourself, Psycho-Cybernetic tranquilizers you already possess are more than sufficient, once you learn to use them.

Overresponse Is a Bad Habit That Can Be Cured

Let us suppose that as you read this, you are sitting quietly in your den. Suddenly, the telephone rings. From habit and experience, this is a signal or stimulus that you have learned to obey. Without taking thought, without making a conscious decision about the matter, you respond to it. You jump up from your comfortable seat and hurry to the telephone. The outside stimulus has had the effect of "moving" you. It has changed your mental set and your position or self-determined course of action. You were all set to spend the hour, sitting quietly and relaxed, reading. You were inwardly organized for this. Now, all this is suddenly changed by your response to the external stimulus in the environment.

The point I wish to make is this. You do not *have* to answer the telephone. You do not have to obey. You can *choose* to totally ignore the telephone. You can, if you choose, continue sitting quietly and relaxed, maintaining your own original state of organization, by *refusing to respond* to the signal.

Get this mental picture clearly in your mind, for it can be quite helpful in overcoming the power of external stimuli to disturb you. See yourself sitting quietly, letting the phone ring, ignoring its signal, unmoved by its command. Although you are *aware* of it, you no longer mind or obey it. Also, get clearly in your mind the fact that the outside signal in itself has no power over you, no power to move you. In the past you have obeyed it, responded to it, purely out of habit. You can, if you wish, form a new habit of not responding.

Also notice that your failure to respond does not consist in doing something, or making an effort, or resisting or fighting, but in doing nothing—in relaxation from doing. You merely relax, ignore the signal, and let its summons go unheeded.

The telephone ringing is a symbolic analogy to any and every other outside stimulus you might habitually give control over to and now choose to very intentionally alter that habit. So-called road rage is nothing more than the giving up control of your own emotional state to an outside stimulus.

Stress brought on by having too much to do—i.e., trying to do too many things at once—is giving up control to the fax machine, the cell phone, the e-mail messages, the person hovering in your office doorway.

How to Condition Yourself for Equanimity

In much the same way that you automatically obey or respond to the ring of the telephone, we all become conditioned to respond in a certain way to various stimuli in our environment.

The word "conditioning" in psychological circles grew out of Pavlov's well-known experiments where he "conditioned" a dog to salivate at the sound of a bell, by ringing it just before presenting food to the dog. This procedure was repeated many times. First, the sound of the bell. A few seconds later, the appearance of food. The dog "learned" to respond to the sound of the bell by salivating in anticipation of the food. Originally, the response made sense. The bell signified that food was forthcoming, and the dog got ready by salivating. However, after the process was repeated a number of times, the dog would continue to salivate whenever the bell was rung, whether or not food was immediately forthcoming. The dog had now become "conditioned" to salivate at the mere sound of the bell. Its response made no sense and served no good purpose, but it continued to respond in the same way out of habit.

There are a great many "bells," or disturbing stimuli, in our various environmental situations, to which we have become conditioned to and to which we continue to respond out of habit, whether or not the response makes any sense. But, my friend, you are *not* a poor, dumb animal who must go through life so unwittingly and easily manipulated and controlled. You are a human being with creative powers, with the power of rational thinking, with the ability to stand up on your hind legs and assert yourself. You must decide to be "worked like a dog" or to be your own person, to be controlled or to be in control. This is a decision with far-reaching consequences. It is the answer to the question, how can I get respect in a disrespectful world?

Many people learn to fear strangers, for example, because of parental admonitions to have nothing to do with strange people. "Do not accept candy from a stranger." "Do not get into a car with a stranger," and so on. The response of avoiding strangers serves a good purpose in small children. But many people continue to feel ill at ease and uncomfortable in the presence of all strangers, even when they know that they come as friends instead of foes. Strangers become "bells" and the learned response becomes fear, avoidance, or the desire to run away.

In counseling sales professionals who are "frozen" and avoiding the task of "prospecting" by every imaginable excuse and contrivance, I frequently uncovered this bit of programming grooved into their servo-mechanism. In counseling men and women who are unable to make new friends or meet and initiate relationships with members of the opposite sex, I often uncovered this same bit of programming.

Still another person may respond to crowds, closed spaces, open spaces, persons in authority such as "the boss," by feelings of fear and anxiety. In each case the crowd, the closed space, the open space, the boss, or whatever acts as a bell that says, "Danger is present, run away, feel afraid." And out of habit, we continue to respond in the accustomed way. We obey the bell. It is time to disconnect these bells.

How to Extinguish Conditioned Responses

We can extinguish the conditioned response if we make a practice of relaxing instead of responding. We can, if we wish, just as in the case of the telephone, learn to ignore the bell and continue to sit quietly and let it ring. A key thought that we can carry with us to use whenever we are confronted by any disturbing stimulus is to say to ourselves, "The telephone is ringing, but I do not *have* to answer it. I can just let it ring." This thought will key in to your mental picture of yourself sitting quietly, relaxed, unresponsive, doing nothing, letting the telephone ring unheeded. It will act as a trigger or clue to call up the same attitude that you had when letting the telephone ring.

It You Cannot Ignore the Response, Delay It

In the process of extinguishing a conditioning, a person may find it difficult, especially at first, to totally ignore a bell, especially if it is rung unexpectedly. In such instances you can accomplish the same final result—extinction of the conditioning—by delaying your response.

A woman, whom we will call Mary S., became anxious and ill at ease in the presence of crowds. She was able, by practicing the foregoing technique, to immunize or tranquilize herself against the disturbing stimuli on most occasions. However, occasionally, the desire to run away, to flee, became almost overpowering.

"Remember Scarlett O'Hara in *Gone with the Wind*?" I asked her. "Her philosophy was, 'I won't worry about that now. I'll worry about it tomorrow.'" She was able to maintain her inner equilibrium and effectively cope with her environment in spite of war, fire, pestilence, and unrequited love by delaying the response.

Delaying the response breaks up and interferes with the automatic workings of conditioning.

"Counting to ten" when you are tempted to become angry is based on the same principle and is very good advice, if you count slowly and in fact actually delay the response, rather than merely holding in your angry shouting or desk pounding. The response in anger consists of more than shouting or desk beating. The tension in your muscles is a response. You cannot feel the emotion of anger or fear if your muscles remain perfectly relaxed. Therefore, if you can delay feeling angry for ten seconds, delay responding at all, you can extinguish the automatic reflex.

Mary S. extinguished her conditioned fear of crowds by delaying her response. When she felt that she simply had to run away, she would say to herself, "Very well, but not this very minute. I will delay leaving the room for two minutes. I can refuse to obey for only two minutes!"

Relaxation Erects a Psychic Screen, or Tranquilizer

It is well to get clearly in your mind the fact that our disturbed feelings—our anger, hostility, fear, anxiety, insecurity—are caused by our own responses, not by externals. Response means tension. Lack of response means relaxation. It has been proved in scientific laboratory experiments that you absolutely cannot feel angry, fearful, anxious, insecure, unsafe as long as your muscles remain perfectly relaxed. All these things are, in essence, our own feelings. Tension in muscles is a preparation for action or a getting ready to respond. Relaxing muscles brings about mental relaxation or a peaceful relaxed attitude. Thus, relaxation is nature's own tranquilizer, which erects a psychic screen or umbrella between you and the disturbing stimulus.

Physical relaxation is a powerful disinhibitor for the same reason. In the last chapter we learned that inhibition results from excessive negative feedback, or rather from our overresponse to negative feedback. Relaxation means no response. Therefore, in your daily practice of relaxation, you are learning disinhibition as well as providing yourself with nature's own do-it-yourself tranquilizer, which you can take with you into your daily activities. Protect yourself from disturbing stimuli by maintaining the relaxed attitude.

Early in his speaking career, the editor of this book would go through a series of rituals to "get up" for the pending performance, including pacing around, without realizing it, adding considerable physical tension to his body. Later in his career, he could often be observed stretched out casually in a chair, even lying on a couch in a room immediately prior to his time on stage, looking to the observer to be completely disinterested in the upcoming task. While he still went through certain mental rituals to ready himself for the performance, he did so in a physically relaxed manner. You too can learn to be motivated, to be energized, to be ready for peak performance without being tense and anxious.

Learn to Use Pre-Performance Rituals to Your Advantage

In several different articles in various issues of *Golf Magazine*, Dr. Richard Coop, author of the book *Mind Over Golf*, has advised players to briefly step back from a shot if they feel negative thoughts boiling up, and to use some physical ritual to regain calm control and reset their concentration. It may be adjusting their glove or tapping their club on the ground. He also teaches developing your own personal preshot routine, as the best way to keep stray thoughts from invading your mind in the middle of your swing. "Bottom-line," Dr. Coop writes, "good players have a consistent routine and poor players don't."

We have a saying in Psycho-Cybernetics training: "Calm mind, calm body; calm body, calm mind." It doesn't matter which end of the thread you start with, physical or mental relaxation, the result is the same.

The trick is to develop a "preshot routine" for whatever you do that calms and relaxes, not heightens anxiety.

Build Yourself a Quiet Room in Your Mind

"Men seek retreats for themselves: houses in the country, sea-shores and mountains; and thou too art wont to desire such things very much," said Marcus Aurelius, "But this is altogether a mark of the most common sort of men, for it is in thy power whenever thou shalt choose to retire into thyself. For nowhere, either with more quiet or more freedom from trouble, does a man retire than into his own soul, particularly when he has within him such thoughts that by looking into them he is immediately in perfect tranquillity; and I affirm that tranquillity is nothing else than the good ordering of the mind. Constantly then give to thyself this retreat, and renew thyself…" (*Meditations of Marcus Aurelius,* translated by George Long, Mount Vernon, N.Y., Peter Pauper Press)

During the last days of World War II someone commented to President Harry Truman that he appeared to bear up under the stress and strain of the presidency better than any previous president, that the job did not appear to have "aged" him or sapped his vitality, and that this was rather remarkable, especially in view of the many problems that confronted him as a wartime president. His answer was, "I have a foxhole in my mind." He went on to say that just as a soldier retreated into his foxhole for protection, rest, and recuperation, he periodically retired into his own mental foxhole, where he allowed nothing to bother him.

I cannot urge you strongly enough to invest time and utilize your imagination to build your own "foxhole in your mind."

Your Own Decompression Chamber

Some people attempt to obtain this benefit by physical relocation. I know one corporate CEO here in New York who has the habit of suddenly disappearing from the office and going to the Bronx Zoo. He leaves behind his cell phone. He is not anywhere someone can come and disturb him. He is lost in the crowds, walking about the zoo, intentionally distracted and inaccessible. This strategy apparently works well for him, as he has risen up the corporate ranks, and become a multimillionaire thanks to his stock options and success at growing companies' profits. However, doesn't it seem a bit inconvenient to have to depart the office and take a cab across the city to walk around the zoo in order to decompress?

It is a much shorter, convenient commute to a readily accessible decompression chamber, constructed within your own imagination. The harried mother, besieged all day by two young children—if one is quiet for a moment, the other is not!—needs only a brief opportunity, possibly their nap time, to step into the decompression chamber she has built in her imagination for recovery. The stressed-out salesperson can stop the car in a parking lot between appointments for a quick visit to his or her decompression chamber.

Each of us needs a quiet room inside the mind, a quiet center within, like the deep of the ocean that is never disturbed, no matter how rough the surface waves may become.

This quiet room within, which is built in imagination, works as a mental and emotional decompression chamber. It depressurizes you from tensions, worry, pressures, stresses, and strains, refreshes you and enables you to return to your work-a-day world better prepared to cope with it.

It is my belief that each personality already has a quiet center within, which is never disturbed and is unmoved, like the mathematical point in the very center of a wheel or axle that remains stationary. What we need to do is to find this quiet center within us and retreat into it periodically for rest, recuperation, and renewed vigor.

One of the most beneficial prescriptions that I have ever given patients is the advice to learn to return to this quiet tranquil center. And one of the best ways that I have found for entering this quiet center is to build for yourself, in imagination, a little mental room. Furnish this room with whatever is most restful and refreshing to you: perhaps beautiful landscapes, if you like paintings; a volume of your favorite verse, if you like poetry. The colors of the walls are your own favorite "pleasant" colors, but should be chosen from the restful hues of blue, light green, yellow, gold. The room is plainly and simply furnished; there are no distracting elements. It is very neat and everything is in order. Simplicity, quietness, beauty are the keynotes. It contains your favorite easy chair. From one small window you can look out and see a beautiful beach. The waves roll in on the beach and retreat, but you cannot hear them, for your room is very, very quiet.

Take as much care in building this room in your imagination as you would in building an actual room. Be thoroughly familiar with every detail. Do not permit the thought that this is childish stop you in your tracks. The power of this technique lies in its careful and thorough construction, its vivid detail, its "realness" as a *place* of retreat rather than just a vague idea.

A Little Vacation Every Day

Whenever you have a few spare moments during the day between appointments, perhaps riding the bus, retire into your quiet room. Whenever you begin to feel tension mounting or feel hurried or harried, retire into your quiet room for a few moments. Just a very few minutes taken from a very busy day in this manner will more than pay for themselves. It is not time wasted, but time invested. Say to yourself, "I am going to rest a bit in my quiet room."

Then, in imagination, see yourself climbing the stairs to your room. Say to yourself, "I am now climbing the stairs. Now I am opening the door. Now I am inside." In imagination notice all the quiet, restful details. See yourself sitting down in your favorite chair, utterly relaxed and at peace with the world. Your room is secure. Nothing can touch you here. There is nothing to worry about. You left your worries at the foot of the stairs. There are no decisions to be made here— no hurry, no bother.

You Need a Certain Amount of Escapism

Yes, this is escapism. Sleep is "escapism" too. Carrying an umbrella in the rain is escapism. Building yourself an actual house where you can retreat from the weather and the elements is escapism. And taking a vacation is escapism. Our nervous system needs a certain amount of escapism. It needs some freedom and protection from the continual bombardment of external stimuli. Your soul and your nervous system need a room for rest, recuperation, and protection every bit as much as your physical body needs a physical house, and for the same reasons. Your mental quiet room gives your nervous system a little vacation every day. For the moment, you mentally "vacate" your work-a-day world of duties, responsibilities, decisions, pressures, and "get away from it all" by mentally retiring into your no-pressure chamber.

Pictures are more impressive to your automatic mechanism than words. Particularly so, if the picture happens to have a strong symbolic meaning. One mental picture that I have found very effective is the following:

On a visit to Yellowstone National Park, I was waiting patiently for the geyser "Old Faithful," which goes off approximately every hour. Suddenly the geyser erupted in a great mass of hissing steam, like a gigantic boiler whose safety plug had blown out. A small boy standing near me, asked his father, "What makes it do that?"

"Well," said his father, "I guess old Mother Earth is like the rest of us. She builds up a certain amount of pressure, and every once in a while just has to blow off steam to stay healthy." Wouldn't it be wonderful, I thought to myself, if we humans could blow off steam harmlessly like that when emotional pressures build up inside us?

I didn't have a geyser or a steam valve in the top of my bead, but I did have an imagination. So I began to use this mental picture when I would retire into my mental quiet room. I would remember Old Faithful, and form a mental picture of emotional steam and pressure coming out the top of my head and evaporating harmlessly. Try this mental picture on yourself when you're wrought up or tense. The ideas of blowing off steam and blowing your top have powerful associations built into your mental machinery.

Incidentally, many psychologists and performance coaches now talk about these same ideas and techniques in the context of recovery.

In The New Psycho-Cybernetics audio program, you will find this discussion continued under that topic.

"Clear" Your Mechanism Before Undertaking a New Problem

If you are using an adding machine or an electronic computer, you must clear the machine of previous problems before undertaking a new one. Otherwise, parts of the old problem or the old situation carry over into the new one—and give you a wrong answer.

This exercise of retiring for a few moments into your quiet room in your mind can accomplish the same sort of clearing of your success mechanism. For that reason, it is very helpful to practice it between tasks, situations, or environments that require different moods, mental adjustments, or mental sets.

A common example of carry-over, or failure to clear your mental machinery, is the following: A business executive carries his work-a-day worries and his work-a-day mood home with him. All day he has been harried, hurried, aggressive, and "set to go." Perhaps he has felt a bit of frustration, which tends to make him irritable. He stops working physically when he goes home. But he carries with him a residue of his aggressiveness, frustration, hurry, and worry. He is still set to go and cannot relax. He is irritable with his wife and family. He keeps thinking about problems at the office, although there is nothing he can do about them.

Insomnia, Rudeness Are Often Emotional Carry-Overs

Many people carry their troubles to bed with them when they should be resting. Mentally and emotionally, they are still trying to do something about a situation, at a time when doing something is not in order.

All during the day we need many different types of emotional and mental organizations. You need a different mood and mental organization for talking with your boss and talking with a customer. And if you have just talked with an irate and irritable customer, you need a change in mind set before talking with a second customer. Otherwise emotional carry-over from the one situation will be inappropriate in dealing with the other.

Emotional Carry-Over Causes Accidents

Insurance companies and other agencies that do research on the cause of accidents have found that emotional carry-over causes many automobile accidents. If the driver has just had a spat with her spouse or boss, if she has just experienced frustration, or if she has just left a situation that called for aggressive behavior, she is much more likely to have an accident. She carries over inappropriate attitudes and emotions into her driving. She is really not angry at the other drivers. She is somewhat like someone who wakes up in the morning from a dream in which she experienced extreme anger. She realizes that the injustice heaped on her happened only in a dream. But she is still angry—period!

Fear can carry over in the same manner.

Carry-Over Is the Opposite of Concentration

The popular television detective Lt. Columbo, played brilliantly by actor Peter Falk, once said, "Sometimes my thoughts—it gets like a traffic jam up here."

Successful performers in all fields know that they cannot function well with a traffic jam going on in their head! In fact, peak performers virtually worship at the altar of "focus" and "concentration," working tirelessly to achieve it, for very good reason: concentration *is* a major key to minute-by-minute success in any endeavor. John Lyons, one of the world's most celebrated trainers of horses and riders, as well as editor of *The Perfect Horse* newsletter, states, "The hardest thing about training horses isn't knowing what to do or having enough strength or courage to do it. It is learning to stay focused." The same statement may be made about golf or selling or parenting or you-name-it; the hardest thing is not the mechanics, it's staying focused. Mr. Lyons went on to say, "If I don't zero in on one thing at a time, I can't help my horse." If you don't zero in on one thing at a time, you cannot help yourself, help a team, or succeed!

Create Your Own Quick Distractions Eraser and Use It as Often as Needed

The visualization I taught for many years, which I called "clearing the calculator," depicted clearing or storage for later work one mathematical problem on the calculator's little screen before you could attempt work on another. Hitting the "clear" button takes problem 1 completely off your "screen." You must do so before addressing problem 2. Many people develop other illustrations and visualizations more useful to them. I've received many letters in which people describe visualizing using an eraser and wiping a chalkboard clean, a sponge to wipe a window clean, even stepping into the shower and rinsing clean. You can call up this mental picture and use it as an eraser in as short a time as a few seconds, such as those five seconds of imposed hesitation before answering the phone.

Olympic champion high-diver Greg Louganis reportedly mentally rehearsed each dive 40 times immediately prior to the dive! In reality, what he was doing was:

1. **Stopping to "clear the calculator."**

2. **Pushing all distractions aside by, in quick succession, replaying a mini-mental movie 1, 2, 3, 4, 5, 6, 7…38, 39, 40 times so that there was nothing left on his screen but the successful mental picture.**

3. **Letting his servo-mechanism deliver the 41st as actual experience.**

Most people never adopt this simple but profoundly effective approach. Instead, they enter into a challenging activity—say, an important meeting at the office—with "traffic jam" (complete with horns blaring, people shouting) going on in their thoughts. They attempt to function without focus! With a whole pot of thought-and-emotional stew boiling over—worries about this or that, a disagreeable conversation with spouse or friend, distraction by things that need to be addressed an hour or two down the road—they give their servo-mechanism fifty different things to do, thus dissipating its power.

An athlete like Louganis must put a firm lid not only on that bubbling stew, but also on another pot on the next burner over, where perhaps thoughts recognizing stiffness or soreness in a limb, tension in a muscle, worry over form all threatens to boil up as well. All of this must first be replaced with single focus, to permit relaxed performance. You, too, need to put the lids firmly on the pots, turn down the heat, and successfully ignore them altogether in favor of concentration on one vivid, successful mental picture at a time.

PRESCRIPTION

Develop your own equivalent of the "clear the calculator" ritual, to erase distractions instantly on command, and practice its use. With practice, it will become more and more effective, so that the desired "clear-headedness" occurs faster and faster, ultimately in an instant. Then, for each situation, you can immediately follow the "erasing" with an appropriate mini-mental movie or even a still or two from the movie, providing *the* mental picture for the servo-mechanism to concentrate all of its powers on at that moment.

Click off Tension, Click on Performance

I was once backstage at a television talk show, chatting with the host of the program. The show's director stuck his head in the "green room" door and said, "One minute."

"Excuse me, Dr. Maltz," the host said. He closed his eyes firmly, snapped his fingers loudly once, stood still and silent for a few seconds, snapped his fingers again, and stood silent again for a few seconds. Then he opened his eyes, smiled, and said "Let's go make show business magic" and walked confidently across the hallway, through the curtains and out onto the stage in front of the audience and the cameras.

After the taping was over, I asked him about what I'd observed. "It's my get-ready ritual," he explained. "Early in my career, it took me twenty, even thirty minutes of hard effort to try and clear my head of everything except the show I was about to do. Gradually I learned how to do it in steps in my mind, then I was able to speed it up. Now I can do it in about 30 seconds."

"What about the finger-snapping?" I asked.

"Those are like clicking on and off a light switch. The first snap triggers the clearing or blanking of my mind, and now that happens just about instantly. The second click triggers a quick series of slides, pictures of me walking out to rousing applause, the audience laughing during the show, a pleasant interview with a guest, and the crew, producer and I congratulating ourselves on another great show at its end." He smiled and added, "You see, I really did read your book years ago."

Calmness Carries Over Too

A helpful aside to all this is that friendliness, love, peace, quiet, and calmness also "carry over."

It is impossible, as we have said, to experience or feel either fear, anger, or anxiety, while completely relaxed, quiet, and composed. Retiring into your quiet room thus becomes an ideal clearance mechanism for emotions and moods. Old emotions evaporate and disappear. At the same time you experience calmness, peacefulness, and a feeling of well-being that will carry over into whatever activities immediately follow. Your quiet time wipes the slate clean so to speak, clears the machine, and gives you a clean new page for the environment to follow.

I practiced the quiet time both immediately before and after surgery. Surgery requires a high degree of concentration, calmness, and control. It would be disastrous to carry over into the surgical situation feelings of hurry, aggressiveness, or personal worries. Therefore, I always deliberately cleared my mental machinery by spending a few moments completely relaxed in my quiet room. On the other hand, the high degree of concentration, purpose, and obliviousness to surroundings, which are so necessary to the surgical situation, would be most inappropriate to a social situation, whether the social situation be an interview in my office or a grand ball. Therefore, upon leaving surgery I also make it a point to spend a couple of minutes in my quiet room, to clear the decks, so to speak, for a new type of action.

Dr. Ira Sharlip, a San Francisco surgeon, talks about running a mental movie from initial incision to final suturing. Dr. Bodell, a hand and joint reconstructive surgeon we interviewed for a video program about Psycho-Cybernetics, told us of creating vivid, detailed mental movies of operations the evening before performing them, so that the perfect operation is installed in his mind and the performance is rote. It seems we are all using nearly identical approaches to create a carry-over of calmness into the operatory.

Build Your Own Psychic Umbrellas

By practicing the techniques in this chapter you can build your own psychic umbrellas, which will screen out disturbing stimuli, bring you more peace of mind, and enable you to perform better. Prepare your own mental tranquilizers, which can be consumed without side effects or expense.

Above all, keep in mind, and hammer it home to yourself, that the *key* to the matter of whether you are disturbed or tranquil, fearful or composed is not the external stimulus, whatever it may be, but your own response and reaction. Your own response is what "makes" you feel fearful, anxious, insecure. If you do not respond at all, but just "let the telephone ring," it is impossible for you to feel disturbed, regardless of what is happening around you.

You are striving to be an actor, not a reactor. Throughout this book we have spoken of reacting and responding appropriately to environmental factors. The human being, however, is not primarily a reactor, but an "actor." We do not merely react and respond, willy-nilly, to whatever environmental factors may be present, like a ship without a captain, that goes whichever way the wind happens to blow. As goal-striving beings we first act. We set our own goal, determine our own course. Then, within the context of this goal-striving structure, we respond and react appropriately, that is, in a manner that furthers our progress and serves our own ends.

If responding and reacting to negative feedback does not take us farther down the road to our own goal or serve our ends, then there is no need to respond at all. And, if response of any kind gets us off course or works against us, then *no* response is the appropriate response.

Your Emotional Stabilizer

In almost any goal-striving situation, our own inner stability is in itself an important goal to maintain. We must be sensitive to negative feedback data that advises us when we are off course, so that we can change direction and go forward. But at the same time, we must keep our own ship afloat and stable. Our ship must not be tossed and rocked and perhaps sunk by every passing wave or even a serious storm. As Prescott Lecky expressed it, "The same attitude must be maintained in spite of environmental changes."

Our letting the telephone ring is a mental attitude that keeps our stability. It keeps us from being tossed about, knocked off course, or shaken up, by every wave or ripple in the environment.

Stop Fighting Straw Men

Still another type of inappropriate response that causes worry, insecurity, and tension is the bad habit of trying to respond emotionally to something that doesn't exist except in our imaginations. Not satisfied with overresponding to actual minor stimuli in the actual environment, many of us create straw men in our imaginations and emotionally respond to our own mental pictures. In addition to negatives that actually exist in the environment, we impose our own negatives: This or that may happen; what if such and such happens. When we worry, we form mental pictures, adverse mental pictures of what may exist in the environment, of what may happen. We then respond to these negative pictures *as if* they were present reality. Remember, your nervous system cannot tell the difference between a real experience and one that is vividly imagined.

"Doing Nothing" Is the Proper Response to an Unreal Problem

Again, you can tranquilize yourself against this sort of disturbance, not by something you do, but by something you don't do: your refusal to respond. As far as your emotions are concerned, the proper response to worry pictures is to totally ignore them. Live emotionally in the present moment. Analyze your environment, become more aware of what actually exists in your environment, and respond and react spontaneously to that. To do this you must give all your attention to what is happening now. You must keep your eye on the ball. Then your response will be appropriate, and you will have no time to notice or respond to a fictitious environment.

Your First Aid Kit

Carry these thoughts with you as a sort of first aid kit:

Inner disturbance, or the opposite of tranquillity, is nearly always caused by overresponse, a too-sensitive alarm reaction. You create a built-in tranquilizer, or psychic screen between yourself and the disturbing stimulus, when you practice "not responding," letting the telephone ring.

You cure old habits of overresponse, you extinguish old conditioned reflexes, when you practice *delaying* the habitual, automatic, and unthinking response.

Relaxation is nature's own tranquilizer. Relaxation is nonresponse. Learn physical relaxation by daily practice. Then, when you need to practice nonresponse in daily activities, just do what you're doing when you relax.

Use the quiet room in your mind, both as a daily tranquilizer to tone down nervous response and as a way to clear your emotional mechanism of carry-over emotions that would be inappropriate in a new situation.

Stop scaring yourself to death with your own mental pictures. Stop fighting straw men. Emotionally, respond only to what *is*—here and now—and ignore the rest.

MENTAL TRAINING EXERCISE

Create in your imagination a vivid mental picture of yourself sitting quietly, composed, unmoved, letting your telephone ring, as outlined earlier in this chapter. Then, in your daily activities carry over the same peaceful, composed, unmoved attitude by remembering this mental picture. Say to yourself, "I am letting the telephone ring" whenever you are tempted to "obey" or respond to a fear-bell or anxiety-bell. Next, use your imagination to practice nonresponse in various sorts of situations: See yourself sitting quietly and unmoved while an associate rants and raves. See yourself going through your daily tasks one by one, calmly, composed, unhurried, in spite of the pressures of a busy day. See yourself maintaining the same constant, stable course, in spite of the various hurry-bells and pressure-bells in your environment. See yourself in various situations that have in the past upset you; only now you remain "set," settled, poised by not responding.

CHAPTER THIRTEEN

How to Turn a Crisis into a Creative Opportunity

I have seen boys on my baseball team go into slumps and never come out, and I have seen others snap right out and come back better than ever. I guess more players defeat themselves than are ever beaten by an opposing team.

—Connie Mack

"*C*lutch player!" "Money player!" Oh, to be able to handle all the pressure that comes your way and still perform!

I knew a young golfer who for many years held the all-time course record for his home course, yet has never even placed in a really big tournament. When playing by himself, with friends, or in small tournaments where the stakes are low, his play is flawless. Yet each time he gets into a big tournament his game deteriorates. In the language of golfdom, "the pressure gets him."

He is not alone in this experience.

In fact, in a popular movie, Kevin Costner played the role of a golfer known to all the professionals as "Tin Cup." He was spectacularly skilled but, under the pressure of big money tournament play, came apart at the seams like a cheap suit in a rainstorm. Many golfers identified with tin cup. Ironically, one of the very best golf instructors and coaches I know about, who is well-known and often called on by top professionals, is unbeatable in friendly, casual, private play but has never been able to make the cut to play for real money.

Many baseball pitchers have pinpoint control until they find themselves in a situation where the chips are down. Then they choke up, lose all control, and appear to have no ability whatever. Casey

Stengel, famous manager of the 1950s New York Yankees, made the comment, "Anybody can hit home runs in batting practice."

On the other hand, many athletes perform better under pressure. The situation itself seems to give them more strength, more power, more finesse. Understanding why "pressure" makes some peoples' performance better while destroying others' performance is key to consistently and reliably being at your best.

As an aside, let me quickly remind you that the golf pro's or baseball pitcher's "coming apart at the seams" does not make him a lousy golfer or a worthless pitcher, does not make either of them a "choker." Such labels, quickly slapped on by the media, by kibitzing fans, even by colleagues are not only reinforcing and damaging, they are fundamentally untrue because a person is never his mistakes. Every one of us is a mistake-maker but also potentially a mistake-breaker. We most certainly possess the capacity to rise above our mistakes. In this case, these players have not yet discovered their true selves, not yet learned how to successfully manage their self-images and servo-mechanisms so as to respond positively to pressure. While what they do not know and have not mastered does control them at the moment, it does not define them, and whether it is of days, months, or years in duration, it can be changed!

People Who Come into Their Own in a Crisis

One basketball player's foul shot average may be significantly better during practice than regular games, and better in regular games than in playoffs, while another exhibits the reverse behavior; performance improves in a playoff, all-or-nothing situation. Almost every NFL team of note has one pass receiver who can be relied on to make a big play or extraordinarily difficult catch in the clutch, when everything depends on that play. Yet he may muff a number of easy receptions earlier in the game. Quarterbacks learn to throw to their clutch receivers when they must, and often also learn to use them minimally at other times.

One salesperson may find himself inarticulate in the presence of an important prospect. His skills desert him. Another salesperson under the same circumstances, may "sell over her head." The challenge of the situation brings out abilities she does not ordinarily possess. (In our book *Zero Resistance Selling*, one of the most important chapters is "How To Sell When You Are in Over Your Head.")

There are students who do extremely well in day-to-day class work, but find their minds a blank when taking an examination. There are other students who are ordinary in class work, but do extremely well on important examinations.

The Secret of the Money Player

The difference between all these persons is not an inherent quality that one has and the other hasn't. It is largely a matter of how they learned to react to crisis situations.

A "crisis" is a situation that can either make you or break you. If you react properly to the crisis, it can give you strength, power, wisdom you do not ordinarily possess. If you react improperly, a crisis can rob you of the skill, control, and ability that you ordinarily have to call on.

The so-called "money player" in sports, in business, or in social activities—the person who comes through in the clutch, who performs better under the stimulus of challenge—is invariably the person who has learned either consciously or unconsciously to react well to crisis situations.

To perform well in a crisis, we need to (1) learn certain skills under conditions where we will not be overmotivated; we need to practice without pressure. (2) We need to learn to react to crisis with an aggressive, rather than a defensive, attitude, to respond to the challenge in the situation rather than to the menace, to keep our positive goal in mind. (3) We need to learn to evaluate so-called "crisis" situations in their true perspective, to avoid making mountains out of molehills or reacting as if every small challenge were a matter of life or death.

In other words, making yourself into a money player is very doable, because it is totally dependent on a relatively short list of attitudes and skills that can be learned, exercised, and developed, and that can be accelerated in development and maintained through other Psycho-Cybernetics Techniques. No one lacks what it takes to be a money player.

Practice Without Pressure

Although we may learn fast, we do not learn well under crisis conditions. Throw a man who can't swim into water over his head, and the crisis itself may give him the power to swim to safety. He learns fast, and manages to swim *somehow*. But he will never learn to become a championship swimmer. The crude inept stroke that he used to rescue himself becomes fixed and it is difficult for him to learn better ways of swimming. Because of his ineptness he may perish in a real crisis where he is required to swim a long distance.

Dr. Edward C. Tolman, psychologist and expert on animal behavior at the University of California, said that both animals and men form "brain maps" or "cognitive maps" of the environment while they are learning. If the motivation is not too intense, if there is not too much of a crisis present in the learning situation, these maps are broad and general. If the animal is overmotivated, the cognitive map is narrow and restricted. It learns just one way of solving the problem. In the future, if this one way happens to be blocked, the animal becomes frustrated and fails to discern alternative routes or detours. It develops a single cut-and-dried, preconceived response and tends to lose the ability to react spontaneously to a new situation. It cannot improvise. It can only follow a set plan.

Consider the young man growing up in a tough ghetto environment, spending his time on the street, interacting with gang members, at risk virtually all the time, in an environment where any hint of fear, weakness or vulnerability may lead to dire consequences. If this is the environment in which he learns all his conflict resolution skills, he will learn only one narrowly defined set of such skills, probably incorporating fiercely aggressive behavior and physical violence. I would suggest you might see this reflected in a man like Mike Tyson, awesomely successful in the boxing ring but horribly unsuccessful in any other setting.

Pressure Retards Learning

Dr. Tolman found that if rats were permitted to *learn* and *practice under noncrisis* conditions, they later performed well in a crisis. For example, if rats were permitted to roam about at will and explore a maze when well fed and with plenty to drink, they did not *appear* to learn anything. Later, however, if the same rats were placed in the maze while hungry, they showed they had learned a great deal by quickly and efficiently going to the goal. Hunger faced these trained rats with a crisis to which they reacted well.

Other rats, forced to learn the maze under the crisis of hunger and thirst, did not do so well. They were overmotivated and their brain maps became narrow. The one "correct" route to the goal became fixated. If this route was blocked, the rats became frustrated and had great difficulty learning a new one.

Fire Drills Teach Crisis Conduct in Noncrisis Situation

People react in the same way. Persons who have to learn how to get out of a burning building will normally require two or three times as long to learn the proper escape route, as they would if no fire were present. Some of them do not learn at all. Overmotivation interferes with reasoning processes. The automatic reaction mechanism is jammed by too much conscious effort, trying too hard. Something akin to purpose tremor develops and the ability to think clearly is lost. The ones who manage somehow to get out of the building have learned a narrow fixated response. Put them in a different building, or change the circumstances slightly, and they react as badly the second time around as the first.

But you can take these same people, let them practice a "dry run" fire drill when there is no fire. Because there is no menace, there is no excessive negative feedback to interfere with clear thinking or correct doing. They practice filing out of the building calmly, efficiently, and correctly. After they have practiced this a number of times, they can be counted on to act the same way when an actual fire breaks out. Their muscles, nerves, and brain have memorized a broad, general, flexible map. The attitude of calmness and clear thinking will carry over from practice drill to actual fire. Moreover, they will have learned something about how to get out of any building or cope with any changed circumstances. They are not committed to a rigid response, but will be able to improvise, to react spontaneously to whatever conditions may be present.

The moral is obvious for either mice or men: Practice without pressure and you will learn more efficiently and be able to perform better in a crisis situation.

Shadow-Boxing for Stability

Famous boxer Gentleman Jim Corbett made the word "shadow-boxing" popular. When asked how he developed the perfect control and timing for his left jab, which he used to cut John L. Sullivan, the Boston Strong-boy, to ribbons, Corbett replied that he had practiced throwing his left at his own image in the mirror more than 10,000 times in preparation for the bout.

Gene Tunney did the same thing. Years before he actually fought Jack Dempsey in the ring, he had fought an imaginary Dempsey more than a hundred times in the privacy of his own room. He secured all the films of old Dempsey fights. He watched them until he knew every one of Dempsey's moves. Then he shadow-boxed. He would imagine that Dempsey was standing before him. When the imaginary Dempsey would make a certain move, he would practice his counter-move.

Billy Graham preached sermons to cypress stumps in a Florida swamp before developing his compelling platform personality with live audiences. Most good public speakers have done the same thing in one way or another. The most common form of shadow-boxing for public speakers is to deliver their speech to their own image in the mirror. One man I know lines up six or eight empty chairs, imagines people sitting in them, and practices his speech on the invisible audience. Another lectured to chickens on his farm!

A female stand-up comedian I know, who asked not to be identified by name, told me that, early in her career, she practiced delivering her routine with full style and emotion as if before a big audience—but actually alone, standing completely naked, in front of three full-length mirrors arranged in an arc in front of her! She reasoned that she never felt more vulnerable and inhibited than being seen naked (which is why she preferred having sex only in a dark room) so if she could stand nude in a lit room looking at her mirrored reflections and still concentrate and deliver her routine there, she'd be able to do it easily fully clothed and thus "protected" in front of an audience. Prior to this conversation I had heard of speakers visualizing their audiences stripped to their underwear so as to be less intimidating, but I'd never heard of a speaker going au naturale!

She uniquely combined "safe" practice with simulated or synthetic pressure.

For the record, she has gone onto become one of the most successful female comedians in the business.

My point is to find a form of shadow-boxing that works for you.

Easy Practice Brings Better Scores

When the great Ben Hogan was playing tournament golf regularly, he kept a golf club in his bedroom, and daily practiced in private, swinging the club correctly and without pressure at an imaginary golf ball. When Hogan was on the links, he would go through the correct motions in his imagination before making a shot, then depend on muscle memory to execute the shot correctly. Virtually all golf instruction today incorporates such relaxed practice and imagination practice.

Shadow-Boxing "Turns on" Self-Expression

The word "express" literally means to push out, exert, show forth. The word "inhibit" means to choke off, restrict. Self-expression is a pushing out, a showing forth, of the powers, talents and abilities of the self. It means turning on your own light and letting it shine. Self-expression is a yes response. Inhibition is a no response. It chokes off self-expression, turns off or dims your light.

In shadow-boxing you practice self-expression with no actual inhibiting factors present. You learn the correct moves. You form a mental map that is retained in memory. A broad, general, flexible map. Then, when you face a crisis, where an actual menace or inhibiting factor is present, you have learned to act calmly and correctly. There is a carryover in your muscles, nerves, and brain from practice to the actual situation. Moreover, because your learning has been relaxed and pressure-free, you will be able to rise to the occasion, extemporize, improvise, act spontaneously. At the same time your shadow-boxing is building a mental image of yourself acting correctly and successfully. The memory of this successful self-image also enables you to perform better.

Dry-Shooting Is the Secret of Good Marksmanship

A novice on the pistol range will quite often find that he can hold the hand gun perfectly still and motionless, as long as he is not trying to shoot. When he aims an empty gun at a target, his hand is steady. When the same gun is loaded and he attempts to make a score, purpose tremor sets in. The gun barrel uncontrollably moves up and down, back and forth, in much the same way that your hand tremors when you attempt to thread a needle (see Chapter 11). Many good pistol coaches recommend lots of dry run target shooting to overcome this condition. The marksman calmly and deliberately aims, cocks, and snaps the hand gun at a target on the wall. Calmly and deliberately he pays attention to just how he is holding the gun, whether it is canted or not, whether he is squeezing or jerking the trigger. He learns good habits calmly. There is no purpose tremor because there is no overcarefulness, no overanxiety for results. After thousands of such dry runs, the novice will find that he can hold the loaded gun, and actually shoot it while maintaining the same mental attitude, and going through the same calm, deliberate physical motions.

Shadow-Boxing Helps You Hit the Ball

I visited a friend of mine one Sunday in a suburb of New York. His 10-year-old son had visions of becoming a big-league baseball star. His fielding was adequate, but he couldn't hit. Each time his father threw the ball across the plate, the boy froze up—and missed it by a foot. I decided to try something. "You're so anxious to hit the ball, and so afraid you won't, that you can't even see it clearly," I said. All that tension and anxiety was interfering with his eyesight and his reflexes; his arm muscles weren't executing the orders from his brain.

"For the next ten pitches," I said, "don't even try to hit the ball. Don't try at all. Keep your bat on your shoulder. But watch the ball very carefully. Keep your eyes on it from the time it leaves your Daddy's hand until it goes by you. Stand easy and loose, and just watch the ball go by."

After ten trials of this, I advised him, "Now for a while, watch the ball go by and keep the bat on your shoulder, but think to yourself you are going to bring the bat around so it will really hit the ball, solidly and dead center." After this, I told him to keep on "feeling the same way" and to keep watching the ball carefully, and to "let" the bat come around and meet the ball, making no attempt to hit it hard. The boy hit the ball. After a few easy hits like this, he was knocking the ball a country mile, and I had a friend for life.

The Salesman Who Practiced "Not Selling"

You can use the same technique to "hit the ball" in selling, teaching, or running a business. A young salesperson complained to me that he froze up when calling on prospects. His one big trouble was his inability to properly reply to the prospect's objections. "When a prospect raises an objection or criticizes my product, I can't think of a thing to say at the time," he said. "Later, I can think of all kinds of good ways to handle the objection."

I told him about shadow-boxing and about the kid who learned to bat by letting the ball go by with the bat on his shoulder. I pointed out that hitting a baseball or thinking on your feet requires good reflexes. Your Automatic Success Mechanism must respond appropriately and automatically. Too much tension, too much motivation, or too much anxiety for results jams the mechanism. "You think of the proper answers later because you're relaxed and the pressure is off. Right now your trouble is you're not responding quickly and spontaneously to the objections your prospects throw at you. In other words, you're not hitting the ball that the prospect throws."

I told him first of all to practice a number of imaginary interviews—actually walking in, introducing himself to a prospect, making his sales pitch—then imagining every possible objection, no matter how screwballish, and answering it out loud. Next, he was to practice "with his bat on his shoulder" on an actual live client. He was to go in with an "empty gun" as far as intents and purposes were concerned. The purpose of the sales interview would not be to sell. He had to resign himself to being satisfied with no order. The purpose of the call would be strictly practice—"bat on the shoulder," "empty gun" practice.

In his own words, this shadow-boxing "worked like a miracle."

As a young medical student I used to shadow-box surgical operations on cadavers. This no-pressure practice taught me much more than technique. It taught a future surgeon calmness, deliberateness, clear thinking, because he had practiced all these things in a situation that was not do-or-die, life-or-death.

How to Make Your "Nerves" Work for You

The word "crisis" comes from a Greek word that means, literally, decisiveness, or point of decision.

A crisis is a fork in the road. One fork holds a promise of a better condition, the other of a worse condition. In medicine, the crisis is a turning point where the patient either gets worse and dies or gets better and lives.

Thus every crisis situation is two-pronged. The relief pitcher who goes into the game in the ninth inning with the score tied and three men on base can become a hero and gain in prestige, or he can become a villain who loses the game. Hugh Casey, who was one of the most successful and the calmest relief pitchers of all time, was once asked what he thought of when he was sent in a game in the middle of a crisis situation.

"I always think about what I a*m going to do, and what I want to happen*," he said, "instead of what the batter is going to do or what may happen to me." He said he concentrated on what he wanted to happen, felt that he could make it happen, and that it usually did.

This same attitude is another important key to reacting well in any crisis situation. If we can maintain an aggressive attitude, react aggressively instead of negatively to threats and crises, the very situation itself can act as a stimulus to release untapped powers.

Keep Your Goal in Mind

The essence of all this is remaining goal-oriented. You keep your own positive goal in mind. You intend to go through the crisis experience to achieve your goal. If you can do this, the crisis situation itself acts as a stimulus that *releases additional power* to help you accomplish your goal. In fact, in many instances, what begins as a crisis ends as yet another opportunity for real progress toward the overriding objectives.

I once visited with a woman who had taken the reins of a very troubled inner city high school as its principal. At the time, she was most unusual, a woman in a "man's job." She was also hip-deep in problems, from teachers who had given up and were just going through the motions to inadequate resources, to kids completely uninvolved in learning, to actual crime and violence. She told me that each day was "crisis city." Two years after taking this position, for which, I might add, there was little competition, she had turned this school around dramatically. Attendance was up, grade averages were up, "bad apples" were plucked and extracted, real learning (not just warehousing) was taking place. The change was so remarkable that school administrators from distant cities came to observe this school and consult with this principal. Again, this was all the more remarkable because it was a woman captaining the turnaround in the late 1960s.

When I asked her how she'd been able to weather the relentless storminess of this environment day after day, she explained that she kept reminding herself that each crisis presented another different opportunity to accomplish something linked to her ultimate objective. Her handling of each problem was an opportunity to gain the trust or grudging respect of a teacher or a student, and she told herself that she would use these as building blocks, constructing her influence and control over this unwieldy organism called a school one brick at a time. At the end of a particularly bad day, she acknowledged to herself that a few bricks she thought had been properly laid had been knocked back out of place, but that it only meant she would need to put them back and get another one in place the next day. When some crisis exploded into her office, she not only asked herself how to solve it, but how to utilize solving it as a means of moving closer toward her vision of what this school was going to be like when it was made over. "It was like a jigsaw puzzle in my mind," she told me. "I had a picture from the box of what it would look like when it was done. Then I had all these loose, scrambled pieces in a pile. Most of the time, I didn't get to methodically search for the next piece. I had one leap out of the pile and demand I try to fit it into the puzzle. Sometimes the piece was on fire and had to be saved before it could be used. Sometimes it was crumbling and had to be taped together. But piece by piece I was still completing a puzzle. The trick was to keep the box handy with the picture of the whole, and not lose sight of it."

If you think about her experience and the words she used to explain her approach, you can clearly see that she was heavily relying on Psycho-Cybernetics for equilibrium in a pressure-cooker situation.

Lecky has said that the purpose of emotion is "re-enforcement," or additional strength, rather than to serve as a sign of weakness. He believed that there was only one basic emotion—excitement—and that excitement manifests itself as fear, anger, courage, etc. depending on our own inner goals at the time, whether we are inwardly organized to conquer a problem, run away from it, or destroy it. "The real problem is not to control emotion, but to control the choice of which tendency shall receive emotional reinforcement." (Prescott Lecky, *Self Consistency, A Theory of Personality*, New York, Island Press)

If your intention or your attitude-goal is to go forward, if it is to make the most of the crisis situation and win out in spite of it, then the excitement of the occasion will *reinforce this* tendency. It will give you more courage, more strength to go forward. If you lose sight of your original goal, and your attitude-goal becomes one of running away from the crisis, of seeking to somehow get past it by evading it, this running-away tendency will also be reinforced, and you will experience fear and anxiety.

Don't Mistake Excitement for Fear

Many people have made the mistake of habitually interpreting the feeling of excitement as fear and anxiety, and therefore interpreting it as a proof of inadequacy.

Any normal person who is intelligent enough to understand the situation becomes excited or nervous just before a crisis situation. Until you direct it toward a goal, this excitement is neither fear, anxiety, courage, confidence, nor anything else other than a stepped-up, reinforced supply of emotional steam in your boiler. It is *not* a sign of weakness. It is a sign of additional strength to be used *in any way you choose*.

PRESCRIPTION

Stop thinking in terms of fear, anxiety or nervousness, and think only in terms of excitement. It is fine to be a bit excited before you step into the spotlight in whatever you do.

Experienced actors know that this feeling of excitement just before a performance is a good token. Many of them deliberately work themselves up emotionally just before going on stage. I've been told by those who would know that even after many years hosting The Tonight Show, Johnny Carson was still so "hyper" backstage that he would sometimes feel nauseous right before the curtains parted and he walked out to deliver his opening monologue. A wonderful man and, for years, one of America's most beloved speakers to sales organizations, the founder of the National Speakers Association, Cavett Robert used to say "Don't try to get rid of the butterflies in your stomach. Just get them to fly in formation."

Many people place their bets at racetracks on the basis of which horse appears to be the most nervous just before going to the post. Trainers also know that a horse that becomes nervous or spirited just before a race will perform better than usual. The term "spirited" is a good one. The excitement that you feel just before a crisis situation is an infusion of spirit and should be so interpreted by you. You do not need to get rid of this; you need to marshall it as a force for your own benefit.

In fact, the absence of this excitement can pose its own problems. Not long ago I met a man on a plane whom I had not seen for several years. In the course of conversation, I asked if he still made as many public speeches as he had in the past. Yes, he said, as a matter of fact he had changed jobs so that he would be able to speak more and now made at least one public speech every day. Knowing his love for public speaking, I commented that it was good he had this type of work. "Yes," he said, "in one way it is good. But in another way it is not so good. I don't make as many good speeches now as I used to. I speak so often that it has become old-hat to me, and I no longer feel that little tingly feeling in the pit of my stomach, which tells me that I am going to do well."

Some people become so excited during an important written examination that they are unable to think clearly or even hold a pencil steadily in their hands. Other people become so aroused under the same circumstances that they perform over their heads; their minds work better and clearer than usual. Memory is sharpened. It is not the excitement per se that makes the difference, but *how it is used*.

What Is the Worst That Can Possibly Happen?

Many people have a tendency to magnify out of all proportion the potential penalty or failure that the crisis situation holds. We use our imaginations against ourselves and make mountains out of molehills.

Or else we do not use our imaginations at all to see what the situation really holds, but habitually and unthinkingly react *as if* every simple opportunity or threat were a life-or-death matter.

If you have ever watched daytime TV soap operas, and I confess I have, you can quickly see a common thread stitching these programs together: crisis after crisis after crisis. But in these dramas, every event represents crisis, and everyone reacts with grossly exaggerated emotions. The perfect home for a ham actor is one of these daytime dramas. You do *not* want to turn your life into one of these soap operas, where every incident, small or large, is greeted with the same gigantic excitement. After all, a traffic accident that is a mere fender-bender and only inconveniences you a bit does not warrant the same level or range of excitement as one that sends you or others to the hospital with life-threatening injuries. In a soap opera, one is the same as the other. You can be more discerning.

I once counseled a woman who was terribly unhappy with her life and everyone in it. Not a day passed without some provocation sparking a bitter argument with spouse, sibling, or neighbor. Her descriptions of these disputes were as dramatic as any soap opera scriptwriter could imagine. She perceived the slightest problem as an epic crisis, the most trivial slight a mammoth assault on her dignity; she even took inclement weather personally. A simple spill of beverage on the carpet was the same to her as a five alarm fire. She had become a drama queen. Such people exist everywhere—in marriages, in the workplace, in political circles—and they are toxic to themselves and to everyone around them. With an inappropriate level of excited response to events and other peoples' behavior, such a person is a stick of TNT tossed into each situation. But remember, to her, her overexcitement is a perfectly appropriate response, and altering that will involve fundamental work with her self-image.

If you face a *real crisis*, you need a lot of excitement. The excitement can be used to good advantage in the crisis situation. However, if you overestimate the danger or the difficulty, if you react to information that is faulty, distorted, or unrealistic, you are likely to call up much more excitement than the occasion calls for. Because the real threat is much less than you have estimated, all this excitement cannot be used appropriately. It cannot be gotten rid of through creative action. Therefore it remains inside you, bottled up, as the jitters. A big

excess of emotional excitement can harm rather than help performance, simply because it is inappropriate.

Philosopher and mathematician Bertrand Russell tells of a technique which he used on himself to good advantage in toning down
excessive excitement:

> When some misfortune threatens, consider seriously and deliberately
> what is the very worst that could possibly happen. Having looked this
> possible misfortune in the face, give yourself sound reasons for thinking
> that after all it would be no such very terrible disaster. Such reasons
> always exist, since at the worst nothing that happens to oneself has any
> cosmic importance. When you have looked for some time steadily at the
> worst possibility and have said to yourself with real conviction, "Well,
> after all, that would not matter so very much," you will find that your
> worry diminishes to a quite extraordinary extent. It may be necessary to
> repeat the process a few times, but in the end, if you have shirked noth-
> ing in facing the worse possible issue, you will find that your worry dis-
> appears altogether and is replaced by a kind of exhilaration. (Bertrand
> Russell, *The Conquest of Happiness*)

I believe it is also important to have the self-image of someone
who responds well to crisis, and is frequently successful at finding
opportunity in adversity. The person who sees himself as "no good in
an emergency" cannot do much with Bertrand Russell's advice.

Life Is Long

Many people allow themselves to be thrown off course by minor or
even imaginary threats, which they insist on interpreting as life-or-
death or do-or-die situations.

To the teenage girl, just spotting her boyfriend or even her
hoped-for-boyfriend sitting and talking amiably with another attractive
girl is of life or death importance. "I just want to die!" she exclaims. We
all know that a few years from that moment, she won't even remember
it or him. Life is long. But many adults keep on behaving like teenagers
their entire lives. Many people allow themselves to be thrown "off
course" by very minor or even imaginary threats, which they insist
upon interpreting as life-or-death, or do-or-die situations.

A sales professional calling on an important prospect may act as
if it were a matter of life or death. If I don't close this account, she tells

herself, I will have wasted months of effort. I'll miss quota. I won't make bonus, and how will I tell my husband we can't take our planned vacation? My sales manager may cut my territory. And so on. The single appointment takes on earthshaking importance. Yet over a year's time, such a muffed opportunity will be offset by solid successes, even by lucky breaks that seemingly deliver new accounts or larger orders from unexpected sources. If this life-or-death sales call occurs in March, it will be part of a blur of past activity by Christmas and, over an entire selling career, of no importance whatsoever. Life is long.

Perhaps this life-or-death feeling that many people experience in any sort of crisis situation, is a heritage from our dim and distant past, when failure to primitive man usually was synonymous with death.

Regardless of its origin, however, the experience of numerous patients has shown that it can be cured by calmly and rationally analyzing the situation. Rather than responding automatically, blindly, and irrationally, ask yourself, "What is the worst that can possibly happen if I fail?" Remind yourself that "Life is long" and seek the perspective of 20/20 hindsight in advance.

The Curtain Will Rise on a Second Act

Close scrutiny will show that most of these everyday so-called crisis situations are not life-or-death matters at all, but *opportunities* to either advance or stay where you are. For example, what is the worst that can happen to the salesperson? She will either get an order and come out better off than she was or she will not get the order and be no worse off than before she made the call. The applicant will either get the job or not. If he fails to get it, he will be in the same position as before he asked.

Few people realize just how potent such a simple change of attitude can be. One salesperson I know doubled his income after he was able to change his attitude from a scared and panicky outlook ("Everything depends on this") to the attitude, "I have everything to gain and nothing to lose."

Walter Pidgeon, the great actor, told how his first public performance was a complete flop. He was scared to death. However, between acts, he reasoned with himself that he had already failed, therefore he had nothing to lose; that if he gave up acting altogether he would be a complete failure as an actor, and therefore he really had nothing to worry about by going back on. He went out in the second act relaxed and confident, and made a big hit.

It seems there's always a second act waiting for you if you calmly organize yourself to take advantage of it.

There was a time when Frank Sinatra's career was so far in the doldrums he couldn't find work. Few remember any of that; Sinatra is remembered as a giant. George Foreman had completely left boxing, was struggling as an evangelist, struggling just to earn sufficient money to feed his family, and was outright laughed at and ridiculed when he began his boxing comeback. During his first act, his personality had been so unpleasant, he had few friends in the media. He talks about how he deliberately mounted his comeback with a very different personality, so as to become a valuable sports personality by the end of the second act, not just a washed-up old boxer. And he succeeded masterfully, ultimately becoming a millionaire thanks to his immense popularity as a commercial spokesperson, public speaker, and sports commentator. A small kitchen appliance company became a giant in short order on the strength of George Foreman's "pitching" its products on TV infomercials and TV home shopping channels in the late 1990s. Regis Philbin had bounced around the TV business, hosting mostly local talk shows in different markets for twenty years, and was widely regarded as a minor player in the industry and by critics, before his syndicated morning show and his hosting the enormously popular "Who Wants to Be a Millionaire?" made him big, and led to a reported $20-million contract with ABC. Regis' second act will make the twenty years that preceded it irrelevant. Former President Jimmy Carter had, by most measurements, a woefully unsuccessful and troubled presidency, was voted out of office after his first term in a landslide, and returned to small-town Plains, Georgia with his tail between his legs, admittedly depressed. But his second act has led to prestige, prominence, influence, and bipartisan respect, and many historians agree that he has been "the best former President."

We can read about "the second act" in the lives of such famous people, but don't lose sight of the fact that most successful but nonfamous people have second acts too. Many a prosperous businessperson has a business bankruptcy in the past that, at its moment, was humiliating and seemed of life-or-death importance. Many a gratified parent with a good relationship with grown son or daughter has a spectacularly rocky patch when the relationship was in shambles to look back on. Many happily married men and women have woefully unsuccessful first marriages and ugly, bitter divorces in their pasts.

For the most part, today's crisis winds up being but one little "blip" on a long life history. For today, there's an immediate second act tomorrow. For this week, there's a second act beginning next Monday. For even the authentic tragedy, there's a second act waiting to be scripted and played out over time.

Remember, above all, that the key to any crisis situation is *you*. Practice and learn the simple techniques of this chapter, and you, like hundreds of others before you, can learn to make crisis work for you by making crisis a creative opportunity.

MENTAL TRAINING EXERCISE

Creating 20/20 hindsight as foresight is yet another immensely valuable and creative use of your imagination. Stop and recall a few situations from your past that seemed of dire, earth-shaking consequence at the time but have proven inconsequential over time. Then project yourself three, four, or five years into the future, looking back on today's event, and consider how you will feel about it and how much impact it will have had on your life.

CHAPTER FOURTEEN

How to Get and Keep "That Winning Feeling"

Slump? I ain't in no slump...I just ain't hitting.
—Yogi Berra

Your powerful servo-mechanism is tele-logical. That is, it operates in terms of goals and end results. Once you give it a definite goal to achieve you can depend on its automatic guidance system to take you to that goal much better than you ever could by conscious thought. You supply the goal by thinking, in terms of end results. Your automatic mechanism then supplies the means whereby. If your muscles need to perform some motion to bring about the end result, your automatic mechanism will guide them much more accurately and delicately than you could by taking thought. If you need ideas, your automatic mechanism will supply them. There are even many who believe that if you need contacts, your servo-mechanism can magnetically attract them.

Whatever the extent of its powers, one thing is certain; it will lie sleepy, lazy, and dormant, if undirected. Note the word "servo"; it is your servant. If not called on, will servants in the mansion polish the silver, prepare high tea, or launder the clothes solely on their own initiative, attempting to anticipate the lord of the manor's wishes? Don't count on it. Also, if the servants employed speak only in an unintelligible foreign tongue and the master speaks only in English, unintelligible to the servant, how much will get accomplished? You see, Psycho-Cybernetics is both the language translator so that you, the master, can communicate with and be understood by your "inner servant," and the means of organizing the "to-do list" directives you give to the inner servant so that they may be brought to fruition.

Think in Terms of Possibilities

You must supply the goal. And to supply a goal capable of activating your creative mechanism, you must think of the end result *in terms of a present possibility*. The possibility of the goal must be seen so clearly that it becomes real to your brain and nervous system. So real, in fact, that the same feelings are evoked as would be present if the goal were already achieved.

This is not as difficult or mystical as it may first appear. You and I do it every day of our lives. What, for example, is worry about possible unfavorable future results, accompanied by feelings of anxiety, inadequacy, or perhaps humiliation? For all practical purposes we experience the very same emotions in advance that would be appropriate if we had already failed. We picture failure to ourselves, not vaguely or in general terms, but vividly and in great detail. We repeat the failure images over and over again to ourselves. We go back in memory and dredge up memory images of past failures.

Remember what has been emphasized earlier: Our brain and nervous system cannot tell the difference between a real experience and one which is vividly imagined. Our automatic creative mechanism always acts and reacts appropriately to the environment, circumstance, or situation. The only information concerning the environment, circumstance, or situation available to it is what *you believe to be true* concerning them.

Your Nervous System Can't Tell "Real Failure" from Imagined Failure

Thus, if we dwell on failure and continually picture failure to ourselves in such vivid detail that it becomes real to our nervous system, we will experience the feelings, even the physical responses, that go with failure.

On the other hand, if we keep our positive goal in mind, and picture it to ourselves so vividly as to make it real, and think of it in terms of an accomplished fact, we will also experience winning feelings: self-confidence, courage, and faith that the outcome will be desirable.

We cannot consciously peek into our creative mechanism and see whether it is geared for success or failure. But we can determine its present set by our feelings. When it is set for success, we experience that winning feeling.

Setting Your Machinery for Success

And if there is one simple secret to the operation of your creative servo-mechanism, it is this: Call up, capture, evoke *the feeling of success*. When you feel successful and self-confident, you will act successfully. When the feeling is strong, you can literally do no wrong.

The winning feeling itself does not *cause* you to operate successfully, but it is more in the nature of a sign or symptom that we are geared for success. It is more like a thermostat, which does not cause the heat in the room but measures it. However, we can use this thermostat in a very practical way. Remember: When you experience that winning feeling, your internal machinery is set for success.

Too much effort to consciously bring about spontaneity is likely to destroy spontaneous action. It is much easier and more effective to simply define your goal or end result. Picture it to yourself clearly and vividly. Then simply capture the feeling you would experience if the desirable goal were already an accomplished fact. Then you are acting spontaneously and creatively. Then you are using the powers of your subconscious mind. Then your internal machinery is geared for success: to guide you in making the correct muscular motions and adjustments, to supply you with creative ideas, and to do whatever else is necessary to make the goal an accomplished fact.

How That Winning Feeling Won a Golf Tournament

Dr. Cary Middlecoff, writing in the April 1956 issue of *Esquire Magazine*, said that The Winning Feeling is the real secret of championship golf. "Four days before I hit my first drive in the Masters last year, I had a feeling I was sure to win that tournament," he said. "I felt that every move I made in getting to the top of my back swing put my muscles in perfect position to hit the ball exactly as I wanted to. And in putting, too, that marvelous feeling came to me. I knew I hadn't changed my grip any, and my feet were in the usual position. But there was *something about the way I felt that gave me a line to the cup just as clearly as if it had been tattooed on my brain. With that feeling all I had to do was swing the clubs and let nature take its course.*"

Middlecoff went on to say that the winning feeling is "everybody's secret of good golf," that when you have it the ball even bounces right for you, and that it seems to control that elusive element called luck.

Before pitching his famous perfect game in the World Series, Don Larsen said that, the night before, he "had the crazy feeling" that he would pitch perfectly the next day.

Today's athletes sometimes talk about this winning feeling as "being in the zone," as entering a time and place and emotional state where they are totally relaxed, totally confident of the outcome. Many times we can sense that they are in the zone just by observation. Recall John Elway's last-minute, end-zone-to-end-zone march that deprived the Cleveland Browns of competing in the Super Bowl—now known to football fans as *The* Drive. Just about everybody who watched *The* Drive looked at each other when it began and nodded; it seemed predestined and inevitable even to Browns fans that *The* Drive was about to occur.

But let's remember that the zone is not a real, physical place, nor is it a sudden change in physical skill or technical capability, nor is it even rationally justified by statistical probabilities or past experience. It is purely an emotional state. In my opinion, it is the complete and utter release of responsibility for hitting a target to the servo-mechanism. It is, in a way, surrender to the servo-mechanism to such a degree that all anxiety, worry, stress, and desperation disappear in an instant, and the person just goes about performing the necessary functions in a calm, businesslike manner.

Much work has gone into finding ways to trigger this emotional state on demand. The popular motivational guru of recent years, Tony Robbins, is reportedly paid huge sums by a handful of top athletes, notably including Andre Agassi and Greg Norman, to teach them such "get into state fast" techniques.

There is truly magic in this winning feeling. It can seemingly cancel out obstacles and impossibilities. It can use errors and mistakes to accomplish success. J. C. Penney tells how he heard his father say on his death bed, "I know Jim will make it." From that time onward, Penney felt that he would succeed somehow, although he had no tangible assets, no money, no education. The chain of J. C. Penney stores was built on many impossible circumstances and discouraging moments. Whenever Penney would get discouraged, however, he would remember the prediction of his father, and he would feel that somehow he could whip the problem facing him.

After making a fortune, he lost it all at an age when most men have long since been retired. He found himself penniless, past his prime, and with little tangible evidence to furnish reason for hope. But again he remembered the words of his father, and soon recaptured the winning feeling, which had now become habitual with him. He rebuilt his fortune and in a few years was operating more stores than ever.

Mr. Penney had as his most concrete foundation, a profound, fundamental belief grooved into his self-image that he was the kind of a person who would make it.

Unfortunately, many people have heard just the opposite from parents or other influences, causing them to give far greater import to the times when they fail than to the times they succeed, gradually becoming convinced that they are the kind of persons who never seem to make it happen.

The simple distinction in self-concept and self-talk should not have its strength and power underestimated.

How That Winning Feeling Made Les Giblin Successful

Les Giblin, founder of the famous Les Giblin Human Relations Clinics and author of the book *How to Have Power and Confidence in Dealing with People*, read the first draft of this chapter, then told me how imagination coupled with that winning feeling had worked like magic in his own career.

Les had been a successful salesperson and sales manager for years. He had done some public relations work and had gained some degree of reputation as an expert in the field of human relations. He liked his work but he wanted to broaden his field. His big interest was people, and after years of study, both theoretical and practical, he thought he had some answers to the problems people often have with other people. He wanted to lecture on human relations. However, his one big obstacle was lack of experience in public speaking. Les told me:

> One night, I was lying in bed thinking of my one big desire. The only experience I had had as a public speaker was addressing small groups of my own salesmen in sales meetings, and a little experience I had had in the Army when I served part-time as an instructor. The very thought of getting up before a big audience scared the wits out of me. I just couldn't imagine myself doing it successfully. Yet, I could talk to my own salesmen with the greatest of ease. I had been able to talk to groups of soldiers without any trouble. Lying there in bed, I recaptured in memory the feeling of success and confidence I had had in talking to these small groups. I remembered all the little incidental details that had accompanied my feeling of poise. Then, in my imagination I pictured myself standing before a huge audience and making a talk on human relations—and at the same time having the same feeling of poise and self-confidence I had had with smaller groups. I pictured to myself in detail just how I would stand. I could feel the pressure of my feet on the floor, I could see the expressions on the people's faces, and I could hear their applause. I saw myself making a talk successfully—going over with a bang.
>
> Something seemed to click in my mind. I felt elated. Right at that moment I felt that I could do it. I had welded the feeling of confidence and success from the past to the picture in my imagination of my career in the future. My feeling of success was so real that I knew right then I could do it. I got what you call 'that winning feeling' and it has never deserted me. Although there seemed to be no door open to me at the time, and the dream seemed impossible, in less than three years time I saw my dream come true—almost in exact detail as I had imagined it and felt it. Because of the fact that I was relatively unknown and because of my lack of experience, no major booking agency wanted me. This didn't deter me. I booked myself, and still do. I have more opportunities for speaking engagements than I can fill.

Les Giblin became known as an authority on human relations. Over two hundred of the largest corporations in America have paid him thousands of dollars to conduct human relations clinics for their employees. His book *How to Have Confidence and Power* has become a classic in the field. And it all started with a picture in his imagination and that winning feeling.

Les' experience demonstrates how we must search our past experiences for signs that the goal we are now tentatively imagining can be achieved. Those signs are almost always there, or the goal would never have occurred to us in the first place. You undoubtedly have "little" past indications that you can do what it is you would most like to do, and if you will look for them and highlight them in your mind, you can begin proving to your self-image that you are in fact qualified to be as you desire to be, secure its acceptance of this as new truth, and send your servo-mechanism hurrying to make it so.

When you shine your spotlight on these Can-Do Indicators and consign everything else to the shadows, your winning feeling will be reflected back and envelope you in its warmth.

Two Men, Two Different Feelings

I once had occasion to observe two men I knew quite well. They had remarkably similar backgrounds, education, intelligence, and skill, both attempting to master a brand new endeavor at the same time. Each was totally unknown to the other, but both observed by me. The details of the task being undertaken are unimportant. Suffice it to say it represented considerable difficulty, offered up considerable frustration, and required considerable patience.

One of these men said to me, "I'll never get this. You know, Max, all my life, everything's been difficult for me. I've had to do everything the hard way. I can't recall ever getting a break. I just don't have it in me to fight my way through this too."

The other fellow said to me, "Max, I'll tell you something. All my life, everything's been difficult for me. Every single thing I now do well, every single thing I can now do effortlessly, and every success I've had, I started out doing it badly and struggled mightily to get from bad to good. If there's one thing I know exactly how to do, it is to go from being a bumbling incompetent to capable. Looks like I'm going to do that again with this."

Which one of these men do you suppose gave up on this goal and walked away empty-handed and unfulfilled? Which do you suppose wound up successful?

This is more than just the old cliché about positive thinking—glass half full versus glass half empty. That's superficial and tends to be consciously forced. This is deeper. Foundational. Right there, in the self-image. How these two men have interpreted their lives, how they feel about themselves. One will see the slightest improvement as encouraging proof that he is again progressing as usual, from ineptness to competence, while the other will see the exact same slight improvement as proof that he is mired in struggle so great and challenge so unyielding he is not up to the task.

Any two people can look at any situation and interpret it quite differently. That's why we have Republicans and Democrats, conservatives and liberals, right-to-life activists and pro-choice activists, and so on. There's room for differences of opinion about you too! If you hold an opinion about yourself that is limiting and inhibiting, try to step out and examine yourself as an outside analyst, then advocate the opposing opinion. The most adept debators can take either side of any argument and win. Try it!

How Science Explains That Winning Feeling

The science of Cybernetics throws new light on just how the winning feeling operates. We have previously shown how electronic servo-mechanisms make use of stored data, comparable to human memory, to "remember" successful actions and repeat them.

Skill learning is largely a matter of trial-and-error practice until a number of hits, or successful actions, have registered in memory.

Cybernetic scientists have built what they call an electronic mouse, which can learn its way through a maze. The first time through the mouse makes numerous errors. It constantly bumps into walls and obstructions. But each time it bumps into an obstruction, it turns 90 degrees and tries again. If it runs into another wall, it makes another turn, and goes forward again. Eventually, after many, many errors, stops and turns, the mouse gets through the open space in the maze. The electronic mouse, however, remembers the successful turns and, the next time through, these successful motions are reproduced, or played back, and the mouse goes through the open space quickly and efficiently.

The object of practice is to make repeated trials, constantly correct errors, until a hit is scored. When a successful pattern of action is performed, the entire action pattern from beginning to end is not only stored in what we call conscious memory, but in our very nerves and tissues. Folk language can be very intuitive and descriptive. When we say, "I had a feeling in my bones that I could do it," we are not far from right. When Dr. Cary Middlecoff says, "There was something about the way I felt that gave me a line to the cup just as clearly as if it had *been tattooed on my brain*," he is, perhaps unknowingly, very aptly describing the latest scientific concept of just what happens in the human mind when we learn, remember, or imagine.

How Your Brain Records Success and Failure

Much research in the workings of the brain has taken place since I wrote the original Psycho-Cybernetics book. But this explanation, condensed from it, remains helpful in understanding how the winning feeling (or failure feeling) comes about: The human cortex is composed of billions of neurons, each with numerous axons (feelers or extension wires), which form synapses (electrical connections) between the neurons. When we think, remember, or imagine, these neurons discharge an electrical current that can be measured. When we learn something or experience something, a pattern of neurons forming a "chain" (or tattooing of a pattern) is set up in brain tissue. This pattern is not in the nature of a physical groove, like a groove in a record (although that analogy is not far off the mark), but more in the nature of an electrical track, the arrangement and electrical connections between various neurons being somewhat similar to a magnetic pattern recorded on a CD. The same neuron may thus be a part of any number of separate and distinct patterns, making the human brain's capacity to learn and remember almost limitless.

These patterns, or engrams, are stored away in brain tissue for future use and are reactivated, or replayed, whenever we remember a past experience.

In short, there *is* a tattooing, or action pattern of engrams, in your brain for every successful action you have ever performed in the past. And, if you can somehow furnish the spark to bring that action pattern into life, or replay it, it will execute itself, and all you'll have to do is "swing the clubs" and "let nature take its course."

When you reactivate successful action patterns out of the past, you also reactivate the winning feeling that accompanied them. By the same token, if you can recapture that winning feeling, you also evoke all the winning actions that accompanied it. View this as a circular process: Feeling begets action, action begets feeling or imagined action, especially memory-based imagined action begets feeling, feeling begets action. Fortunately, it doesn't matter much where in that loop you strike the spark.

Build Success Patterns into Your Gray Matter

Dr. Elliott, when President of Harvard, once made a speech on what he called "The Habit of Success." Many failures in elementary schools, he said, were due to the fact that students were not given at the very beginning a sufficient amount of work at which they *could succeed*, and thus never had an opportunity to develop the "Atmosphere of Success," or what we call the winning feeling. Students, he said, who had never *experienced* success early in their school life, had no chance to develop the "habit of success," the habitual feeling of faith and confidence in undertaking new work. He urged that teachers arrange work in the early grades so as to ensure that students *experienced success*. The work should be well within the ability of the student, yet interesting enough to arouse enthusiasm and motivation. These small successes, said Dr. Elliott, would give students the "feel of success," which would be a valuable ally in all future undertakings.

When a quarterback is injured and removed from the game, and the second stringer who's been warming the bench is rushed in, the astute coach tries to give him easy plays with a high probability of success, even if small, in order to establish a sense of success, a rhythm—to spark that winning feeling. Rather than having him attempt a pass down field or over the middle that might result in a gain of 10, 20, or 30 yards but is difficult to complete, the play might be a little swing pass, almost sideways, that may result in a gain of only 2 or 3 yards but has a very high probability of being successfully completed.

A top salesman I know in the printing industry habitually arranges his schedule so that his first two sales calls of each day are in "friendly territory." He visits clients where he knows he will be welcomed, where he writes business repetitively, where there is a high likelihood of being asked to bid a job or even immediately take an order or, at the very least, he'll be treated respectfully and courteously. Then he moves on to cold calling on possible new accounts where the welcome may not be nearly as warm, or visiting the tough customers who are ultra-price-conscious, where he is frequently outbid. He tells me he wants a winning feeling already in place before testing his patience and persistence. His sales manager says, "Small victories lead to big victories."

Fred DeLuca, the founder of the Subway sandwich shop chain, a champion of micro business launches, counsels, "Make pennies first." It is easier to envision making dollars if you've made pennies, easier to envision making thousands if you've made hundreds.

What you might call the small victory process is the natural evolution of things. Crawl. Stand by holding onto something. Stand independently. Toddle forward by holding onto something. Walk. Having mastered walking, it's a bit easier to believe you can ride a bicycle. Having ridden a bicycle, it's easier to picture yourself riding a motorcycle.

We can acquire the habit of success or rhythm of success, we can build into our gray matter patterns and feelings of success at any time and at any age by following Dr. Elliott's advice to teachers, the savvy coach's strategy for the inexperienced quarterback, the printing sales rep's trick for starting each day. If we are habitually frustrated by failure, we are very apt to acquire habitual feelings of failure, which color all new undertakings. But by arranging things so that we can succeed in little things, we can build an atmosphere of success that will carry over into larger undertakings. We can gradually undertake more difficult tasks, and after succeeding in them, be in a position to undertake something even more challenging. Success is literally built on success and there is much truth in the saying, "Nothing succeeds like success."

Obviously, as adults we are eager to speed up this process. To accelerate success. To have such a good foundation in place we can even trigger our winning feeling on command. The experienced quarterback who has been parked on the bench for weeks needs and wants to turn on his winning feeling in an instant, when suddenly needed in a game, without requiring the gentle, patient build-up of small victories. This acceleration must be created totally through imagination, not actuality. In the Theater Of The Mind rather than the arena of real experience. Because synthetic and actual experience have virtually identical impact, this can be done.

How to Play Back Your Own
Built-In Success Patterns

Everyone has at some time or another been successful in the past. It does not have to have been a big success. It might have been something as unimportant as standing up to the school bully and beating him; winning a race in grammar school, winning the sack race at the office picnic, winning out over a teenage rival for the affections of a girl-friend. Or it might be the memory of a successful sale, your most successful business deal, or winning first prize for the best cake at the county fair. *What* you succeeded in is not so important as the feeling of success that attended it. All you need is an experience where you succeeded in doing what you wanted to, in achieving what you set out to achieve, and something that brought you some feeling of satisfaction.

Go back in memory and relive those successful experiences. In your imagination revive the entire picture in as much detail as you can. In your mind's eye, see not only the main event but all the little incidental things that accompanied your success. What sounds were there? What about your environment? What else was happening around you at the time? What objects were present? What time of year was it? Were you cold or hot? And so forth. The more detailed you can make it, the better. If you can remember in sufficient detail just what happened when you were successful at some time in the past, you will find yourself feeling just as you felt then. Try particularly to remember your feelings at the time. If you can remember your feelings from the past, they will be reactivated in the present. You will find yourself feeling self-confident, because self-confidence is built on memories of past successes.

Now, after arousing this general feeling of success, apply it in your thoughts to the important sale, conference, speech, business, golf tournament, rodeo competition, whatever you are engaged in *now*. Use your creative imagination to picture to yourself just how you would act and just how you would feel if you had *already succeeded*.

Positive and Constructive Worry

Mentally, begin to play with the idea of complete and inevitable success. Don't force yourself. Don't attempt to coerce your mind. Don't try to use effort or willpower to bring about the desired conviction. Just do what you do when you worry, only "worry" about a positive goal and a desirable outcome, rather than about a negative goal and an undesirable outcome.

Don't begin by trying to force yourself to have absolute faith in the desired success. This is too big a bite for you to mentally digest at first. Use "gradualness." Begin to think about the desired end result as you do when you worry about the future. When you worry, you do not attempt to convince yourself that the outcome will be undesirable. Instead, you begin gradually. You usually begin with "suppose." "Just suppose such and such a thing happens," you mentally say to yourself. You repeat this idea over and over to yourself. You play with it. Next comes the idea of possibility. "Well, after all," you say, "such a thing *is* possible." It could happen. Next, comes mental imagery. You begin to picture to yourself all the various negative possibilities. You play these imaginative pictures over and over to yourself, adding small details and refinements. As the pictures become more and more real to you, appropriate feelings begin to manifest themselves, just as if the imagined outcome had already happened. And this is the way that fear and anxiety develop.

How to Cultivate Faith and Courage

Faith and courage are developed in exactly the same way. Only your goals are different. If you are going to spend time in worry, why not worry constructively? Begin by outlining and defining to yourself the most desirable possible outcome. Begin with your "suppose." "Suppose the best possible outcome did actually come about?" Next, remind yourself that after all this could happen. Not that it will happen, at this stage, but only that it could. Remind yourself that, after all, such a good and desirable outcome is possible.

You can mentally accept and digest these gradual doses of optimism and faith. After having thought of the desired end result as a definite possibility, begin to imagine what the desirable outcome would be like. Go over these mental pictures and delineate details and refinements. Play them over and over to yourself. As your mental images become more detailed, as they are repeated over and over again, you will find that *more appropriate feelings* are beginning to manifest themselves, just as if the favorable outcome had already happened. This time the appropriate feelings will be those of faith, self-confidence, courage—or all of them wrapped up into one package, That Winning Feeling.

Don't Take Counsel of Your Fears

General George Patton, the hell-for-leather, "Old Blood and Guts" general of World War II fame, was once asked if he ever experienced fear before a battle. Yes, he said, he often experienced fear just before an important engagement and sometimes during a battle, but, he added, "I never take counsel of my fears."

If you experience negative failure feelings—fear and anxiety— before an important undertaking, as everyone does from time to time, it should not be taken as a sure sign that you will fail. It all depends on how you react to them and what attitude you take toward them. If you listen to them, obey them, and take counsel of them, you will probably perform badly. But this need not be true.

First of all, it is important to understand that failure feelings— fear, anxiety, lack of self-confidence—do not spring from a heavenly oracle. They are not written in the stars. They are not holy gospel. Nor are they intimations of a set and decided fate that means that failure is decreed and decided. They originate from your own mind. They are indicative only of *attitudes of mind within* you, not of external facts that are rigged against you. They mean only that you are underestimating your own abilities, overestimating and exaggerating the nature of the difficulty before you, and that you are reactivating memories of past failures rather than memories of past successes. That is *all* that they mean and all that they signify. They do not pertain to or represent the truth concerning future events, but only your own mental attitude about the future event.

Knowing this, you are free to accept or reject these negative failure feelings, to obey them and take counsel of them, or to ignore their advice and go ahead. Moreover, you are in a position to use them for your own benefit.

Accept Negative Feelings as a Challenge

If we react to negative feelings aggressively and positively, they become challenges that automatically arouse more power and more ability within us. The ideas of difficulty, threat, and menace arouse additional strength within us if we react to them aggressively rather than passively. In the last chapter we saw that a certain amount of excitement, if interpreted correctly and employed correctly, helps rather than hinders performance. It all depends on the individual and his or her attitudes, whether negative feelings are used as assets or liabilities.

React Aggressively to Your Own Negative Advice

Everyone has known individuals who can be discouraged and defeated by the advice from others that "you can't do it." On the other hand, there are people who rise to the occasion and become more determined than ever to succeed when given the same advice. An associate of industrialist Henry J. Kaiser's said, "If you don't want Henry to do a thing, you had better not make the mistake of telling him it can't be done, or that he can't do it—for he will then do it or bust."

It is not only possible, but entirely practicable, to react in the same aggressive, positive manner to the "negative advice" of our own feelings as we can and should when the negative advice comes from others.

Overcome Evil with Good

Feelings cannot be directly controlled by willpower. They cannot be voluntarily made to order or turned on and off like a faucet. If they cannot be commanded, however, they can be wooed. If they cannot be controlled by a direct act of will, they can be controlled indirectly.

A bad feeling is not dispelled by conscious effort or willpower. It can be dispelled, however, by another feeling. If we cannot drive out a negative feeling by making a frontal assault on it, we can accomplish the same result by substituting a positive feeling. Remember that feeling follows imagery. Feeling coincides with, and is appropriate to, what our nervous system accepts as real or the truth about environment. Whenever we find ourselves experiencing undesirable feelings, we should not concentrate on the undesirable feeling, even to the extent of driving it out. Instead, we should immediately concentrate on positive imagery, on filling the mind with wholesome, positive, desirable images, imaginations, and memories. If we do this, the negative feelings take care of themselves. They simply evaporate. We develop new feeling-tones appropriate to the new imagery.

If, on the other hand, we concentrate only on driving out or attacking worry thoughts, we necessarily must concentrate on negatives. And even if we are successful in driving out one worry thought, a new one, or even several new ones, are likely to rush in, since the general mental atmosphere is still negative. Jesus warned us about sweeping the mind clean of one demon, only to have seven new ones move in, if we left the house empty. He also advised us not to resist evil, but to overcome evil with good.

The Substitution Method of Curing Worry

Dr. Matthew Chappell, a modern psychologist, recommends exactly the same thing in his book *How to Control Worry*. We are worriers because we practice worrying until we become adept at it, says Dr. Chappell. We habitually indulge in negative imagery out of the past and in anticipating the future. This worry creates tension. The worrier then makes an effort to stop worrying and is caught in a vicious cycle. Effort increases tension. Tension provides a worrying atmosphere. The only cure for worry, he says, is to make a habit out of immediately substituting pleasant, wholesome, mental images, for unpleasant worry images. Each time you find yourself worrying, use this as a signal to immediately fill the mind with pleasant mental pictures out of the past or in anticipating pleasant future experiences. In time worry will defeat itself because it becomes a stimulus for practicing antiworrying. The worrier's job, says Dr. Chappell, is not to overcome some particular source of worry, but to change mental habits. As long as the mind is set or geared in a passive, defeatist, "I hope nothing happens" sort of attitude, there will always be something to worry about.

When I was a medical student I remember being called on by the professor to orally answer questions on the subject of pathology.

Somehow, I was filled with fear and anxiety when I stood up to face the other students, and I couldn't answer the questions properly. Yet, on other occasions, when I looked into the microscope at a slide and answered the typewritten questions before me, I was a different person. I was relaxed, confident, and sure of myself because I knew my subject. I had that winning feeling and did very well.

As the semester progressed I took stock of myself and when I stood up to answer questions I pretended I didn't see an audience but was looking through a microscope. I was relaxed and substituted that winning feeling for the negative feeling when quizzed orally. At the end of the semester I did very well in both oral and written examinations.

The negative feeling had finally become a sort of bell that created a conditioned reflex to arouse that winning feeling.

Today, I lecture and speak with ease at any gathering in any part of the world, because I am relaxed and know what I am talking about when I do speak. More than that, I bring others into the conversation and make them feel relaxed too.

The Choice Is Up to You

Within you is a vast mental storehouse of past experiences and feelings, both failures and successes. Like inactive recordings on tape, these experiences and feelings are recorded on the neural engrams of your gray matter. There are recordings of stories with happy endings, and recordings of stories with unhappy endings. One is as true as the other. One is as real as the other. The choice is up to you as to which you select for playback.

Another interesting scientific finding about these engrams is that they can be changed or modified, somewhat as a tape recording may be changed by dubbing in additional material, or by replacing an old recording with a new one.

These recordings in the human brain tend to change slightly each time they are played back. They take on some of the tone and temper of our present mood, thinking and attitudes toward them. We now know that not only does the past influence the present, but that the present clearly influences the past. In other words, we are neither doomed nor damned by the past. Our present thinking, our present mental habits, our attitudes towards past experiences, and our attitudes toward the future—all have an influence on old recordings. The old can be changed, modified, replaced by our present thinking.

Old Recordings Can Be Changed

Another interesting finding is that the more a given recording or engram is activated or replayed, the more potent it becomes. The permanence of engrams is derived from synaptic efficacy (the efficiency and ease of connections between the individual neurons that make up the chain) and further that synaptic efficiency improves with use and diminishes with disuse. Here again, we have good scientific ground for forgetting and ignoring those unhappy experiences from the past and concentrating on the happy and pleasant. By so doing, we strengthen those engrams having to do with success and happiness and weaken those having to do with failure and unhappiness.

How We Manufacture Feelings or "State"

When a family member or friend dies, we recall many past memories involving this person. We tend to set aside most of the bad memories and not only recall, but improve on and magnify the good ones. An uncle who was often sullen and distant and hypercritical but occasionally warm and witty is transformed into the life of the party and a great encourager who will be sadly missed at every future family occasion. A sister you were quite content to see only two or three times a year at holidays and never missed or thought of much in between is now a confidante you'll miss talking to everyday. This is all part of the mourning feeling. It is manufactured by choosing to replay only certain recordings, to completely forget about others, and even to modify the recordings played. History is literally rewritten to permit the mourning feeling we believe to be appropriate, based on everything programmed into our own self-image about the kind of person we are and how we should behave in these circumstances.

I remember attending a funeral where the brother of the deceased, who had been estranged from his brother for years following a very bitter war over the family business, stood up and spoke for nearly fifteen minutes, delivering an emotionally moving eulogy that had the halo glowing brightly over the coffin and left no dry eyes in the house. A few weeks later, I encountered him in a neighborhood coffee shop and we sat down together to talk. I gingerly said, "Bill, I know all about the bad feelings between you and your brother and I wonder, how did you find it in you to be so gracious at his memorial ceremony?"

His answer reveals the chief secret to how we manufacture our feelings! He answered, "I'm the kind of person who never speaks ill of the dead."

The phrase "I am the kind of person who [fill in the bank]" is incredibly revealing and incredibly powerful. It reveals what is at the core, not the circumference, of the self-image, to which all other thought, feeling, action, and outcome must conform. It also reveals exactly how you can lock in and assure the emergence of a winning feeling whenever it is appropriate.

MENTAL TRAINING EXERCISE

Change negative self-talk, the voice of the Automatic Failure Mechanism, to a positive affirmation: "I am the kind of person who..." Repeat the affirmation as a personal mantra until it becomes an automatic response to any sliver of self-doubt that slips through the door! Here are a few examples:

I am the kind of person who ...

effectively plans the day ahead, sets goals, and accomplishes them.

listens carefully, then communicates confidently and persuasively.

takes the initiative in solving problems and suggesting ideas.

stays calm under pressure.

prefers fresh fruit and other healthy foods to "junk food."

CHAPTER FIFTEEN

More Years of Life and More Life in Your Years

We age not by years but by events
and our emotional reactions to them.

—Dr. Arnold Hutschnecker

T he search for the fountain of youth ... Does every human being have a built-in fountain of youth? Can the Success Mechanism keep you young?

Does the Failure Mechanism accelerate the "aging process"?

Woody Allen said, "I do not want to achieve immortality through my work. I want to achieve immortality by not dying." At my age, I identify with his statement. In fact, I'd gladly trade away whatever legacy I have thanks to my Psycho-Cybernetics work for another decade of comparative youth. But I have lived a very vibrant, healthy, interesting, and rewarding life without significant loss of vitality, activity, or acuity in my later years, so I have no complaint. I believe I have done so in large part by aggressively working on my psychological health and letting it take care of my physical health.

I posit that the role of emotional well-being in antiaging or longevity medicine will only expand and grow and become more accepted, respected and prominent in the years to come.

Truths That Cannot Yet Be Proven Are Nonetheless Useful

William James once said that everyone, scientists included, develops his own over-beliefs concerning known facts, which the facts themselves do not justify. As a practical measure, these "over-beliefs" are not only permissible, but necessary. Our assumption of a future goal, which sometimes we cannot see, is what dictates our present actions and our "practical conduct." Columbus had to assume that a great land mass lay to the westward before he could discover it. Otherwise he would not have sailed at all and, having sailed, would not have known whether to set his course to the south, east, north, or west.

Scientific research is possible only because of faith in assumptions. Research experiments are not helter-skelter or aimless, but directed and goal-oriented. The scientist must first set up a hypothetical truth, a hypothesis based not on fact but on implications, before being able to know which experiments to make or where to look for facts that may prove or disprove the hypothetical truth.

In this last chapter I want to share with you some of my own over-beliefs, hypotheses, and philosophy, not as a M.D., but as a man. As Dr. Hans Selye has said, certain "truths" cannot be used by medicine, but can be used by the patient.

Life Force: The Secret of Healing and the Secret of Youth

I believe that the physical body, including the physical brain and nervous system, is machine-like, composed of numerous smaller mechanisms, all purposeful, or goal-directed. I do not believe, however, that a human is a machine. I believe that the essence of humans is *that which* animates this machine, that which inhabits the machine, directs and controls it, and uses it as a vehicle. Humans are not machines, any more than electricity is the wire over which it flows or the motor that it turns. I believe that the essence of humanity is extraphysical.

For many years individual scientists—psychologists, physiologists, biologists—have suspected that there was some sort of universal "energy" or vitality that ran the human machine. They also suspected that the amount of this energy available and the way it was utilized explained why some individuals were more resistant to disease than others, why some individuals aged faster than others, and why some hardy individuals lived longer than others. It was also fairly obvious that the source of this basic energy—whatever it might be—was something other than the surface energy we obtain from the food we eat. Caloric energy does not explain why one individual can snap back quickly from a serious operation, withstand long continued stress situations, or outlive another. We speak of such persons as having a "strong constitution."

The strong constitution exhibited by individuals who live long and live well seems linked to elements over which we have considerable control, not the least of which is the never-ending setting and resetting of goals, so that we have something meaningful to live for.

A very famous professional speaker, on the circuit for three decades, was finally beginning to feel burn-out, not so much toward the speaking itself as to the grind of incessant travel with all its inherent frustrations, the endless blur of nights in innocuous hotel rooms. Friends mentioned that they could see the travel was aging him. He was on the verge of quitting his profession, which he actually loved and arguably required to have meaning and purpose. About the same time, probably in anticipation of retirement, he had taken up golf and became fascinated with, even addicted to the game, and reasonably adept at it. One day, on yet another lengthy flight, a new goal popped into his head: to play on at least one famous golf course in every state of the union. He began mulling this idea over in his imagination. Seeing himself being photographed after hitting a hole in one at the famously difficult Pebble Beach. Chuckling at being in the real rough on a golf course in rural Alaska.

The mulling over became increasingly serious, until he found himself thinking about it often over the ensuing days. He decided to test it by taking his clubs on his next ten-day trip and scheduling rounds of golf between his engagements. Not surprisingly, he found himself looking forward to the next day's travel rather than dreading it. Locked on this new target, he has uncovered a whole new level of passion and energy for securing speaking engagements in locations where there are golf courses he wants to play. He has not only extended and breathed new life into his career, he has quite likely extended and breathed new life into his life.

This occurred some six or seven years ago and, as of this writing, at age 73, this speaker/golfer is going strong. It seems he has the life force or elan vital of a much younger man.

Are you older or younger than your chronological years? The counting itself is arguably arbitrary. After all, if our calendars put 15 months instead of 12 months into each year, you'd be celebrating a different year's birthday this time around. That smaller number might very well convince your self-image of a different truth about your age, and you might very well feel and act differently. We all know people who are 35 going on 65, and 65 going on 35. I suppose something less extreme is desirable. But regardless of pondering about age itself, we all seek to tap more life force.

Science Discovers the Life Force

This life force was established as a scientific fact by Dr. Hans Selye of the University of Montreal. Since 1936 Dr. Selye has studied the problems of stress. Clinically and in numerous laboratory experiments and studies, Dr. Selye has proved the existence of a basic life force, which he calls "adaptation energy." Throughout life, from the cradle to the grave, we are daily called on to adapt to stress situations. Even the process of living itself constitutes stress—or continual adaptation. Dr. Selye has found that the human body contains various defense mechanisms (local adaptation syndromes or LAS), which defend against specific stress, and a general defense mechanism (general adaptation syndrome or GAS), which defends against nonspecific stress. "Stress" includes anything that requires adaptation or adjustment, such as extremes of heat or cold, invasion by disease germs, emotional tension, the wear and tear of living, or the so-called aging process.

"The term *adaptation energy*," says Dr. Selye, "has been coined for that which is consumed during continued adaptive work, to indicate that it is something different from the caloric energy we receive from food, but this is only a name, and we still have no precise concept of what this energy might be. Further research along these lines would seem to hold great promise, since here we appear to touch upon the fundamentals of aging." (Hans Selye, *The Stress of Life*)

Dr. Selye has written twelve books and hundreds of articles explaining his clinical studies and his stress concept of health and disease. It would be a disservice to him for me to try to prove his case here. Suffice it to say that his findings are recognized by medical experts the world over. And if you wish to learn more of the work that led to his findings, I suggest that you read Dr. Selye's book written for laymen, *The Stress of Life*.

To me, the really important thing that Dr. Selye has proved is that the body itself is equipped to maintain itself in health, to cure itself of disease, and to remain youthful by successfully coping with those factors that bring about what we call old age. Not only has he proved that the body is capable of curing itself, but that in the final analysis that is the only sort of cure there is. Drugs, surgery, and various therapies work largely by either stimulating the body's own defense mechanism when it is deficient, or toning it down when it is excessive. The adaptation energy itself is what finally overcomes the disease, heals the wound or burn, or wins out over other stressors.

Is This the Secret of Youth?

This elan vital, life force, or adaptation energy—call it what you will—manifests itself in many ways. The energy that heals a wound *is the same* energy that keeps all our other body organs functioning. When this energy is at an optimum all our organs function better, we feel good, wounds heal faster, we are more resistant to disease, we recover from any sort of stress faster, we feel and act younger, and in fact biologically we are younger. It is thus possible to correlate the various manifestations of this life force and to assume that *whatever works to make more of this life force available to us,* whatever opens to us a greater influx of life stuff, whatever helps us utilize it better—helps us "all over."

We may conclude that whatever nonspecific therapy aids wounds to heal faster might also make us feel younger. Whatever nonspecific therapy helps us overcome aches and pains might, for example, improve eyesight. And this is precisely the direction that medical research is now taking and that appears most promising.

Science's Search for the Elixir of Youth

In the original edition of this book, in this chapter, I wrote at length about some medical research and promising "medical miracles" coming to the forefront at the time (1960). I think you would find it interesting to revisit those comments, in light of what has actually transpired now, more than forty years later. What is unwaveringly true, regardless of changes in the specifics, is that the search for the elusive fountain of youth never ends. Today, human growth hormone (HGH) injections are much the rage among Hollywood celebrities, wealthy executives, and aging athletes, and many over-the-counter nostrums purporting to mimic the effects of these injections populate the shelves of health food stores and pharmacies alike. Perhaps you've read about or use DHEA nutritional supplements, testosterone patches. On and on.

Diet, exercise, certain herbal and nutritional supplements, as well as drug therapies all have influence, and there will undoubtedly be many exciting discoveries and breakthroughs to come. We have, of course, made huge strides in medically extending physical life, but are less successful regarding quality of life.

I have been more intrigued with psychological life extension and improvement. In bridging the two—physical and psychological—I once searched for other factors, or common denominators, that might explain why the surgical wounds of some patients heal faster than others. The medicine used for this purpose worked better for some people than for others. This in itself was food for thought, because the results obtained in mice were practically uniform. Ordinarily, mice do not worry or become frustrated. Frustration and emotional stress can be induced in mice, however, by immobilizing them so that they cannot have freedom of movement. Immobilization frustrates any animal. Laboratory experiments have shown that under the emotional stress of frustration, very minor wounds may heal faster, but any real injury is made worse and healing sometimes made impossible. It has also been established that the adrenal glands react in very much the same way to emotional stress and to the stress of physical tissue damage.

How the Failure Mechanism Injures You

Thus it might be said that frustration and emotional stress (those factors we have previously described as the failure mechanism) literally add insult to injury whenever the physical body suffers damage. If the physical damage is very slight, some emotional stress may stimulate the defense mechanism into activity, but if there is any real or actual physical injury, emotional stress adds to it and makes it worse. This knowledge gives us reason to pause and think. If aging is brought about by a using up of our adaptation energy, as most experts in the field seem to think, then our indulging ourselves in the negative components of the Failure Mechanism can literally make us old before our time by using up that energy faster.

What Is the Secret of Rapid Healers?

Among my human patients who did not receive the serum, some individuals responded to surgery just as well as the average patient who did receive it. Differences in age, diet, pulse rate, blood pressure, etc. simply did not explain why. There was, however, one easily recognizable characteristic that all the rapid healers had in common.

They were optimistic, cheerful positive thinkers who not only expected to get well in a hurry, but invariably had some compelling *reason or need* to get well quick. They had something to look forward to and not only something to live for, but something to get well for. "I've got to get back on the job." "I've got to get out of here so I can accomplish my goal."

In short, they epitomized those characteristics and attitudes that I have previously described as the Success Mechanism.

Thoughts Bring Organic as Well as Functional Changes

We do know this much: Mental attitudes can influence the body's healing mechanisms. Placebos or sugar pills (capsules containing inert ingredients) have long been a medical mystery. They contain no medicine of any kind that could bring about a cure. Yet when placebos are given to a control group in order to test the effectiveness of a new drug, the group receiving the phony pills nearly always shows *some* improvement, and quite often as much as the group receiving the medicine. Students receiving placebos actually showed more immunization against colds than the group receiving a new cold medicine.

During World War II the Royal Canadian Navy tested a new drug for seasickness. Group 1 received the new drug, and Group 2 received sugar pills. Of those groups, only 13% suffered from seasickness, while 30% of Group 3, which received nothing, got sick.

Visible Results from Invisible Medicine

Patients receiving placebos *must not be told* that the treatment is phony, if it is to be effective. *They believe* they are receiving legitimate medicine that will bring about a cure. To write off placebos as merely due to suggestions explains nothing. More reasonable is the conclusion that in taking the "medicine," some sort of expectation of improvement is aroused, a goal-image of health is set up in the mind, and the creative mechanism works through the body's own healing mechanism to accomplish the goal.

The so-called placebo effect is now common knowledge, a powerful form of autosuggestion aided and abetted by convincing physical props. But this is more than another set of evidence that the servo-mechanism is unable to distinguish synthetic from real; this is evidence that the servo-mechanism can even bring about restorative physical changes without the assistance of actual medicine!

Do We Sometimes Think Ourselves into Old Age?

We may do something very similar but in reverse, when we unconsciously expect to get old at a certain age.

At the 1951 International Gerontological Congress at St. Louis, Dr. Raphael Ginzberg, of Cherokee, Iowa, stated that the traditional idea that a person is supposed to grow old and useless around seventy is responsible in large measure for persons' growing old at that age, and that in a more enlightened future we might regard seventy as middle age. We are now, in 2001, rapidly approaching the time and place where 50 replaces 40 as life's midpoint, and 70 or even 80 will be looked upon as 60 was in 1950.

It begs the chicken-egg debate: Which comes first, changing reality governing expectations, or expectations governing changing reality? In truth it is both, and we can move toward the targets of longer life and enhanced quality of life from either direction.

At least two ways suggest themselves as to how we may think ourselves into old age. In expecting to grow old at a given age we may unconsciously set up a negative goal image for our servo-mechanism to accomplish. Or, in expecting old age and fearing its onset, we may unwittingly do those very things necessary to bring it about. We begin to taper off on both physical and mental activity. Cutting out practically all vigorous physical activity, we tend to lose some of the flexibility of our joints. Lack of exercise causes our capillaries to constrict and virtually disappear, and the supply of life-giving blood through our tissues is drastically curtailed. Vigorous exercise is necessary to dilate the capillaries that feed all body tissues and remove waste products. Dr. Selye has cultivated animal cell cultures within a living animal's body by implanting a hollow tube. For some unknown reason biologically new and young cells form inside this tube. Untended, however, they die within a month. However, if the fluid in the tube is washed daily, and waste products removed, the cells live indefinitely. They remain eternally young and neither age nor die. Dr. Selye suggests that this may be the mechanism of aging and that, if so, old age can be postponed by slowing down the rate of waste production or by helping the system to get rid of waste. In the human body the capillaries are the channels through which waste is removed. It has definitely been established that lack of exercise and inactivity literally "dries up" the capillaries.

Expectation and Engagement Means Life

When we decide to curtail mental and social activities, we stultify ourselves. We become set in our ways, bored, and give up our great expectations.

I have no doubt but that you could take a healthy man of 30 and within five years make an old man of him if you could somehow convince him that he was now old, that all physical activity was dangerous, and that mental activity was futile. If you could induce him to sit in a rocking chair all day, give up all his dreams for the future, give up all interest in new ideas, and regard himself as washed up, worthless, unimportant and nonproductive, I am sure that you could experimentally create an old man.

Dr. John Schindler, in his book *How to Live 365 Days a Year* (Prentice-Hall, Inc., Englewood Cliffs, N.J.), pointed out what he believed to be six basic needs that every human being has:

1. The Need for Love
2. The Need for Security

3. The Need for Creative Expression
4. The Need for Recognition
5. The Need for New Experiences
6. The Need for Self-Esteem

To these six, I would add another basic need: *the need for more life*, the need to look forward to tomorrow and to the future with gladness and anticipation. You might think of this as expectation and engagement.

Look Forward and Live

This brings me to another of my over-beliefs.

I believe that life itself is adaptive, that life is not just an end in itself, but a means to an end. Life is one of the means we are privileged to use in various ways to achieve important goals. We can see this principle operating in all forms of life, from the amoeba to man. The polar bear, for example, *needs* a thick fur coat to survive in a cold environment. It needs protective coloration to stalk game and hide from enemies. The life force acts as a means to these ends and provides the polar bear with a white fur coat. These adaptations of life to deal with problems in the environment are almost infinite, and there is no point in continuing to enumerate them. I merely want to point out a principle in order to draw a conclusion.

If life adapts itself in so many varied forms to act as a means toward an end, is it not reasonable to assume that if we place ourselves in the sort of goal-situation where *more life* is needed, that we will receive more life?

If we think of humans as goal strivers, we can think of adaptation energy or Life Force as the propelling fuel or energy that drives us forward toward our goal. A stored automobile needs no gasoline in the tank. And a goal striver with no goals doesn't really need much Life Force.

I believe that we establish this need by looking forward to the future with joy and anticipation, when we expect to enjoy tomorrow, and, above all, when we have something important (to us) to do and somewhere to go.

Create a Need for More Life

Creativity is certainly one of the characteristics of the Life Force. And the essence of creativity is a looking forward toward a goal. Creative people need more Life Force. And actuary tables seem to confirm that they get it. As a group, creative workers—research scientists, inventors, painters, writers, philosophers—not only live longer but remain productive longer than noncreative workers. Michelangelo did some of his best painting when past 80; Goethe wrote Faust when past 80; Edison was still inventing at 90; Picasso, past 75, dominated the art world; Wright at 90 was still considered the most creative architect; Shaw was still writing plays at 90.

One of the most visible poster boys for eternal youth is entertainment industry entrepreneur, Dick Clark. People marvel and joke about his boyish look, his never seeming to age. Is he drinking some water or taking some pill we don't know about? No, he is not. Is there some genetic edge involved? Probably, but that alone cannot explain the phenomenon we see. If you learn much about Mr. Clark, you will discover he is one of the busiest, most diversified, most innovative impresarios in all of the entertainment industry. He has, as they say, many irons in the fire, with no sign or suggestion of cutting back.

This is not to suggest youthfulness requires continued work until you are carried out of your workplace by your pall bearers. For some people, any form of retirement could be anathema. But the secret is positive expectations and engagement, not necessarily in the same vocation you have built your career in or at the same pace. There are endless options for staying out of the proverbial rocking chair.

I began my career as a writer and lecturer on Psycho-Cybernetics at age 61, after already having a long, varied, and colorful career. I remained active in both arenas for quite some time, sometimes performing a surgery in New York during the day, then flying to Los Angeles for a lecture that same night. At an age when too many men and women are thinking of stopping and fossilizing, I began anew, doing something that fascinated me. In my case, I have been very fortunate, as it has led to published books, lecturing, and meeting and corresponding with many fascinating people, fans of Psycho-Cybernetics, including Hollywood personalities like Jane Fonda, civic leaders like Nancy Reagan, even Salvador Dali, who presented me with his own original painting depicting the essence of Psycho-Cybernetics. But even if my "work" had not led to this kind of public acceptance and recognition, I would still be a happy and fulfilled man, engaged in activity meaningful to me and to others, setting and progressing toward goals. There is absolutely no rational reason that you cannot do the same.

This is why I tell my patients to develop a nostalgia for the future, instead of for the past, if they want to remain productive and vital. Develop an enthusiasm for life, create a need for more life, and you will receive more life.

Have you ever wondered why so many actors and actresses manage to look far younger than their years, and present a youthful appearance at age 50 and beyond? Could it not be that these people have a *need* to look young, that they are interested in maintaining their appearance, and simply do not give up the goal of staying young, as most of us do when we reach the middle years?

"We age, not by years, but by events and our emotional reactions to them," says Dr. Arnold A. Hutschnecker. "The physiologist Rubner observed that peasant women who work as cheap labor in the fields in some parts of the world are given to early withering of the face, but they suffer no loss of physical strength and endurance. Here is an example of specialization in aging. We can reason that these women have relinquished their competitive role as women. They have resigned themselves to the life of the working bee, which needs no beauty of face but only physical competence." (Arnold A. Hutschnecker, *The Will to Live*, rev. ed., Englewood Cliffs, N.J., Prentice Hall, Inc.)

Hutschnecker also comments on how widowhood ages some women, but not others. "If the widow feels that her life has come to an end and she has nothing to live for, her attitude gives outward evidence—in her gradual withering, her graying hair. Another woman, actually older, begins to blossom. She may enter into the competition for a new husband, or she may embark on a career in business, or she may do no more than busy herself with an interest for which perhaps she has not had the leisure until now." (Ibid.) Faith, courage, interest, optimism, looking forward bring us new life and more life. Futility, pessimism, frustration, living in the past are not only characteristic of old age; they contribute to it.

Retire from a Job, but Never Retire from Life

Many people go downhill rapidly after retirement. They feel that their active productive life is completed and their job is done. They have nothing to look forward to; they become bored, inactive, and they often suffer a loss of self-esteem because they feel left out of things— not important anymore. They develop a self-image of uselessness, worthlessness, being "worn out," a hanger-on. And a great many die within a year or so after retirement.

It is not retiring from a job that kills these people; it is retiring from life. It is the feeling of uselessness, of being washed up, the dampening of self-esteem, courage, and self-confidence, which our present attitudes of society help to encourage. We need to know that these are outmoded and unscientific concepts. Some fifty years ago psychologists thought that man's mental power peaked at the age of 25, and then began a gradual decline. The latest findings show that a man reaches his peak mentally somewhere around the age of 35 and *maintains the same level* until well past 70. Such nonsense as "you can't teach an old dog new tricks" still persists despite the fact that numerous researchers have shown that learning ability is about as good at 70 as it is at 17.

We are always about pluses and minuses. The young person embarking on a business career may have the advantages of great physical energy and stamina, a wide-open and uncluttered mind, intense curiosity, adventurousness, and a sharp and facile mind. A much older person competing in the same business arena may have far less physical stamina and may wrestle with certain physical difficulties; he or she may have certain built-up biases that block creativity, and may be risk-averse and conservative, less mentally quick. However, the young buck lacks experience, emotional maturity, confidence built on competence, and credibility with others. The elder statesman has much more relevant experience—in some cultures still revered as wisdom—to draw on in making important decisions and in recovering from mistakes. Each has a different list of pluses and minuses.

In business, if either is especially astute, they will counter their minuses with associates or advisors, much like a president constructs a cabinet. Lacking access to such an advisory committee made up of actual persons, a person can develop a "roundtable" in his or her own fertile imagination and solicit advice from any expert.

My point is that, at any age, even confronted with any adversity, tragedy, handicap, illness, people can determine how they are going to respond and, with regard to the symptoms and exhibitions of aging, their determined emotional responses may have at least as much to do with their actual life experience of the moment as their biological calendar or genetics or medicine. If you accept this to any great degree, then you should have additional motivation for mastering the concepts and techniques of Psycho-Cybernetics, to stay younger than your years.

Why I Believe in Miracles

While confessing my over-beliefs, I might as well make a clean breast of it and say that I believe in miracles. Medical science does not pretend to know why the various mechanisms within the body perform as they do. We know a little bit about the how and something about what happens. We can describe what happens and how the mechanisms function when the body heals a cut. But description is not explanation, no matter in what technical terms it may be couched. I still do not understand why or even the ultimate how when a cut finger heals itself.

I do not understand the power of the Life Force, which operates the mechanisms of healing, nor do I understand how that force is applied or just what makes it work. I do not understand the intelligence that created the mechanisms, nor just how some directing intelligence operates them.

Dr. Alexis Carrel, in writing of his personal observations of instantaneous healings at Lourdes, said that the only explanation he could make as a medical doctor was that the body's own natural healing processes, which normally operate over a period of time to bring about healing, were somehow speeded up under the influence of intense faith.

If miracles, as Dr. Carrel says, are accomplished by the acceleration of, or the intensifying of, natural healing processes and powers within the body, then I witness a small miracle every time I see a surgical wound heal itself by growing new tissue. Whether it requires two minutes, two weeks, or two months makes no difference insofar as I can see. I still witness some power at work that I do not understand.

Medical Science, Faith, Life, All Come from Same Source

Dubois, the famous French surgeon, had a large sign in his operating room: "The Surgeon dresses the wound, God heals it."

The same might be said of any type of medication, from antibiotics to cough drops. Yet I cannot understand how rational persons can forego medical help because they believe it inconsistent with their faith. I believe that medical skill and medical discoveries are made possible by the same Intelligence, the same Life Force, that operates through the media of faith healing. And for this reason I can see no possible conflict between medical science and religion. Medical healing and faith healing both derive from the same source and should work together.

No father who saw a mad dog attacking his child would stand idly by and say, "I must do nothing because I must prove my faith." He would not refuse the assistance of a neighbor who brought a club or a gun. Yet, if you reduce the size of the mad dog trillions of times and call it a bacteria or a virus, the same father may refuse the help of his doctor-neighbor who brings a tool in the form of a capsule, a scalpel, or a syringe.

Don't Place Limitations on Life

Which brings me to my parting thought. In the Bible we are told that when the prophet was in the desert and hungry, God lowered a sheet from the heavens containing food. Only to the prophet it didn't look much like good food. It was unclean and contained all sorts of crawling things. Whereupon God rebuked him, admonishing him not to call unclean that which God had offered.

Some doctors and scientists today still turn up their noses at whatever smacks of faith or religion. Some religionists have the same attitude, suspicion, and revulsion concerning anything scientific. The biased lack of cooperation is everywhere and repugnant to me. Doctors of chiropractic and medicine choose to feud rather than recognize the value and validity of their respective contributions and work together for the good of their patients. Psychiatrists, psychologists, and academia sneer at self-help, yet the anecdotal and documented evidence of hundreds of thousands of people being genuinely and profoundly assisted by books like these is so overwhelming and consistent no sane person would prosecute against it. So why not embrace it? When a professional therapist angrily criticizes the "pop-psych" author or "guru" who appears on "Oprah" or even the Home Shopping Network, is the rebuke genuine or ego- and jealousy-driven?

While all these sources war with each other and deny each other legitimacy, you need not be caught up in their petty differences. You have the freedom to seek out and "mix 'n match" whatever works best for you. Do not close your mind to any potential benefit or assistance. Use your own rational thought. Test hypotheses for yourself.

Everyone's real goal, as I said in the beginning, is for more life—more living. Whatever your definition of happiness may be, you will *experience* happiness only as you experience more life. More living means among other things more accomplishment, the attainment of worthwhile goals, more love experienced and given, more health and enjoyment, more happiness for both yourself and others.

I believe that there is *one life*, one ultimate source, but that this *one life* has many channels of expression and manifests itself in many forms. If we are to get more living out of life, we should not limit the channels through which Life may come to us. We must accept it, whether it comes in the form of science, religion, psychology, or what not.

Another important channel is other people. Let us not refuse the help, happiness, and joy that others may bring us, or that we can give to them. Let us not be too proud to accept help from others, nor too callous to give it. Let us not say "unclean" just because the form of the gift may not coincide with our prejudices or our ideas of self-importance.

The Best Self-Image of All

Finally, let us not limit our acceptance of Life by our own feelings of unworthiness. God has offered us forgiveness and the peace of mind and happiness that come from self-acceptance. It is an insult to our Creator to turn our backs on these gifts or to say that His creation—humanity—is so "unclean" that he is not worthy or important or capable. The most adequate and realistic self-image of all is to conceive of yourself as "made in the image of God." "You cannot believe yourself the image of God, deeply and sincerely, with full conviction, and not receive a new source of strength and power," says Dr. Frank G. Slaughter.

The ideas and exercises in this book have helped many of my patients get more living out of life. It is my hope, and my belief, that they will do the same for you.

CHAPTER SIXTEEN

True Stories of Lives Changed Using Psycho-Cybernetics

The Case of the
Least-Likely-to-Succeed Stockbroker

Cella Quinn was born with a gift, an advantage: far above-average intelligence. She is a MENSA member, an association of people with IQ in the top 2% of the entire population. But this "gift" was of little use to her for quite some time, thanks to other birth disadvantages. She was born with a severe cleft lip and palate, a birth defect that is a split in the roof of the mouth and the upper lip, and that produces "mangled" speech. It is often accompanied by a deformed nose. Cella described hers as looking like "a Quonset hut with one corner of the roof collapsed." The crude, minimal surgery of the time did not help her speech. Her speech was so unintelligible to many, she carried a pad and pencil with her to communicate with. Her jaw, teeth, and face often ached. Cella had a very difficult time in school; other children picked on her, and even teachers presumed her stupid.

"When you can't speak," Cella said, "people think you are stupid. My family, teachers, other children thought so and even I started to believe it."

She was 16 when she left home, catching a bus to the nearest big city, with $44 in her pocket. She had no plan, no idea where she was going; she only knew she had to escape where she was. She got a dish-

washer job at a drug store lunch counter, she was able to rent a basement room from a black woman who worked as a prostitute. This
woman encouraged Cella to improve herself, to continue her education and to push to do something with her life. In conversations, Cella
learned that the woman owned real estate and even invested in stocks,
something that both surprised her and motivated her.

A dentist, who stopped for coffee each morning at the Walgreens
lunch counter, got a note passed to him one morning from Cella. It
read: "My teeth hurt so much. I can only pay you $5 a month. Will
you help me?" The dentist arranged for her to receive surgeries and
subsequent dental care, at a total cost of over $3,000. Cella remembers
bursting into tears over the sum. However, she worked at multiple
jobs, paid those bills, paid to attend business school to become a secretary, and saved up to pay for plastic surgery for her nose. Then she
worked her way through the University of Nebraska, obtaining a
degree in journalism after twelve years. For the next seven years, she
worked in Lincoln, Nebraska as a reporter. An ad for a trainee for
Merrill Lynch intrigued her. She soon began a career with Merrill
Lynch. Somewhat to their surprise, she did well and after seven years,
she was recruited by Smith-Barney and made a vice-president.

Cella Quinn went on to achieve truly extraordinary success as a
stock broker, investment advisor, ultimately as president of her own
investment firm. Her personal lifestyle has mirrored that of the rich
and famous, complete with a mansion with a swimming pool in its living room, luxury automobiles, civic leadership, and security.

How did this woman manage to persevere through so many disadvantages and hardships to achieve such success?

She says her conversion was never easy. "My self-image was terrible, but due to a combination of necessity, an occasional push from
someone else, and gradually discovering abilities, I moved ahead."
Early in her selling career, she consulted a psychiatrist to improve her
self-esteem. He told her she was not "stupid" as she believed; in fact,
to the contrary, she was extremely intelligent, and he urged her to take
the MENSA examination—and she passed!

She discovered the original edition of this book, *s* while still
working at Walgreens, and says it was pivotal in getting her to pursue
and obtain plastic surgery. She also credits the book with giving her
the courage to seek therapy. Finally, she began to understand that she

need not be held back by any of her childhood traumas, and that she could take pride and confidence from the progress she had made. "Dr. Maltz' ideas made it possible for me to go from an 88-cent-an-hour dishwasher to owning my own investment firm," says Cella Quinn.

Regardless of the impetus, the important point is that Cella Quinn tested the "truths" about herself and discovered they were not true at all!

Be inspired by this example and test every believed but limiting "truth" in your self-image's inventory. You too may very well discover some of the most inhibiting are not true at all.

The Case of the Professor's "F"

"I was flunking out of college and contemplating suicide when I first read *Psycho-Cybernetics*, and it literally turned my life around."

That dramatic statement comes from college professor, professional speaker, author, and successful businessman Marshall Reddick. Mr. Reddick says that, at age 20, he was struggling just to stay in college, and believed he lacked the intelligence necessary to make it to graduation, let alone to go farther toward success in life. He was also painfully shy, a representation of his poor self-image and near total absence of self-confidence.

After reading *Psycho-Cybernetics*, he began experimenting with some of its simplest, most basic prescriptions and techniques. "I began to re-program myself," he says. "For example, I placed little notes all around me, in my pockets, on my mirror, in my car, 'reminding' me that I was a confident person and a capable person. Sure enough, after just 21 days, I started to feel and behave differently."

Marshall Reddick went on with a successful academic career: obtaining his Bachelor's Degree in Business and Economics, a Master's Degree in Business from Colorado State University, his Ph.D. in Business from Texas Tech University, and a three year tenure as Professor of Business and Economics at California State University. "I had all my students read and then write a report on *Psycho-Cybernetics*," Reddick says, "and I still recommend the book today."

Today, Mr. Reddick is a much-in-demand professional speaker, and has earned the Certified Speaking Professional (CSP) designation from the National Speakers Association. His seminar company has been presenting programs on time management, negotiations, and peak performance for corporate clients worldwide since 1975.

Isn't it remarkable that a failing student can metamorphose into a stellar student, earn a Ph.D., and step to the other side of the desk as professor, from such simple techniques? Self-made multi-millionaire W. Clement Stone has a favorite saying: "Little hinges swing big doors." It has many profound applications, and this is one of them—that frequently little tests of "truths" imbedded in the self-image, little experiments in exercising new control over one's thoughts can swing open huge doorways to rapid and dramatic personal growth.

It isn't necessarily the size of the idea but the size of the opportunity that governs the result. By experimenting with even the simplest of the ideas found in *Psycho-Cybernetics*, you too may make amazing self-discoveries.

The Case of the Alcoholic's Daughter

I am a professional speaker. The other day, as I was getting ready to leave my office to deliver a keynote address for a large association's luncheon, my eyes went to the bookcase in my office—where one book stands out from all the others. Soft cover, tattered in places, used and worn. It takes me back to 1960 °

I was working my way through Lamar University in Beaumont, Texas by being the "girl Friday" for a prestigious law firm. The managing partner became my mentor. I know today that he saw the low self-esteem in that 19-year-old girl. In one of our meetings that year, he handed a copy of Psycho-Cybernetics to me to read. If he said it was worthwhile, then it was, and I digested its contents that very week. Maxwell Maltz offered me tools to "re-engineer" my thoughts and feelings about myself, in ways that had never occurred to me.

For the first 16 years of my life, my father was a trouble-shooter for a huge manufacturing company, and they must have had a lot of troubles because we moved every year, sometimes twice in the same year, coast to coast and back again, 17 schools in 12 years. On weekends, after traveling all week, my Dad came home and crawled into a bottle. My Mom was rarely able to leave the house and, as the eldest of four children, I became her legs. I was the one who got the utilities connected each time we moved, got bills paid, groceries purchased. Yet, in her eyes, I never quite did anything well enough. With this as background, I was attempting to function effectively in the world of work, and struggling obviously enough that my employer handed me this book about the self-image.

The first year that I was given Psycho-Cybernetics, I read it five times. Over the next five years, I re-read it several times each year. Maxwell Maltz became my encourager. He not only opened the door to a new way of living for me, but he birthed a lifelong interest in mind-body studies that directed my career and brought me a lifetime of fulfillment. Today, I speak to audiences all over the country on issues of self-esteem and communication. I know firsthand that we cannot connect with others until we connect with ourselves.

Peggy Collins traveled from law firm clerk to a top producer in real estate selling to Senior Vice-President of a banking institution before embarking on her current career as a professional speaker and workshop leader, with an impressive corporate client list including Mobil Oil, Frito-Lay, Burger King, and the J.C. Penney Corporation. Her story reinforces the important fact that the past need not predict the future. It is a well-known psychological fact that children of alcoholics face significant and special problems. But depending on your definition of "dysfunctional family," nearly everyone has one! Each person must rise above childhood experiences or adverse adult experiences to take control of his or her own personality, beginning now and moving forward.

One of American business' favorite speakers, Joel Weldon, gave a speech for many years titled "Jet Pilots Don't Use Rearview Mirrors." We must all stop looking in our rearview mirrors and focus on the present moment and the future.

The Case of the Rodeo Cowboys

When Doug Butler agreed to take the reins as coach of the Cal-Poly, Pomona (California State Polytechnic University) rodeo team in the fall of 1969, they occupied last place in the western region of the National Intercollegiate Rodeo Association. One of the students in Doug's horseshoeing class, a top rodeo cowboy stuck on this last-place team, urged Doug to step in as coach, insisting that the team had more ability than they were demonstrating.

"I had recently read Dr. Maltz' *Psycho-Cybernetics*, was impressed by it, and working to apply its methods in my life. I felt the methods could be used to coach rodeo athletes, although I had never heard of the techniques being used for that purpose," Doug Butler recalled. "Later I discovered that Gary Leffew was using these methods to coach students in his bull-riding school, but at the time I thought I was breaking new ground."

Doug developed a plan for turning the team around, including new rules, training disciplines, a code of behavior for the athletes, and use of *Psycho-Cybernetics* as a text for personal improvement. The director of the University's Animal Science department, a former professional hockey player, agreed to support the plan. Doug then met with the rodeo team members and made it clear he would not accept the coaching responsibilities unless they would agree to all of his conditions. The rules included no alcohol, no tobacco, no drug use, good grades, even a well-groomed appearance, and participation in a rigorous practice schedule at the college rodeo arena two days a week, supplemented by daily mental practice.

Doug led an aggressive program of physical and mental conditioning. "Three days a week we worked out at the gym starting at 6:30 AM. We used weight training machines, did calisthenics and ran wind sprints. As we cooled down, we would discuss insights from our study of *Psycho-Cybernetics*. Everybody had a copy of the book and read it and re-read it. Each team member would practice visualizing his own champion performance, and would share their detailed descriptions of these imagined experiences with each other."

By late spring of 1970, the team had moved from the basement to the second place in the division, behind a team that featured a future six-time world champion cowboy. As the team's image, performance, and record improved, rodeo athlete scholarships became available for students for the very first time.

"The students presented me with an engraved silver belt buckle and a standing ovation at the year-end banquet. I still wear the buckle and will always treasure the great 'Psycho-Cybernetics' experience we shared. And every one of these team members has gone on to become successful in their chosen professions."

Doug Butler has his Ph.D. from Cornell University in veterinary anatomy and equine nutrition, is one of only 500 Certified

Journeyman Farriers, was three times a member of the North American Horseshoeing Team, and is the author of over 30 books and tapes on horseshoeing and horse foot care. In 1980, he won the North American Challenge Cup Horseshoeing Contest. In 1997, he was inducted into the International Horseshoeing Hall of Fame. And in 1999, he won the Journalism Award from the American Farriers Association. Today, Doug conducts classes, teaching blacksmiths to apply visualization techniques to be more efficient and competent craftsmen. He also speaks to business groups, associations and corporate audiences on "The Cowboy Code," dealing with character, leadership, and self-mastery. He says that his continued use of the techniques of *Psycho-Cybernetics* "has steered him towards successful accomplishment of every goal."

As you can see, it doesn't matter what your occupation or vocation is—even rodeo rider—the principles, concepts, and techniques of *Psycho-Cybernetics* are reliable tools for achieving peak performance. Also, as the story of Doug's team illustrates, it doesn't matter what your starting point may be. Even if, like his team, you are in last place, in disarray, absent focus, self-discipline, or self-confidence, all that can change at your own determination. No collection of circumstances founded on past experience need remain in control of your present or your future.

The Case of the Woman Who Could Not Walk

"Dear Dr. Maltz—please let me express to you my feelings of gratitude for your book *Psycho-Cybernetics*," so began a letter much like thousands of others received in Dr. Maltz' office over the years. However, this letter went on to describe a truly amazing story …

> What I am about to share with you is very personal and charged with emotion. When I think of how one paperback book has changed my whole life, is it any wonder I want to tell you my story, hoping it may help others.
>
> My life began in Providence, Kentucky on October 1, 1924, as a healthy, normal 9 pound baby girl. I was stricken with Muscular Dystrophy at age 10. I recall overhearing the doctor telling my parents that they might as well take me out of school as I had less than one year to live. This etched fear deep into me. Gradual changes took place in my motor abilities. I began to stumble, soon it became difficult to walk. Then I began to expe-

rience great difficulty using my hands. With loving and understanding, I began a journey that would span 20 years, trying to cope with this progressive disease, this shadow of doom, MD.

Many summers were spent in hospitals, in body casts, in therapy. Finally specially built shoes with steel braces attached were provided to help me walk. My whole body was showing signs of weakness. Tasks that were so simple for others were great frustrations for me. Still, in spite of numerous obstacles, I managed to complete my education, which included college. Then came thirteen years teaching school. At the age of 25, I was told I must undergo an operation on both ankles or risk spending the remainder of my life in a wheelchair. After suffering these operations, almost a year of confinement in casts and wheelchair, I had to learn to walk again. It was months before I could stand for periods of time. Several years before I was able to return to work.

Even though, for the most part, the operations were a success, mental scars remained, and they became a greater handicap to me than did my physical disabilities. I lacked self-confidence, self-esteem and self-reliance. I seemed to have lost a sense of direction and a purpose in living.

We will interrupt only for a moment to make this important point: It does not matter how or by what series of events a person loses the purpose for living, and with it self-esteem and self-confidence. It happens to tens of thousands of people, thousands of different ways. It certainly does not require severe physical handicaps or trauma to wind up in this very same emotional state. However, the pathway out of this darkness, into the light, is the same regardless of what brought on the darkness in the first place.

The letter continues...

Well-meaning friends and my family tried to help me. Inspirational booklets, books, and a desperate search into all types of philosophy filled every waking moment. I investigated everything from Buddhism to Transcendental Meditation. I even delved into some of the Ancient Vedas. One day while browsing in a bookstore, my eye caught sight of a book titled *Psycho-Cybernetics*. The title aroused my curiosity. I was told by the clerk in the store that she simply couldn't keep enough copies on hand, that it was one of the best-selling books in her store. That was all I needed to hear. I bought a copy and found that I couldn't lay it down. For the first time in my life I began to gain an insight into my own behavior.

When I finished the book, I decided that someday I would meet the author. I didn't know how this meeting could come about, but I knew I must have the opportunity to tell Dr. Maltz of my appreciation.

Over a period of years, *Psycho-Cybernetics* has served as an action manual for me. My attitude has changed from the negative to "a winning feeling." What now appears to be a miracle to others is simply my working to change my own self-image.

I have become somewhat of a medical phenomenon. Every doctor that has examined me has said that I do not have the physical muscle ability to walk. From a medical standpoint there seems to be no logical explanation for the fact that I do walk. I was recently named "Handicapped Professional Woman of the Year" at the District-4 Pilot International Convention. This award is jointly sponsored by Pilot and the President's Committee on Employment for the Handicapped. I have just been appointed to Governor Askew's sub-committee on information and press relations on employment of the handicapped here in Florida.

Through my work in television, I have had the good fortune and pleasure of working with many well-known personalities. Among the notables was—you, Dr. Maltz.

I have come to know what it is to live a fulfilling, useful and happy life.

Jeanne Sanders

Jeanne and her husband Peter became good friends of Max and Anne Maltz.

About her, Dr. Maltz once wrote, "Sooner or later in life, every person must face catastrophe. Each person then chooses to rise above it, no matter how Herculean the effort required, or to succumb to it. How can Jeanne Sanders walk and drive a car without the muscle capability and strength required to do so, according to all medical experts? Because of the muscle strength of her self-image, which cannot be so readily seen or medically evaluated."

It is significant that Jeanne Sanders noted that she used *Psycho-Cybernetics* as an "action manual." Unlike philosophical writings and unlike scores of other self-improvement books, *Psycho-Cybernetics* emphasizes things to *do*, not just things to think. This is important, because it is the constructive doing that yields results.

Dr. Maltz frequently told a story about the man who spent hours each and every day, in privacy, in a quiet room, eyes closed, meticulously visualizing such events as winning the lottery or being made Chief Executive Officer of a giant corporation, and then captaining its affairs from his plush penthouse office with floor-to-ceiling windows overlooking all of Manhattan, or of enjoying a honeymoon with a beautiful woman on a sunny tropical beach. This man engaged in these visualizations day after day, month after month, for a number of years before finally giving up in disgust, proclaiming to anyone who would listen that all this "self-help mumbo-jumbo" was bunk. The problem was, this fellow never once purchased a lottery ticket, applied for a better position, or asked a young woman out to dinner!

Psycho-Cybernetics can be of little value if only read, then relegated to a bookshelf. But if used with purpose and direction and determination as Jeanne Sanders did, it can liberate you to live a most fulfilling life.

Vocabulary

Automatic Success Mechanism (ASM, aka Success Mechanism). Refers to the servo-mechanism when directed to perform as a success mechanism, i.e., when stimulated by specific, positive targets (goals) and by Psycho-Cybernetics techniques.

Course Correction. Refers to the "zig zag" means by which virtually all targets are reached.

Critic Within, The. Refers to the voice of the AFM, Automatic Failure Mechanism; reinforcement of self-doubt, inferiority, unhealthy self-image via negative, self-critical self-talk.

Cybernetics. Control processes in electrical, mechanical or biological systems, notably including the negative-feedback-to-positive-results loop. Evolved in large part from guided-missile technology.

Deja Vu Effect. Typically defined as the illusion of having already experienced something actually being experienced for the first time. The "Deja Vu Effect" is the ease of doing something as it occurs in close replication of imagination practice and mental rehearsal.

Elan Vital. "Enthusiasm for the essence of life." In Dr. Maltz' writings the term "aliveness" is frequently used to mean experiencing elan vital.

Kind Eyes. Compassion for oneself. The opposite of self-criticism.

Mental Rehearsal. The use of the imagination to rehearse a function, process conversation, etc. in vivid and specific detail, repetitively, so that it may occur as rehearsed.

Servo-Mechanism (aka Creative Mechanism). Refers to the "inner computer" combining memory search and retrieval, creative thinking, problem solving, providing self-confidence, and many other functions. Performs as directed through conscious, rational thought, deliberate use of imagination, and automatic repetition of learned behavior in congruence with/controlled by the self-image.

Synthetic Experience. The product of mental rehearsal, meaning that the artificial or imagination-made experience is nearly as good as actual successful experience.

Target. Synonym for clearly defined, specific goal, whether of a behavioral or outcome nature.

Theater of the Mind. The exact process for mental rehearsal developed and prescribed by Dr. Maltz; a "place" created in your imagination where you "go" for purposes of relaxation, mental rehearsal, and to view "mental movies" you create, direct and star in.

Visualization. Commonly used term for use of the imagination in a purposeful manner.

Recommended Reading

Psycho-Cybernetics (Original Edition) by Dr. Maxwell Maltz. While approximately 60% of this book duplicates content from the original, updated in some cases, having read this book you are likely to find also reading the original unabridged edition interesting and enlightening. It is a classic that belongs in everyone's success library.

Magic Power of Self-Image by Dr. Maxwell Maltz. Dr. Maltz's second book, a practical guide to applying Psycho-Cybernetics, and further exploration of self-image psychology.

Zero Resistance Selling by Dr. Maxwell Maltz, Foundation, and co-authors Kennedy, Brooks, Paul, Oechsli and Yellen. The first and only book ever published specifically for sales professionals, based on Psycho-Cybernetics.

List of Books Referred to Throughout This Book

Anatomy of an Illness/Cousins
Body, Mind, Spirit/Worcester*
Battling the Inner Dummy/ Weiner, Hefter
Better Golf without Practice/ Morrison*
Bright Air, Brilliant Fire/ Edelman
Conquest of Happiness/Russell*
Do One Thing Different/ O'Hanlon
From Panic to Power/Bassett
Golf's Mental Hazards/Shapiro
How to Live 365 Days a Year/Schindler*
How to Think Like Leonardo da Vinci/Gelb
How to Make $25,000.00 a Year in Selling/Roth*
How to Control Worry/Chappell*
How to Have Confidence and Power in Dealing with People/Giblin
Human Use of Human Beings/Weiner*
Inner Game of Golf/Gallwey
Inner Game of Tennis/Gallwey
Liberating Everyday Genius/Jacobsen
Making the Most of Your Life/Web, Morgan*

Mind over Golf/Coop
Prescription for Anxiety/Weatherhead*
Profiles of Power and Success/Lundrum
Psychology of Invention/Rossman*
Revolution from Within: A Book of Self-Esteem/Steinheim
Secrets of Successful Selling/Murphy*
Self-Consistency, A Theory of Personality/Lecky*
Six Pillars of Self-Esteem/Branden
Sparks of Human Genius/Root-Bernstein
Stress of Life/Selye
Success Is an Inside Job/Milteer
The Mental Athlete:
    Inner Training for Peak Performance/Parker, Foster
Think and Grow Rich/Hill
Think Outside the Box/Vance
The Will to Live/Hutschnecker*
Wake Up and Live/Brande

---

*Titles marked with this asterisk (*) may be out of print; however, you may find them at libraries. Titles *not* marked with the asterisk are contemporary books currently available at most booksellers.

Additional Resources

These are some of the people you met in *The New Pyscho-Cybernetics:*

WILLIAM BROOKS
The Brooks Group
Reference:
www.psycho-cybernetics.com
www.arizonaspeakersbureau.com

DOUG BUTLER
Doug Butler Enterprises
253 Grey Rock Road
LaPorte, Co. 80535
www.cowboycode.com

PEGGY COLLINS
The People Connection
333 Inwood Village
Dallas, Texas 75209
www.thepeopleconnection.com

LEE MILTEER
www.psycho-cybernetics.com
www.arizonaspeakersbureau.com

JEFF PAUL
Hidden Profits Advertising, Inc.
www.psycho-cybernetics.com
www.arizonaspeakersbureau.com

JOE POLISH
Piranha Marketing, Inc.
512 E. Southern Ave., Suite C
Tempe, AZ 85282
www.thegeniusnetwork.com

CELLA QUINN
Cella Quinn Investment Services
10908 Forrest Drive
Omaha, Nebraska 68144

**MARSHALL REDDICK,
   Ph.D.**
1750 Ocean Blvd. #1405
Long Beach, Ca. 90802

PAUL G. STOLTZ, Ph.D.
Peak Learning Inc.
2650 Skyview Trail
San Luis Obispo, Ca. 93405
www.peaklearning.com

MICHAEL VANCE
Creative Thinking Association
   of America
16600 Sprague Road, Suite 120
Cleveland OH 44130

Free Audio-Cassette Tape from the
Psycho-Cybernetics Foundation

As a purchaser of this book, you are entitled to a **free** audio cassette tape introducing advanced Psycho-Cybernetics concepts, "Your Introduction to 'Zero Resistance Living.'" Simply photocopy and complete the form below (no need to tear a page out of your book) or put the same information on a piece of paper and FAX it to 602-269-3113.

Name _____

Address _____

City, State, Zip _____

Phone _____

FAX _____

E-mail Address _____

Free Articles and Back Issues of the Foundation's
'Zero Resistance Living' Newsletter

A collection of past issues of *The Zero Resistance Living Letter* and other essays, articles, and book excerpts and reviews related to Psycho-Cybernetics is available at www.psycho-cybernetics.com. free of charge.

About the Authors

Dr. Maxwell Maltz received his baccalaureate in science from Columbia University in 1921 and his doctorate in medicine from the College of Physicians and Surgeons of Columbia University in 1923. After postgraduate work in plastic surgery in Europe, Dr. Maltz was appointed to head several departments of reparative surgery in New York hospitals. He became a prominent international lecturer on his specialty and on the psychological aspects of plastic surgery, and he published two books on these subjects: *New Faces, New Futures* and *Dr. Pygmalion.* He developed a very successful private practice in New York and treated patients who came to him from all over the world, including many celebrities.

In the 1950s, Dr. Maltz became increasingly fascinated by the number of people who came to him requesting surgery, who had greatly exaggerated "mental pictures" of their physical deformities, and whose unhappiness or insecurities remained unchanged even after he gave them the new faces they desired. In 1960, after nearly a decade of counseling hundreds of such patients, extensive research on everything from missile guidance technology to hypnosis, and testing his evolving "success conditioning" on athletes, salespeople, and others, he published his findings and then radical ideas in the first edition of *Psycho-Cybernetics.*

The book was an instant bestseller, and Dr. Maltz was sought out by corporations, athletes, entertainers, even religious organizations, as a speaker, seminar presenter, and private coach. His book's fans ranged from Jane Fonda to Vince Lombardi's Green Bay Packers. Even the famous artist Salvador Dali presented him with an original painting depicting the self-image emerging from darkness into light.

Dr. Maltz authored several other books about Psycho-Cybernetics, as well as three novels, even an off-Broadway play, and amassed a wealth of "case history" material, lecture and seminar notes, audio and film recordings—all now in the archives of The Psycho-Cybernetics Foundation. Although Dr. Maltz passed away at age 76, his legacy is thriving; in fact, his works have grown in popularity, almost entirely through word of mouth. Additional information about all Dr. Maltz's work is available at www.psycho-cybernetics.com.

Dan S. Kennedy is a marketing consultant, professional speaker, author of nine books, and successful businessman. As a speaker, he has addressed over 200,000 people a year for each of the past nine years, frequently and repeatedly appearing on programs with former U.S. Presidents, Generals Norman Schwarzkopf and Colin Powell, broadcasters Larry King and Paul Harvey, entertainers, athletes, coaches, business leaders, and fellow speakers like Zig Ziglar, Brian Tracy, Jim Rohn, and Tom Hopkins. His books include *No Rules: 21 Lies and Myths about Success* and *The Ultimate Marketing Plan.* Mr. Kennedy is also a lifelong student and practitioner of Psycho-Cybernetics, CEO of The Psycho-Cybernetics Foundation, author of THE NEW PSYCHO-CYBERNETICS audio program, and co-author of the Psycho-Cybernetics–based book for sales professionals: *Zero Resistance Selling.* Additional information about Mr. Kennedy's work is available at www.dankennedy.com.

The Artist's Gift

In 1966, the famous and celebrated artist Salvador Dali created a painting depicting his experience with *Psycho-Cybernetics*, which he presented as a gift to Maxwell Maltz. Upon Salvador Dali's death in 1989, all the rights were bequeathed and transferred to Maxwell and Anne Maltz, and the work was subsequently issued a copyright in March of 1993, to the Maltzess', titled "Darkness and Light."

Unfortunately, the Psycho-Cybernetics Foundation is unaware of the location of the painting or in whose possession it may be. Thus, the photos and photocopies available for reproduction here do not even approach doing it justice.

Here is Dr. Maltz's description of the painting, based on his conversation with Salvador Dali when first presented with the painting.

> In the center of this painting is a world divided into two parts. The left is a world in shadow from frustration. Here, in the middle, you have a man's image, shrunken to the size of a small potato, moving away from reality, toward the black angel of destruction. Below you see a ship without any sails about to capsize in the rough seas of frustration. Now, the other half of man's inner world is of sunlight, of confidence. Here, man's image is ten feet tall and is walking toward the sun. Below you see a ship in calm waters about to reach port. And what is this port? Peace of mind! We can learn to walk away from this shadow world of frustration into the dawn of a new world, through confidence.

In one interview, Dr. Maltz said, "Dali's gift to me is the gift each person can give to themselves. It is important that we understand that the port of peace of mind cannot be reached by moving away from reality. Any form of simple escapism can only alleviate frustration temporarily as an aspirin may alleviate the symptoms of headache. Only by moving aggressively toward reality—which means uncovering hidden truths about yourself—can you truly have peace of mind."

Above all else Psycho-Cybernetics is about the search for truth: your true potential, your true personality, your true desires and aspirations, your true talents and abilities, your true character.

INDEX